# *Burgundy Stars*

Also by William Echikson

*Lighting the Night: Revolution in Eastern Europe*

# Burgundy

# Stars

★ ★ ★

## *A Year in the Life of a Great French Restaurant*

William Echikson

*Little, Brown and Company*
*Boston ★ New York ★ Toronto ★ London*

FIRST EDITION

Excerpt from "Old Burgundy in the Decor and at the Table," by Patricia Wells, in *International Herald Tribune,* March 15, 1991.

*Photograph acknowledgments: Henry Horenstein—pp. x, 1, 2, 34, 48, 63, 64, 73, 74, 90, 103, 104, 120, 149, 150, 170, 195, 196, 215, 226, 273, 274, 297, 298, 307, 308; Christian Viougard—p. 216; Pierre Boulat—p. 254.*

LIBRARY OF CONGRESS CATALOGING-IN-PUBLICATION DATA

Echikson, William.
Burgundy stars : a year in the life of a great French restaurant / William Echikson. — 1st ed.
p. cm.
ISBN 0-316-19993-1
1. Loiseau, Bernard, 1951– . 2. La Côte d'Or (Restaurant) 3. Cooks—France—Biography. 4. Burgundy (France)—Social life and customs. I. Title.
TX649.L65E27 1995
641.5'09444—dc20 94-24260

10 9 8 7 6 5 4 3 2 1

MV-NY

Designed by Jeanne Abboud

*Published simultaneously in Canada by Little, Brown & Company (Canada) Limited*

PRINTED IN THE UNITED STATES OF AMERICA

*To Anu and Sam, the first Burgundy Stars*

*And in memory of my recently departed grandmother, Fanny Gross. She was my first guide to the mysteries and joys of great food.*

★ ★ ★

# Contents

★ ★ ★

# Prologue

*The menu*

When I travel, I like to read restaurant menus. How else to work up an appetite? What better way to discover a destination? At the beginning of January 1991, my parents, my wife, and I decided to spend a weekend in Burgundy. We left Paris early one cold Saturday. In the morning, we visited the medieval village of Vézelay, with its remarkable Romanesque abbey, then drove through the lush countryside until we arrived in the nondescript town of Saulieu.

It seemed a good place for a short break. Across the street, a large sign identified a restaurant run by a chef named Bernard Loiseau. I remembered a colleague telling me about Loiseau's cooking. We walked up to the front door, where the menu was posted. The least expensive dinner cost 580 francs, about $100. Too expensive, we agreed. We went in anyway, just to take a look. I told the receptionist how much my journalist friend had enjoyed eating at the restaurant. Then Bernard arrived.

The chef had just turned forty, but nothing about him except his bald head seemed middle-aged. Instead of walking normally, he seemed to jump a little with each step. His broad shoulders and robust build suggested a bull charging full speed ahead, without regard for anything blocking his way. But when Bernard extended his hand in greeting, all the animal-like intensity vanished. His face lit up in a magnetic, infectious, and unforgettable smile.

"Look at this," he began, pointing to his sparkling new dining rooms and garden. "We just finished the renovation."

His impassioned monologue continued without pause for more than ten minutes. As his smile became broader and broader, Bernard explained how he had come to Saulieu more than a decade before. In this country that prides itself as the undisputed maker and shaper of global tastes, he had vowed to produce a gastronomic paradise. He had just poured 15 million francs, almost $3 million, into building his new dining rooms and garden.

"Three million dollars?" I interrupted.

"Yes," he said. "All the great chefs are doing the same. The client asks for it and Michelin asks for it."

"Michelin?" I asked.

"Yes," he answered, "the Michelin Guide."

Bernard's obsession surprised me. I had heard about the Michelin Guide. But I didn't know that chefs were ready to risk millions of dollars to impress the Michelin critics and obtain a better rating.

On my return to Paris, I telephoned a business editor in London and described my meeting. Would there be a story in this chef's gigantic investment in search of gastronomic fame and fortune? Yes, the editor said. A short article appeared the next week. I sent it to Bernard and moved on to other subjects.

But in the following months, Bernard kept reappearing in my mind. French newspapers were full of pessimistic stories about the collapse of a dream for a united Europe, an economic crisis costing thousands of jobs each week, and farmers taking their frustrations out by burning Uncle Sam in effigy. Jean-Paul Sartre, the philosopher who invented the idea of existentialism, would have identified the symptoms of "malaise." Judging by opinion polls, a country that long prided itself on being a light to the world worried whether it would be able to stand up to the cruel economic and political competition ahead in the post–Cold War world.

In one endeavor, however, France continued to reign supreme: gastronomy and the good life. The Germans had bested the French in 1940, but the German expression for enjoying life remains to live "like God in France." France is still the arbiter of good taste. The French do not just eat well; they take the activity of pleasurable nourishment and transform it into a high cultural event. Of all the chefs in France, Bernard seemed the most colorful. And of all the regions in France, Burgundy seemed the most beautiful. Bernard and Burgundy told the story of France's special talent for joie de vivre and, just as important, illustrated a universal quest for perfection.

*Burgundy Stars* could not have been written without Bernard Loiseau's full cooperation. He did not ask to edit or change any of the narrative, even when it described many of his less admirable characteristics, his impulsiveness, impetuosity, and egotism. He never hid his worries and anxieties. He even was open about his disastrous first marriage. So this is not a fairy-tale account of haute cuisine. All the twists and turns of Bernard's quest for culinary perfection are presented, unvarnished. My goal is to expose the grit, sweat, and emotion behind the glamour of gastronomic excellence.

For Bernard and his fellow Frenchmen, the business of providing pleasure is more than a business. It is an emotion that lies somewhere between deep love and religious zeal. Only such faith permitted these practitioners to withstand France's steady industrialization and urbanization. It was a lesson that Bernard never tired of impressing on his staff, whom he badgered, exhorted, and teased to work harder and do better.

Money never seemed a major motivation. From the owner-chef to the nonpaid apprentice to the simple peasant cheese maker, everyone involved in Bernard Loiseau's restaurant often repeated the same phrases: "We could earn much more working in an office." "We don't count the hours we put in." "For the best result, you cannot count the hours."

As France urbanizes and develops, some worry that it will lose its special French flavor. To obtain regular, year-round deliveries, Bernard used frog legs that came from Greece and tomatoes from Spain; even his famous Burgundy mustard was made from imported Canadian mustard seeds. And yet, I came away from my year in rural France with renewed optimism. Bernard managed to take time-honored traditions and adapt them to new times. Many of the artisans I met were doing the same. There was the vegetable producer who turned out leeks and turnips while using computers and mobile phones to run his farm. Or the young enthusiastic vintner who vowed to improve his family's ancestral vineyards by avoiding fertilizer.

The miracle of France is how it has been able to thrive and modernize while withstanding global homogenization. Few other countries combine the ease of modern American-style technology with the comfort of traditional Europe. It is possible to shop in a *hypermarché,* bigger than any American supermarket, and find the finest gastronomic delicacies just a few rows away from tires and electrical supplies. It's also possible to wake up and walk across the street into the neighborhood boulangerie to buy fresh, hot croissants. Convenient frozen food is making inroads, but frozen *pithiviers de poisson* or *mousseline de saumon* has nothing to do with TV dinners.

In many ways, the story that follows is not about cuisine. It is about a country trying to maintain and improve upon its traditions. Above all, it is about an individual pursuing perfection. For a little while, forget high cholesterol and the stress of urban living. Dip in and enjoy the special French joie de vivre. Remember what Bernard insisted I do.

Eat and enjoy!

*At table*

# CHAPTER 1

★ ★ ★

# *Shooting for Stars*

*Eric Rousseau, senior waiter and cheese hunter*

BERNARD LOISEAU, Bernard "the Bird," is flying mad.

In his immaculate white chef's tunic and apron, he stands in front of his cramped nest of a kitchen. Behind, a staff of twenty-five *chefs de partie, sous chefs, commis,* and *apprentis* rush about, the meat team to his left, the fish side to his right, and the pastry chef squeezed into a corner. Savory smells mingle in the air. Copper pans and porcelain plates ring in harmony.

A dish of scallops arrives for final inspection. It forms a sumptuous symphony of colors, plump golden nuggets of fresh shellfish swimming in a rich black sea of truffles. But Bernard, beak quivering and brown eyes flickering, spots a speck of sauce on the side of the plate. Agitated, he shoots his arms up and down in the air like flapping wings.

"*Attention, attention!*" Bernard remonstrates. "Look at this."

The frazzled sous chef takes back the plate and searches for something wrong. Carefully, as if holding a baby, he wipes the edge of the dish. He checks that the scallops are golden, glazed two minutes and not a second more. He places his hands on the dish to gauge the temperature and pokes his finger in a bit of sauce. Then he returns it for Bernard's approval.

The dish now looks perfect, to everyone except Bernard. Another speck of misplaced sauce is still bothering him.

"My poor friend," Bernard says, with a giant sigh, his flapping wings reaching takeoff speed. "This work is not worth three stars."

Three stars!

The conversation is closed. Finished. *Terminé.* Every member of the harried kitchen staff understands. Bernard Loiseau is obsessed with stars. Bernard, mind you, is not a superstitious creature. For him, the stars that count are not up in the sky. They are in the ultimate gastronomic bible, the Michelin Red Guide.

It was September 1990. A decade earlier, Bernard had bought the restaurant-hotel La Côte d'Or in the small Burgundy farm town of Saulieu, 150 miles southeast of Paris. He arrived as a skinny, insecure, but energetic and gregarious youngster. Now, a few months shy of forty, he had lost half of his hair and his frame had filled out. But he was as quick as ever to flash a brilliant smile, to take childlike delight in the smallest pleasures, and to display an exacting enthusiasm for perfection. "I live at a hundred and fifty miles an hour," he often said. One moment he launched into a tirade against his employees. The next he broke out into a giant smile and heaped generous praise on them.

Bernard liked to compare himself in the kitchen to a maestro, leading a team of talented artists to produce beautiful music. His role better resembled a general in wartime. Historians prefer this analogy. When kitchens first were organized in princely homes, chefs drew from the military example, and to this day, the kitchen staff is called a brigade.

During meals, General Bernard stood at the front of the kitchen and barked out commands. The assistant chefs responded with a chorus of "*OUIIiiiii, Chef*" that would satisfy even the most hardened marine officer. A grunt who disobeyed faced martial punishment. Bernard was a sweet and generous man who genuinely loved his staff. But in the heat of a hectic Saturday evening dinner, Bernard told an errant chef successively that he was a *nul, con,* or even a *pauvre con*—a zero, an idiot, and, ultimately, a stupid fucking idiot. Instead of being able to enjoy his afternoon siesta, the *pauvre con* stayed in the kitchen and cleaned up.

Like most great chefs, Bernard almost never grilled meat, broiled fish, or put anything in the oven. He directed the show. He was the creator, dreaming up the recipes and making sure the final result tasted sublime. In most French kitchens, the key figure is the number-two man, called the *chef de cuisine.* This is the person who runs the kitchen, who orders supplies, who perfects the menu, and who directs all the preparation. As owner-chef, Bernard had many other things besides cooking to worry about, obtaining loans from the banks, running the hotel, and dealing with the press. These days, star chefs are often away from the restaurants on promotional tours. A good chef de cuisine makes sure no one notices the absence.

At La Côte d'Or, the chef de cuisine was Patrick Bertron, a reserved, taciturn figure. Where Bernard screamed, Patrick mumbled. Where Bernard had the innate charisma of a general, Patrick had the talent of the perfect staff sergeant. Bernard outlined the big picture. Patrick executed. Patrick had started at La Côte d'Or a decade before. Now Bernard said that Patrick "could cook Loiseau better than Loiseau himself." But of course, managing a restaurant takes more than mere cooking talent.

By most measurements, Bernard and Patrick had already succeeded in turning his La Côte d'Or restaurant into a culinary paradise. Michelin's main competitor, Gault-Millau, had awarded La Côte d'Or 19.5 points out of a possible 20, its highest rating. Regular clients included President François Mitterrand, actor Alain Delon, and the Baron de Rothschild. Critics raved about his inventive, light cooking featuring bright vegetable sauces. They compared a Bernard Loiseau creation to the beauty of the surrounding Burgundy landscape, its famous vineyards ablaze in the ruby red of the autumn harvest and its gentle hills alive with rich velvet-green carpets of grass punctuated by large stretches of golden sunflowers.

Only one thing still was missing: Michelin's highest ranking and the ultimate symbol of culinary excellence, three stars.

Bernard's restaurant, La Côte d'Or, had two Michelin stars. To thrive, Bernard was convinced, he needed to win the precious third. Michelin's standards are so rigorous that of the nearly four thousand restaurants mentioned in the French guide's previous edition, only nineteen merited the supreme accolade—three-star "cooking worth a special journey." In all the rest of Europe, only twelve restaurants had won three. One star is considered "a good place to stop." Two stars merit "a detour." Three stars are "worth a special journey" across the country, from Paris to Lyons or the Côte d'Azur to the Pyrenees, to pay at least $100 a person, and often $200 or more, for a superb meal.

Despite Bernard's talent, his drive, and his energy, customers remained scarce. This September lunchtime, even though the sun still warmed the golden countryside, he would serve just a handful of diners. Come winter, Bernard knew La Côte d'Or would be empty. The only way he could be sure that Parisians—not to mention Americans, Japanese, and Germans—would go out of their way to visit him was to receive Michelin's decree that he was "worth a special journey."

"I often watched the snow falling by the window, and wondered 'Why aren't people coming here?'" he said. "There were even people who walked up to the front door, opened their Michelin Guides, saw there were not enough stars—and left."

Bernard's Burgundy colleague Marc Meneau had already won his third Michelin star at L'Espérance, in Saint-Père-sous-Vézelay. The year afterward, Meneau's restaurant sales jumped by 30 percent. L'Espérance now earned twice as much as Bernard's La Côte d'Or.

"The Japanese, the Americans, all the foreigners, they only come if you have a third star," Bernard told visitors. "For them, France means the Eiffel Tower, Cartier, and three Michelin stars."

Every March, France holds its breath when the new guide is published. At most, one or two new restaurants are awarded the precious third star. Often, none are. The rare three-star winner suddenly finds himself on the cover of glossy magazines and a regular guest on the television shows where the French celebrate the art of cooking by talking about it in mouthwatering detail. Reservations pour in from as far away as Tokyo and Los Angeles. Proposals arrive to write cookbooks and to make lucrative television appearances, along with contracts to market everything from table linens and bathrobes to jams and frozen food.

A national treasure, the three-star winner receives as many medals and decorations as General de Gaulle did during World War II. Three-star seigniors such as Paul Bocuse, Pierre Troisgros, and Michel Guérard mean as much to the French as basketball stars Shaquille O'Neal, Patrick Ewing, and Charles Barkley do to Americans. These members of the culinary Hall of Fame are celebrities who earn their stardom by scoring slam dunks with dishes such as Paul Bocuse's *loup en croûte farci d'une mousse de homard,* sea bass stuffed with lobster mousse and covered with puff pastry.

Bernard had long chased the demanding Michelin standard. At the age of sixteen he dropped out of school and apprenticed at the Troisgros restaurant, in Roanne, a manufacturing city in central France. Troisgros was a two-star Michelin operation run by the Troisgros brothers, Pierre and Jean. On March 1, 1968, Bernard began peeling potatoes and cutting carrots. Two weeks later, the new Michelin Guide was issued. Troisgros had won its third star. The entire restaurant celebrated with champagne. From that moment, the apprentice was addicted.

"I was too young and too dumb to know what it was all about," he later recalled. "But I said to myself, *Wow!* Celebrities suddenly were coming to eat and there was a click in my head. I said, *Someday I'm going to get three stars.*"

To aspire to three Michelin stars takes a special character: creative, durable, and, *mais oui,* a bit crazy. Chefs called the Michelin passion a "sacred fire." For years, Bernard lived on a financial and emotional razor's edge. No girlie pinups adorned his bachelor's bedroom in Saulieu on La Côte d'Or's second floor. Instead, he hung a picture of the two Troisgros brothers, smiling at a giant cow placed between them. Before descending into the kitchen each morning, he stood before the picture.

"I will get my third star," he repeated to himself.

Burgundy was an appropriate setting for Bernard's struggle for gastronomic perfection. The region is best described as France's stomach. Both geographically and psychologically, Burgundy bridges the hardworking, industrial north and the earthy south. It is a land of festivals and folk traditions, joviality and hearty living.

In the popular image, residents of the rich, robust region tend to have large, round, red faces—and big, burly appetites. The cuisine is *plantureuse,* a lusty word meaning ripe, hearty, abundant. Burgundy is a land famous for snails and mustard, wild pigeon and quail, fine Charolais beef, plump Bresse chickens, and pungent Epoisses cheese. When villages gather to celebrate holidays at giant banquets called *potées,* they belt out drinking songs such as "*Joyeux Enfants de la Bourgogne,*" "*Chevaliers de la Table Ronde,*" and, above all, "*Je suis fier d'être Bourguignon*" (I Am Proud to Be a Burgundian).

The pleasurable excesses are balanced by a spiritual disposition. During the Middle Ages, Burgundy flourished as a center of Christianity. A Benedictine monastery founded in 910 in Cluny, near Mâcon, developed into one of the medieval world's religious and intellectual capitals. By the beginning of the twelfth century, the Benedictines controlled more than sixteen hundred monasteries and ten thousand monks throughout Europe. It took forty years to complete the Cluny headquarters; the world's greatest artists assembled to paint the walls with scenes from the lives of the saints, all in glowing shades of deep red and blue. The Romanesque basilica was the largest in Christendom until St. Peter's in Rome was completed five centuries later. Other remarkable churches rose in Vézelay, Tournus, and Paray-le-Monial. As they built, Burgundy architects invented rib vaulting and the flying buttress, which paved the way for soaring Gothic cathedrals.

Later, Burgundy's dukes held sway over large tracts of Western Europe. Under Philip the Good in the fifteenth century, the Burgundian court was an independent dukedom, with domains stretching from the Low Countries to the borders of Provence, incorporating Alsace, Lorraine, Luxembourg, Picardy, Flanders, Brabant, and Holland. The capital, Dijon, became a global leader in the arts. An appetite for luxury and splendor spread down from the court to the merchants and wealthy lawyers of the towns. Talented craftsmen from the Low Countries introduced architectural flourishes such as the bright roofs of colored tiles in geometric patterns found on the famous Hôtel-Dieu in Beaune.

The greatest luxuries of this fertile land were food and wine. In Dijon, Duke Philip himself added a stupendous kitchen to his palace, the better to serve his guests. It consisted of four gigantic stone fireplaces. The duke issued edicts to safeguard the quality of the region's wines and sent gifts of the bounty to popes and kings. He also is considered responsible for the first written "menu," when, for a banquet held in 1457, he displayed a placard listing the dishes to be served. Gingerbread and mustard, two of the region's great gastronomic specialties, became associated at this time with Burgundy. The gingerbread came from Flanders, and the mustard, brought by the Romans, was appreciated by

Duke Philip, who would give away barrels of the condiment to guests. "Some built a hearth in their kitchen," commented the gastronome Curnonsky. "The dukes of Burgundy made a kitchen from their hearth."

This formidable Burgundian empire did not last long. By the end of the sixteenth century, the Bourbons had won back from Philip's successors almost all the duchy's territories for the House of France. In 1477, Louis XI annexed Burgundy, and German and Swiss troops occupied the capital, Dijon. Louis informed his new subjects that they were "of the crown and kingdom," and from that point, Burgundy was relegated to the sidelines of history. Today Dijon is a provincial backwater, with fewer than two hundred thousand inhabitants. Unlike romanticized, prettified Provence or suave, sophisticated Paris, Burgundy is a country of green rolling hills, slow, meandering canals, sparkling lakes, virgin forests, and fabled vines. Farmhouses, their stone giving off a soft golden glow, mingle with magnificent Romanesque churches and glittering Renaissance châteaux topped with colorful checkerboard roofs.

As hearty and sensuous as Burgundians are with both food and life, they also are modest, sensitive, and reflective. Many of the boisterous drinking songs, so linked with the region in the popular imagination, were created for turn-of-the-century Paris cabarets. Despite their medieval costumes, the famous Chevaliers du Tastevin actually date only from 1935. They started their chapters in the Clos Vougeot as a way of promoting Burgundy wine and attracting tourists. Compared with the rest of the country, Burgundy boasts a higher proportion of farmers, winegrowers, craftsmen, traders, and family-run enterprises. Life's rhythms are rooted in the soil, seasons, and cycles of nature. Here one hears the low moan of every cow, the bleat of every sheep, the crow of every rooster. Rustic and rural, Burgundy represents traditional France, what the French themselves call *la France profonde*—deep France.

Burgundy always has been solid Michelin three-star country. Under famed chef Alexandre Dumaine, La Côte d'Or possessed the magical three stars in the 1950s and 1960s. By the time young Bernard arrived, in 1975, the restaurant had suffered long years of neglect. The kitchen that once prided itself on using only the freshest ingredients was reduced to serving canned lobster bisque. A few chopped onions, a little cognac, and a spoonful of cream were mixed in to add flavor. Imagine: haute cuisine à la Campbell's Soup!

A new generation of chefs now was working hard to revive Burgundy's gastronomic reputation. Within sight of the famed vineyards in the village of Chagny, Jacques Lameloise produced impeccable, traditional three-star cuisine at his family-run Lameloise restaurant, a solid bourgeois establishment. In a park and stream with the famous Romanesque basilica of Vézelay in the background, Marc Meneau was awarded three stars for his L'Espérance. A little farther to the north, in Joigny, the Lorain father-and-son team, Michel and Jean-Michel, gained three stars by constructing a mini-Versailles palace called A La Côte Saint-Jacques. Bernard was motivated by these competitors. While he struggled, his rivals profited from the 1980s luxury boom. Meneau built a spectacular hacienda in the Caribbean, where he escaped from the cold Burgundy winters.

Bernard owned no property except La Côte d'Or. He lived right above the dining room, in one small room. The bathroom and shower were down at the end of the hallway. To make ends meet, Bernard kept his restaurant open seven days a week, every day of the year. Meneau and others closed their establishment for several weeks a year.

Unlike these successful chefs, Bernard did not inherit his restaurant from his parents or attend an expensive cooking or hotel management school. When he was appointed chef at La Côte d'Or at the tender age of twenty-four, he was just an employee at a celebrated Hall of Fame establishment, a bit faded at the edges but still a veritable shrine.

Dumaine's ghost hovered over Bernard, both a beacon and a curse. A painting of the old master stared down from the center of the main dining room. Pictures, newspaper clippings, and menus of his most renowned meals decorated the walls. Never before in French gastronomic history had a restaurant fallen from three Michelin stars to none and recovered. Restoring a shrine to its lost glory was considered an impossible task. The comparisons with the bygone days were too severe, the present never good enough when set against the golden memories.

Bernard flailed and flapped. He replaced the canned lobster bisque with the real thing and discovered to his amazement that some clients preferred the packaged industrial stuff. Worse, the veterans in the kitchen and dining room refused to accept him. Dumaine's old receptionist, Madame Rancin, dressed in peasant garb and wore a dirty red wig. She sat down next to diners and asked them, "What do you think of the young guy?"

Without waiting for an answer, she snapped her hands in a guillotine-sharp action across her throat.

"Not much," she replied.

"I used to work my ass off all day long and then go up to my room to cry for most of the night," Bernard recalled. "I was so sad and frustrated." One day, he had too much. "I came down in the morning and called the entire staff together. 'Take a good look at my face,' I told them, 'because it's here to stay, so you'd better get used to it. Now either do that or get out.'"

Within a few months, the rookie had fired Madame Rancin and the rest of Dumaine's veterans.

Bernard plotted and planned how to regain La Côte d'Ors past fame. Year after year, he redecorated his hotel, added chefs, and tested his gastronomic creations on any intrepid visitors. "We are the best, the *best!*" the cheerleader in him would chant to his young and energetic staff. La Côte d'Or won its first star in 1977 and its second in 1981.

Since then, nothing. Bernard became more and more desperate to win the third star.

This was the crucial year. Nearly forty, Bernard was at the peak of his powers. His cooking style had matured. His family life was stable. At the cost of three million dollars, he planned to rebuild his kitchen and construct new dining rooms. Many of his staff had been with him for more than five years, and the team was poised. But Bernard worried that if Michelin passed him by, he would lose his momentum and his best workers would begin to move on. Worse, without three stars, he risked being unable to pay back his mounting debts.

Another serving of scallops in truffle sauce is placed before him. This time, no errant specks of sauce are visible on the plate. Bernard breaks the gentle, soothing melody of the hissing ovens and frying pan, banging a loud bell, not once, but three times in short succession, *whack, whack,* and *whack!!!* A tuxedoed waiter, out of breath, comes running. Bernard pushes the serving of *coquilles Saint Jacques à la crème de truffes* into his waiting hands. The transaction takes only a second, but Bernard thinks it is a second too long.

"Get going," he yells. "One more moment and it won't be three stars."

★ ★ ★

Below, in the wine cellar, Lyonel Leconte wipes dust off vintage bottles of wine, ensuring that nothing mars their presentation. At this particular moment, Lyonel has some mundane worries: his teeth, which give off a deep violet glow, the result of wine chiseling away at the gums. Later in the afternoon, he plans to see a dentist. The week before, the dentist filled six cavities. Lyonel fears a couple more are on their way. Novocain and fillings make it difficult to absorb the taste of delicately fermented grapes. For a sommelier, bad teeth are like tennis elbow, a disabling injury that comes with the passion.

Lyonel feared being put out of action just now, before the start of a big tasting season. In the upcoming year, he was responsible for filling a new, larger wine cellar. From a present stock of 433 labels and 12,000 bottles, he planned to expand the list to 660 wines and 17,000 or 18,000 bottles. That meant frequent tasting trips to vineyards. Burgundy grands crus—the elite first growths—must be stored for at least five years before being opened. Ask any Wall Street financier—this is a bad business proposition. Lyonel was prepared to spend nearly half a million dollars stocking his new cave. If he made many mistakes, he could ruin Bernard's Michelin dream.

Ever since monks planted vineyards along the golden stretch of the Saône River between Dijon and Beaune, the image of Burgundy has been tied to its world-renowned wines: Gevrey-Chambertin, Meursault, Nuits-St.-Georges, and, above all, the world's most expensive and celebrated vintage, Romanée-Conti. Bernard's restaurant was named La Côte d'Or, the Gold Coast, in reverence for the land where these famous vintages are produced.

Burgundy growers became greedy in the heady 1980s. The price of even the middling grands crus skyrocketed to more than forty dollars a bottle wholesale. Growers began adding more and more sugar to speed fermentation, letting their vines "piss" ever-greater quantities of juice. Lyonel often compared the nouveaux riches growers to Arab oil sheiks. They became wealthy because they owned valuable land, not because they possessed real talent as vintners. In his opinion, only 5 percent of premier cru Burgundy warranted the high-quality label.

Until recently, almost all top Burgundies were bottled by merchants, who bought grapes, mixed them, and produced a consistent, if average, wine. Now small farmers were bottling their own wine. Some bottles were good, some bad, but the good were much better than the best merchant bottles. This made life more complicated for the sommelier, who needed to visit vineyards and find the best young growers. Beyond the known names, many an excellent find could be discovered up in the hills around Beaune, Hautes-Côtes de Nuits, and Hautes-Côtes de Beaune, attractive, affordable bottles that would impress the most demanding of diners while sparing even the richest restaurant from bankruptcy.

Lyonel, only twenty-six years old, had a sharp, chiseled face set off by a nose that went far down into a wineglass. He was born in the village of Germolles, between Gilly and Rully, two well-known Burgundy towns on the Côte Châlonnaise. His father ran a small company that built warehouses for winegrowers and served as a chevalier of the local wine-tasting society. One of the first photos in his album is of a family meal. At the center of the table stands a bottle of Mercurey, 1959. Two-year-old Lyonel sits in his proud father's lap.

His mother worked at the reception of a simple restaurant called Auberge de Camp Romain, a place that served hearty *coq au vin* and *boeuf bourguignon.* When he was sixteen, Lyonel got his start working summers as a waiter. He attended the *lycée viticole,* literally a wine high school, in Mâcon. There he studied chemistry and other sciences in addition to viticulture.

Unlike Bernard and most of the other employees at La Côte d'Or, who had never finished high school, Lyonel was a graduate of the University of Bordeaux, where he had majored in marketing and commerce. Lyonel didn't plan to become a sommelier, and certainly not a sommelier in Burgundy. He hoped to set up a catering company with his father, who would be responsible for the food while Lyonel would be responsible for the wine. But in 1987 his father was killed in a car accident, and his dream of founding a family business collapsed.

Lyonel took an internship at a two-star Michelin restaurant, La Bonne Etape, in Château Arnoux, in Provence. The staff sommelier conceived an immediate hatred for this young, ambitious student. He put him to work washing dishes. After two weeks, Lyonel quit. He was saved when a former professor helped him find a summer job at La Côte d'Or. When he arrived in Saulieu, on July 1, 1987, a petite blond receptionist named Christine greeted him at the front door. Two weeks later, the restaurant's chief sommelier left in a huff. By the time the summer was over, Christine was his fiancée and Bernard had asked him to stay on. There was only one condition: he must go to England and improve his English. Lyonel left for three months at Le Gavroche, in London. He hated every moment of the experience. "I learned more about Danish and Swedish women than about wine," he joked.

On his return to Saulieu, Christine told him she was pregnant. They married and now had two children, a two-year-old daughter, Charlotte, and a newborn named Louise. Christine quit her job at La Côte d'Or to take care of them. Like the waiters, Lyonel was paid on a tips basis. Few diners meant less in his pockets. Not surprisingly, he worried about the high price of wines frightening away customers.

He was thin and angular, a studious, ambitious, and tense young man—some would say too studious, too ambitious, and too tense. He kept a meticulous archive of his life in his bathroom, the only place in his small apartment with enough free space to contain the bookshelves. His photo albums and press clippings started at birth and followed him through every stage of his life. They showed hours of work put in, grooming his image and attempting to promote himself. He stored volumes and volumes about wine in his living room. Like many other sommeliers, Lyonel sometimes seemed to forget that drinking wine should be above all a pleasure, not part of a university doctoral course in chemistry.

"Lyonel is a damned good taster, the best," Bernard boasted to guests. In private, though, he added, "Lyonel is not a barrel of laughs."

"Lyonel has a one-track mind, wine, wine, and wine," his colleagues complained. "He is obsessed. A war could be going on outside, but the most important thing to Lyonel would remain wine."

"I am a monk about wine," Lyonel admitted.

Bringing La Côte d'Or's wine cellar up to three-star quality would tax the most experienced sommelier. Lyonel worried that he was too young for the task. Michelin prefers maturity, which it associates with stability and regularity. Throughout France's restaurant business, age is respected. Most chefs worked at least a decade, moving slowly up the formal ladder in the brigade, from commis to chef de partie to sous chef and finally chef. Lyonel's clothing was designed to make him appear more mature. In his sommelier's black tuxedo jacket and apron, with his slicked-back hair and a brooch of grapes pinned on his chest, Lyonel looked ten years older than his actual age.

Lyonel's personal goal this year was to win the title Best Young Sommelier in France. The year before, he had been named Burgundy's Best Young Sommelier. But he finished only fifth in the national contest, a debacle he dubbed his Waterloo.

The Best Young Sommelier competition's age limit was twenty-six. That meant this year was the last in which Lyonel was eligible to compete. The contest would take place the following October in the champagne capital of Reims. Lyonel would have to complete a written test on wine theory. He would have to know the details of each grape variety, the pinot noir, the chardonnay, the gamay, the cabernet, and all the others. He would be presented with a menu and asked to suggest a wine for each course. He even would have to answer detailed questions about champagne, liqueurs, and such culinary accompaniments as cigars and mineral water, which are regulated in France. Lyonel was expected to know from what source each is extracted and what ministerial decree authorized them.

At the competition, he would stand before a crowd of approximately five hundred connoisseurs. About fifty full glasses would be placed before him. Slowly, he would have to take each by its stem, swirl the wine beneath his nose, swish it down his waiting mouth, and identify the vintage.

Lyonel picks up a bottle, a red 1987 Volnay, places it in a straw basket for presentation, and brings it from the cellar to the dining room. Ceremoniously, he presents the bottle to a table of four diners. They nod in recognition. In two swift movements, Lyonel cuts away the foil and pulls out the cork. He pours a little wine into a glass, his fingers curled delicately around the stem, raises it to his nose, and takes a whiff. The wine smells fresh and clear, full of fruit. He takes a taste. Perfect. Only now does he offer a taste to the head of the table. The customer approves. Lyonel then serves the rest of the table. When everyone sips the wine and smiles in pleasure, Lyonel smiles back, an impish grin revealing his ruby-red gums.

He has to leave or he will miss his dentist's appointment. So he leaves his assistant, Emmanuel, to pour refills. Bad teeth aside, Lyonel savored the prospect of becoming the best young sommelier in the best wine-producing country in the world.

"It's our Olympics," Lyonel told Emmanuel, "our three stars."

★ ★ ★

Eric Rousseau stands at the front of the kitchen, a spoon in his hand, looking at two little bowls of yogurt, one made of cow's milk, the other of goat's milk.

His black and white waiter's tuxedo uniform highlights movie-star good looks. A BL logo for "Bernard Loiseau" is sewn on his chest.

Eric tastes the cow's milk yogurt. Ordinary, he judges.

Then he scoops up a small spoonful of fresh, creamy white goat's milk yogurt, swirling it like a glass of wine, inhaling its fresh odor and examining its texture. Slowly, luxuriously, he tastes.

Spectacular, he pronounces.

Showing little emotion, he stops his boss, maître d'hôtel Hubert Couilloud, and asks him to taste it.

"Not bad," Hubert says. From Hubert, an understated and measured man, this judgment represents a compliment. On La Côte d'Or's menu, Eric would soon replace the cow's milk yogurt with goat's milk yogurt.

In the quest for the magical third Michelin star, Bernard gave each employee at La Côte d'Or responsibility for a particular task. Eric was the restaurant's chief cheese taster.

The assignment was no joke. In her book *The Food Lover's Guide to France,* the American food critic Patricia Wells had lambasted La Côte d'Or's cheese platter. "The cheese tray was a bit embarrassing," Wells wrote, "an Epoisses that wasn't well aged, but chalky in the center; a local fresh goat cheese that was simply insipid; and a Vacherin so bland it tasted as though it could have been made of skim milk."

Eric thought Patricia Wells exaggerated. He said she was afflicted with the American disease: an inability to relax and enjoy herself. "Her articles about food are like academic treatises," he said.

Bernard didn't care. "An embarrassing cheese tray!" he shouted. "This cannot last. We must have the *best* cheese tray in France."

Bernard ordered Eric to find the best Burgundy cheeses. I do not want to know how much it costs or what happens to your cholesterol level, he said. Just find the best cheeses. During the next few months, Eric planned to spend much of his time on the road visiting the region's peasant farmers, sampling hundreds of cheeses.

Yogurt tasting was the easy part of the assignment. Yogurt was served only for breakfast at la Côte d'Or, and few Frenchmen eat a serious breakfast. They start the day with a cup of coffee and a croissant, nothing more.

Cheese was different. Bernard loved cheese and considered no meal complete without it. Cheese was served at lunch and dinner as a full course unto itself, after the main dish and before the dessert. The tremendous variety of French cheeses testifies to the natural bounty of the countryside. Charles de Gaulle cited the prodigious number of hard, soft, and medium rounds produced in France—more than four hundred by his reckoning—as proof of the difficulty in ruling such a fractious, individualistic people. After Germany crushed France in World War II, Winston Churchill proclaimed that any country that produced so much cheese could never perish.

Each region has its own specialty, some pungent, some soft, all delicious. The secret is rooted in the land. Austere Auvergne produces sharp and tangy blue cheese. The clean Alpine air favors mild, hard varieties such as Tomme. Bountiful Burgundy concentrates on rich, pungent concoctions, the creamy Chaource, the delicate Cîteaux, and, above all, the rich-smelling Epoisses, which is aged in the fiery local alcohol called marc. Burgundy also makes several goat cheeses of various shapes and sizes. One is nicknamed *bouton de culotte,* trouser button, for its size, little more than a mouthful. Cheese is essential in preparing the special Burgundy popover, a *choux* pastry specialty called *gougère,* whose delicate, unassertive flavor makes a wonderful accompaniment to a full-bodied Burgundy wine. Eric's cheese-tasting excursions would take place on his days off work as a waiter.

In many countries, serving food is treated as a menial job suitable only for students and women. In France, it is viewed as a skilled profession, particularly at an aspiring first-class Michelin restaurant. La Côte d'Or waiters dressed in military fashion, wearing uniforms to signify their rank. Apprentices donned white tuxedos. Full-tenured waiters wore black and white tuxedos. The apprentices brought food from the kitchen into the dining room. They did not serve any dishes. That was the exclusive job of the waiters, who glided up to the table and placed the work of art before the diner. Most of them had completed internships in England so that they could speak passable English. They were sophisticated and suave—and proud of their calling.

Hubert, the maître d'hôtel, directed the action, standing at the head of the dining room. From this perch, he could supervise the entire restaurant. His uniform of gray striped pants and a tailcoat confirmed his preeminent position. Hubert's job was to make sure no hitch disturbed the meal. If he spotted the least error, the least problem, he intervened. The key was to be present when needed, but never to be imposing or obsequious. Service at La Côte d'Or was like theater. Hubert's waiters were actors who communicated through eye contact and head signals, in total silence. They always were ready with an unforced smile and easy manner to allow the audience of diners to relax.

Eric was La Côte d'Or's senior waiter, one of Bernard's first hires and one of the few members of the La Côte d'Or team to come from the region. He had been born in Brazey-en-Morvan, a hamlet just outside of Saulieu. Eric's mother ran a small village grocery store, and his father was a construction worker. As a child, he wouldn't go near La Côte d'Or, then run by the august Dumaine. His parents told him the restaurant was for the rich.

When Eric first walked into La Côte d'Or after graduating from the hotel school in nearby Semur-en-Auxois, he was afraid. Bernard succeeded in putting him at ease. In French, there are two forms of *you,* the formal *vous* and the informal *tu.* Eric always used *vous* with his professors, and he expected to do the same with Bernard, his boss. But after two meetings, Bernard insisted on *tu.*

The thirty-three-year-old Eric considered himself a veteran and was proud of his work. But he was worried. He and his wife, Claude, had two young children. They were pouring all their savings into building a new house in Saulieu. Until he succeeded on his crucial cheese mission and repaired the damage from Patricia Well's damning review, Bernard would make his life miserable.

"I love and hate Bernard," Eric said with marked affection. "You can never forget that he is emotional about everything. He gives you responsibility, then never lets up until you do your work perfectly."

★ ★ ★

Dominique Loiseau hovers in the reception room, feeling out of place. In La Côte d'Or's male world, she is the only visible woman.

Ever since cooks began cooking professionally in France, and especially since the invention of the restaurant, in the eighteenth century, men have dominated the trade. Women were even shut out of cookbook writing. The earliest French recipe collections date from around 1300, but it was not until 1829 that a woman published a cookbook. Fewer women still write cookbooks in France than in Germany or Italy. In French professional high schools for chefs and restaurant personnel, fewer than a fifth of the students are women. Perhaps the most telling statistic of all is that of the 488 chefs to win a Michelin star in 1990, only twelve were women.

In the opinion of Bernard and most other French chefs, women should stay out of the kitchen. They say the work is too hot and hard for them. Bernard insisted that directing a great restaurant's brigade of two dozen or more chefs takes an imposing physical presence. "You have to give a *coup de pied,* a kick in the ass," Bernard liked to say, "and women just don't have that authority."

Fine French restaurants also frown on the idea of waitresses. Serving food is considered a man's job, and no woman except for Dominique worked in La Côte d'Or's dining room. Serious French gastronomes regard miniskirts as distracting. They think women should stay behind the reception desk and far away from handling food.

A longtime exception to this general rule were the so-called mothers working in small, informal family restaurants, mostly in France's second city, Lyons. These were located on obscure backstreets, with a limited amount of room in both the kitchen and the dining room, little staff, little decor, and little pretension. For most French, the *mères lyonnaises* evoke images of pots simmering on the stove, with old-fashioned specialties such as *pot-au-feu, blanquette de veau,* and *boeuf mode.* Sometimes the husband helped out by serving; other times, the tough, truculent mothers did everything themselves. Unfortunately, these generous purveyors of rich, traditional cooking slowly have died off. The most famous of the mothers, Mère Brazier, stirred her last stew in 1977. No one has replaced her.

A few feminist pioneers have since broken into the exclusive world of haute cuisine. In the late 1970s, a slight twenty-year-old *demoiselle* with girlish bangs named Dominique Versini—alias Olympe for her Olympian talents—opened a luxury restaurant near Montparnasse, in Paris. With her cheerful inventiveness, she veered away from academic, rule-bound male cooking to pioneer an instinctive feminine haute cuisine. She was hailed as the discovery of the year and even won two Michelin stars. But she never won three stars, and the chauvinists fought back with fury.

They said that her cooking was flighty—on one day, off another—and that her combinations were too exotic. Italian-inspired ravioli, no matter how ethereal, lacked the punch of true three-star cooking.

An intrepid American woman named Nathalie once tried to break the unwritten rules of haute cuisine. She took an apprenticeship in the kitchen at La Côte d'Or. A few days after starting, she dared offer her fellow chefs some advice about improving kitchen procedures. Instead of saying thank you, her colleagues responded with crude jokes about her physical appearance. The lewd comments continued until Nathalie burst into tears. She quit soon afterward and went back home.

Dominique was tougher. She didn't work in the kitchen, and as Bernard's wife she enjoyed the authority of *la patronne*. She also relied on a subtle brand of sex appeal. At the age of thirty-eight, Dominique was full of the French female's *je ne sais quoi* allure and possessed formidable willpower. Her iron self-discipline permitted her to keep a strict diet, even while surrounded by the splendors of haute cuisine. She often had only a cup of coffee for lunch. Today, she was wearing one of her favorite outfits: a bright red suit that clung to her and showed up her thin figure. Dominique went nowhere without her lipstick and perfume. Not a single wisp of her straight brown hair, cut short and strict, ever seemed out of place.

Her appearance revealed that she was a Parisian export, not a Burgundian local. This was a problem. While Bernard dreamt of stars, Dominique worried about her future in Saulieu. In Paris, she had forged a career as a successful journalist at the restaurant magazine *L'Hôtellerie*. She was the author of a book about kitchen sanitation, a technical book, to be sure, but a standard text for restaurants and in its fourth printing. Within the small world of Parisian gastronomy, Dominique Brunet—she signed her books and articles with her maiden name—was a renowned figure.

Dominique dreaded sacrificing her career. What would she do in Saulieu? What role would she have at La Côte d'Or?

For the first three years of her marriage, Dominique avoided answering these tough questions by commuting to Burgundy on weekends. Each Friday evening, she made the two-and-a-half-hour drive to Saulieu from her small, well-appointed apartment in Paris. She hated life in Bernard's bachelor quarters, a studio above the restaurant's dining room. The couple ate all their meals in the restaurant with the staff.

"Bernard is so obsessed with his restaurant that he doesn't care how he lives," she complained. "The apartment is so old and run-down that the electricity often goes out and the water cuts off."

Clients, particularly American tourists, asked her, "How do you keep so thin?" The question made Dominique smile. She was three months pregnant. It would be her second child. Her daughter, Bérangère, was a year old. When Dominique told Bernard the good news, his mouth opened half in pleasure and half in surprise. Although he wanted a family, he didn't want to worry about a pregnant wife just when he was gearing up for his assault on the Michelin fortress. But Dominique was approaching forty. She felt her biological clock running and told Bernard this was her last chance to have a second child.

Ever since Bérangère's birth, Dominique had lobbied Bernard to buy a house where the family could settle down. Her new pregnancy increased her determination to move. But every piece of property she saw for sale in Saulieu was in terrible shape, almost as run-down as their apartment above the restaurant. Eric, Hubert, and most of the other longtime waiters at La Côte d'Or had ended up building new houses.

One day the doorman mentioned that a big, bourgeois, turn-of-the-century mansion located at the edge of town might be available for about $150,000. Dominique bought it. Bernard was both happy and frightened that she was settling in Saulieu. The restaurant was struggling financially, and he feared that they couldn't afford a new house. He also worried about whether Dominique would appreciate life in the provinces. Often in the evenings, he found her in tears.

"What's wrong?" he would ask.

"I can't live here," she would tell him. "Every time I walk into the restaurant, I wonder, What am I going to do here, how am I going to make my place? You already have been here for ten years, with the same staff. They have their system and they aren't ready to listen to someone who has never worked in a hotel, who is a Parisian and, above all, a woman."

At the end of each meal at La Côte d'Or, Dominique toured the tables, engaging the clients in sweet small talk. When she spoke about the splendors of Burgundy, giving advice about where to buy great bottles of wine or what abbeys to visit, she showed no sign of her distress. She looked and sounded like the ever-charming hostess. She wanted to stay and settle in Saulieu. But Paris beckoned. The coming year would be decisive. Either she would be able to carve out a life for herself in this provincial village or she would have to resign herself again to an unhappy commuter marriage.

★ ★ ★

Back in the kitchen, Larry Knez peels potatoes. Through most of the day, from eight in the morning until midnight, he peels potatoes, a total of at least fifty pounds. When he isn't peeling potatoes, he is plucking parsley leaves, cutting shallots, cleaning mushrooms, defeathering partridges and wild ducks, or performing any of the other myriad, tiresome, and lonely tasks demanded by haute cuisine. The secret behind La Côte d'Or's great cooking was not an artistic temperament. It was perfecting the repetitive tasks of plucking, peeling, and cutting so that the potato cubes were perfectly square and the carrot slices perfectly round. An astounding amount of labor went into producing culinary perfection. At La Côte d'Or, some twenty-five cooks labored in the kitchen, one chef for every two diners.

Larry had just arrived from his home on Long Island. He had already worked in restaurants for more than a decade. Unfortunately, his experience was in American restaurants. That didn't count to his French colleagues. In the authoritarian, hierarchical world of a French kitchen, Larry was on the bottom. He was a *stagaire,* an intern. He toiled all day peeling potatoes and cutting carrots for free—not for even a single centime.

It was tough to become a nonpaid stagaire at La Côte d'Or. Bernard received about two thousand applicants a year. They came from all over the world, Belgium, Germany, England, Japan, and the United States. Bernard liked to have an American in the kitchen. An English-speaker was useful for American or British clients. There was already an English chef, Michael Caines. Bernard liked to boast that a United Nations worked in the kitchen. To him, this was a sign of his importance. "Everybody in the world wants to learn from Loiseau," he said.

As Bernard's fame spread, the number of applications for internships increased. So many applications now poured in that Bernard had begun asking short-term interns to pay him for the privilege of working in his kitchen. The fee came to $1,000 a week. Generally, paying interns had a job in another restaurant or hotel, and their employers paid the tuition as an investment. They stayed for only a week or two.

Nonpaid stagaires such as Larry volunteered for longer periods, usually three months. At the end of their stint, most received a certificate of recognition and were sent on their way. If they were talented, they could rise to commis. Translated, commis means galley slave. The title fits. At La Côte d'Or, commis worked five and a half days a week, for up to twelve hours a day, with only the brief afternoon siesta. Their salary was about $400 a month.

Larry's goal was to become a commis.

The twenty-nine-year-old Larry didn't look like the fresh-faced American G.I. of French dreams. He was short, swarthy, muscular, and mustachioed, a product of Long Island's working-class south shore. His mother was French, his father Croat. They met in Paris after the war and moved across the Atlantic, where they both worked in the restaurant trade, she as a receptionist at the Fox Hollow Inn, in the Long Island suburbs, and he as a waiter at the Riverside Cafe, in Brooklyn. When Larry was eleven years old and in seventh grade, they divorced. His mother took him and his brother back to France. They settled in Paris, with his grandmother. "The school was racist," Larry remembered. "Sometimes my classmates would say, 'Oh, you're just a dirty American.' "

After four months, the family returned to Long Island. His mother took a job at a French restaurant called Le Petit Paris. She often worked in the evenings. Larry learned to cook as a teenager because otherwise he and his brother would often have gone without dinner. He preferred cooking to studying. When the teacher asked all the students to prepare something for a party in ninth-grade French class, Larry made chocolate eclairs. He won first prize.

Larry started working in restaurants when he was fourteen years old. His mother helped him get his first job. Le Petit Paris, in Babylon in the Great South Bay Shopping

Center, produced Americanized versions of traditional Burgundy specialties: *canard à l'orange, boeuf bourguignon,* and *coq au vin.* Larry washed dishes. He wasn't even allowed to melt the cheese on the onion soup.

By sixteen, Larry had worked his way up to pantry man at an Italian restaurant called Capriccio, in Jericho, just off the Long Island Expressway. The restaurant wasn't known for its food. It won fleeting fame instead as a watering hole of pop singer Billy Joel. Larry still was not allowed to cook. He prepared cold dishes.

His big break came at Sal's Pizza, in Rockville Center. OK, he admitted, pizza was a long way from haute cuisine. Still, he succeeded in transforming a greasy spoon into a popular nightspot. Larry added to the menu, and the pizzeria soon took on overtones of a trattoria. One day, he went to the movies and, to his great pleasure, overheard the cashier tell a colleague, "The pizzeria must have a new cook. The food used to be horrible. Now it's great."

Larry's father didn't like the idea of his becoming a chef. As a former waiter, he knew firsthand about the eccentric restaurant world. Once a diner complained that his steak was tough. Larry's father brought the dish back to the kitchen. The chef threw it on the floor, jumped on it, and pronounced the flattened meat "tender." "Why not be a mechanic?" his father asked Larry. "Chefs are crazy."

Larry was a little crazy, and he didn't listen to his father. He cooked in a series of restaurants, in Los Angeles at La Maison du Caviar and then in New York at the ritzy Hudson River Club. The next step was France. For a budding chef, the choice was natural. "In France, gastronomy is a way of life," Larry often said. "In America, it's just a pastime."

Larry stayed a few weeks with his grandmother in Paris. Then some cousins in Normandy offered him a job in their pâtisserie. Every day, he was up at three in the morning to begin baking baguettes. It was a good job, and he enjoyed it. But Larry wanted to learn more than baking. He picked up his Michelin Guide and wrote to all the two- and three-star restaurants.

His résumé arrived at the perfect moment. La Côte d'Or's previous American intern, another New Yorker, named David, was returning to the States to work at the Restaurant Bouley, in Manhattan. Larry received a response from Bernard at the beginning of September. A position was waiting for him in Saulieu—if he came right away.

Larry took the train to Saulieu. When he arrived, he was shocked. Guests lived in luxury in the hotel, the kitchen staff in poverty in cramped rooms above the kitchen, reached by climbing a dark staircase. The light fixture in the hallway was broken, the wallpaper was peeling, and the paint was chipped. The staff rooms contained a desk, a wardrobe, a washstand, and a creaky bed covered by a sagging mattress. A bathroom and shower were down at the end of the hall. "When we tried to fix the rooms up, the stagaires left them a mess," Bernard told him. Compared with other accommodations in the restaurant world, Larry had to admit, these were not bad. In Paris, stagaires received no lodging, and elsewhere in the provinces, rooms often came without a washstand.

Meals served to the staff were not elegant, either. Guests enjoyed gastronomic perfection. The staff ate leftovers, usually a stew, prepared each day by an intern. A dark room with creaking wooden furniture served as the dining room. Everyone stuffed themselves, buffet-style, shoveling the food down in order to get back to work.

Work started at eight in the morning. Lunch break came at eleven. By eleven forty-five, the staff was back behind the ovens, working all out until four in the afternoon. A three-hour siesta followed. Then came the staff dinner and the start of the evening service. The tension never let up for two full hours. During busy Saturday evenings, Larry figured he sweated off ten pounds. Weekdays, of course, were calmer.

Although Larry was hardworking, talented, and spoke good French, his young colleagues mocked him. By his advanced age of nearly thirty, a French cooking hopeful should be at least a chef de partie or sous chef, not a low stagaire. Most promising French chefs work one or two years as an apprentis and commis in a few good restaurants, perhaps a one-star, then a two-star, before finally reaching a three-star.

After this Tour de France, they rise to chef de partie, and, if lucky, after a few more years to sous chef. Since they start as young as sixteen, they are still only thirty years old. Patrick, the chef de cuisine, had worked for a decade at La Côte d'Or, and he was a year younger than Larry.

No French bosses would let an untested American near the oven or grill. Whenever Larry tried to help out, his colleagues yelled at him, "You stupid, arrogant American. Don't you know your place?" Within the kitchen, he no longer was addressed as Larry. His derogatory nickname became *l'Américain.*

Larry's chief tormentor was Michael Caines, a black Englishman. Michael was a rising star in the kitchen, the head of the meat section. At twenty-three he was six years younger than Larry, and unlike the experience of the raw, ambitious American, Michael's was all haute cuisine. He had started out as an apprentice at the Grosvenor House, in London, and continued his training with French expatriate Raymond Blanc at his two-star Michelin restaurant, Le Manoir, near Oxford. Michael was a strong, supple man of Jamaican ancestry. He sported a small mustache, designed to make him look older and more mature. When he cooked, he wielded the frying pan with grace and control, like a basketball star on his way to a dunk.

Michael decided he needed experience in France. Blanc recommended him to his friend Bernard, and an offer was made. At La Côte d'Or, Michael displayed an impressive talent and soon was named chef de partie of the fish section before rising to head of the meat section. Michael earned about $1,000 a month. He was able to escape the grubby apprentice rooms and rent an apartment in Saulieu.

Off the job, Michael liked Larry and often invited the American to his place for a drink. They would discuss the future of Anglo-Saxon cuisine. At work, however, Michael badgered him. In a French kitchen, a superior may curse out an apprentice as much as he wants. The lowly apprentice better not reply.

"Larry, you've got to learn to shut up," Michael said. "Listen when somebody tells you something."

Larry's meager supply of money was running out. Some evenings he would retreat to his room without joining his fellow workers for a nightcap at the Café du Nord. He couldn't spare the change for a beer. Instead, he would curl up in his bed with a book.

On the train from Paris, Larry had met a designer who had a job in nearby Montbard. He began writing her letters. She never answered. On his one day off a week in Saulieu, the American walked the streets girl watching. When he saw an overweight, unattractive blonde in short hot pants walk by, he snickered, "That's the prettiest girl in this town."

Most of all, Larry was frustrated because he had no real responsibility in the kitchen. Because there were few customers, he spent much of his time off on the side with little to do. One day, Bernard saw Larry standing around. Either you get your ass in motion, he told the American, or you're gone. "It got so bad that all of us started to fight to peel potatoes," Larry said.

But when Larry displayed too much enthusiasm and energy, he found himself in even more trouble. At one lunch,

American chefs Emile LeGasse and Charley Trotter arrived from Chicago. They came with Larry Stone, the first American to win the award Best Sommelier in the World. They were on a gastronomic tour of France, and Bernard was eager to impress them. After they finished eating, Larry came out of the kitchen, introduced himself, and struck up a conversation with his fellow Americans. Bernard was shocked. In his opinion, a stagaire never should be so forward.

"What's this American doing here?" he asked Patrick.

Despite all the craziness, Larry admired Bernard and his grueling perfectionism. He put up with the long hours, the poor living conditions, and the stress-filled working environment, all without complaint, because he believed it was the only way for him to become a top-ranking chef.

"It's perfection," he said. "You can see, with Bernard, every plate that goes out has to be perfect. If it ain't perfect, then it's not three stars."

# CHAPTER 2

★ ★ ★

# *Rags to Riches*

*The kitchen*

BERNARD liked to say he started life in grinding poverty. He told visitors that his parents' apartment didn't even have a shower. To bathe, he went to the municipal baths. In school, Bernard said, he was the class dunce. He dropped out at age sixteen and went to work as a chef apprentice. By presenting his childhood in this fashion, Bernard turned his life story into a dramatic success story. "I started with nothing but a toothbrush," he says.

The reality was more mundane. Bernard was born on January 13, 1951, in Clermont-Ferrand, an industrial city of 150,000 in the middle of France. The Loiseau apartment was located at 28 Avenue Franklin Delano Roosevelt (many streets in France are named after the liberating American president). It was a comfortable, middle-class street, and the third-floor apartment had four medium-size rooms and a balcony. It didn't have a shower or toilet, but a majority of French apartments at the time didn't either. For someone who would later try to fly so high, Bernard spent a youth that occupied the comfortable middle ground, neither rural peasant nor urban sophisticated, neither poor nor rich, and neither ambitious nor complacent.

"We were average," said his father, Pierre Loiseau.

Clermont-Ferrand is famous for one reason: as the home of the Michelin Tire Company, publisher of the famous Red Guide. In Clermont-Ferrand, Bernard grew up in the shadow of the Michelin myth. He went to school with the Michelin children, and his younger brother, Rémy, later would become a computer programmer at one of the Michelin factories.

For centuries, the Loiseaus had been butchers. Then Bernard's grandfather was drafted in World War I, wounded at Verdun, and awarded a Legion of Honor. Afterward, he became a cavalier for a duke in the Loire Valley. Martial glory was won more easily in the bloody but victorious First

World War than in the disastrous second. German armies beat the French so quickly in 1940 that seventeen-year-old Pierre Loiseau never had a chance to enlist. After the Allies freed France, in 1944, Pierre attended cavalry school, hoping to live up to the image of his courageous father. But he flunked the oral test and was refused an army commission. He settled in Clermont-Ferrand, where he became a hat salesman for a local firm.

The family of Edith Loiseau, née Rullier, was already established in the city. The Rulliers emigrated from the southern region of Ardèche at the beginning of the century. Edith's father owned a charcuterie. The Charcuterie Rullier was known as the best in town for foie gras, pig's feet, and other delicacies. It was located on the Rue de Gras—the Street of Fat—in the heart of the Old Town, and there was always a long line waiting to be served in front of the Rullier store.

Like their son, both parents were energetic and enthusiastic. In his youth, Pierre Loiseau was a strong soccer player. Even after he and Edith retired and became grandparents, the elder Loiseaus would set off on long bicycle treks into the mountains south of Clermont-Ferrand. They rode all day, some fifty miles, stopping only for a picnic lunch. At night, they picked a hotel with a good restaurant and enjoyed a feast. The next day, they reversed their route and rode back home. In the family photo album, the smiling couple stands with their bicycles on the peak of a mountain. One of Edith Loiseau's proudest mementos is a clipping from the local newspaper showing that she had finished first in a local thirty-five-mile bicycle race.

Bernard inherited this passion for sports. In eighth grade, he was named captain of the school soccer team. A picture of him at age twelve shows a solid boy in high-top Converse sneakers presenting a trophy to his school director. As the eldest of three children, Bernard became the natural leader for his brother, Rémy, two years his junior, and his sister,

Catherine, seven years younger. All the Loiseau youngsters attended private Roman Catholic schools. Bernard enrolled in Ecole Macillon. By the time he attended, morning Mass was optional and the school provided a general, highly respected education. One thing Bernard didn't do was study. He wasn't a bad student, just an underachiever. His grades, on the French scale of 0 to 20, were between 7 and 10. He was worst at math, best at writing. Anything theoretical such as philosophy bored him. In the middle of the 1960s, Bernard was stuck in the rigid and repressed atmosphere of an all-boys church school. Most of the teachers were priests. He did not rebel. He just lost interest in school.

At age sixteen, Bernard needed to pass an exam in order to continue studying. He failed.

"Dad, I want to work," Bernard told his father.

"All you're good for is cooking," his father said.

There couldn't have been a worse insult.

"My parents wanted a professor, a doctor, a lawyer, certainly not a cook," Bernard remembered. "A chef was like a gas station attendant."

Bernard insisted that his call to the kitchen was not inevitable. "It came to me little by little," he explained. Unlike many of the other grand names of haute cuisine—Bocuse, Troisgros, Guérard, not to mention his nearby rivals Marc Meneau and Jean-Michel Lorain—he was never in line to inherit a restaurant. When Bernard talked about other successful chefs, he always seemed to mention, part out of regret, part out of envy, "Oh, he got a head start because of his family." Being born into a family of restaurateurs provides a gigantic advantage. You learn the art from birth. You don't have to worry about getting banks to back your dreams. You just concentrate on cooking.

But Bernard was not as deprived as he would have us believe. Like most French children, he ate like a prince at home. His mother was still a fantastic cook, whipping up delicious mushroom tarts, succulent legs of lamb, and other tempting classic dishes of French country cuisine. From her, Bernard learned the all-important lesson that great cooking comes straight from the land's bounty.

On their vacations, the Loiseaus gathered at a family country home in the simple spa town of La Bourboule, high in the Massif Central mountains, even more isolated than the deepest reaches of Burgundy. During long walks in the forest, Pierre Loiseau taught his children the serious and subtle science of mushroom picking. The other favorite family pastime was hunting—not game, but crayfish. Early in the morning, Bernard, Rémy, and Catherine would march off into the nearby forests with their father. They headed for the banks of a small river to picnic and prepare to catch crayfish.

Pierre would tie a box with string, dunk it into the water, and wait until nightfall, when the crayfish would stir. Pull the string one second too early and the trap would remain empty, one second too late and the crayfish would all escape. Bernard always had trouble waiting for the right moment.

"Let's go, let's go, it's time," he would repeat.

"Patience, have a little patience," Pierre would respond.

At around eight, the sun began to set and the crayfish appeared. Pierre gave the signal.

"*On y va,*" he screamed. "Let's go."

Bernard pulled the string, shutting the trap.

*Thwhack.*

"We've got them," Bernard shouted.

The exercise was illegal—expensive permits were required to hunt crayfish—so the Loiseaus sneaked back home, fearful of being caught by a guard from a nearby campsite. All the way, Pierre kept shushing his loud, voluble son. Edith steamed the shellfish in white wine and *échalotes,* and the family feasted. Bernard always ate the most.

For both Pierre and Bernard Loiseau, "crayfish hunting was like poetry."

★ ★ ★

During Bernard's childhood, his father spent weeks at a time away from home, driving from small town to small town, peddling his company's hats. As in America, much folklore has grown up in France around the traveling salesman and his way of life. But an essential difference separates the American salesman from the French *vendeur:* the French salesman lives to eat as much as sell. Pierre scheduled his stopovers around the best restaurants. In particular, he made sure to end the day in Roanne, an undistinguished city of forty-one thousand.

"There was no reason to visit Roanne," Pierre said, "except for Troisgros."

There still is no good reason to visit Roanne except to eat in the Troisgros restaurant. It stands across the street from the Roanne train station. Today it is acknowledged as one of France's finest three-star establishments, enlarged to grandiose red-lacquered proportions. But when Pierre began frequenting it in the early 1950s, it was a modest, unstarred family bistro under the guidance of Jean-Baptiste "Papa" Troisgros.

The front room was a standard working-class café where locals congregated each afternoon for aperitifs. Salesmen gathered there to eat together at one long table. The atmosphere was hearty and good-natured, the cooking was homestyle and generous. Papa Troisgros took pleasure showing a bon vivant face to his customers, describing dishes about to arrive and accepting compliments for dishes already consumed. He often sat down at the salesmen's table and, since he had come originally from Burgundy, enjoyed a sip of a good Volnay or Gevrey-Chambertin.

"Troisgros wasn't fancy or expensive," Pierre recalled. "But the food was fabulous."

When Bernard set out to become a chef, his father called Papa Troisgros and asked if his son could become an apprentice. All the positions were filled for the upcoming year, so Bernard went to work for a cousin who had a pastry shop in Clermont-Ferrand. Since he had no car, every morning, no matter the rain, snow, or fog, Bernard would set off on a bicycle to bake fresh breakfast croissants at five in the morning.

Making French pastry is an exacting art—meringue, sugar, and flour are not the most durable construction materials. Impetuous Bernard displayed neither talent nor patience.

"I wanted to do more than just pastry," Bernard said. "It was all show, no substance, painting with a small brush instead of a large brush."

When an apprenticeship finally opened up at Troisgros, Bernard left for Roanne. Papa Troisgros's two talented sons, Pierre and Jean, both of whom had trained at a three-star restaurant, ran the kitchen. Their cooking had already earned two Michelin stars, and in the rarefied world of haute cuisine, critics considered them comers.

Bernard's apprenticeship at Troisgros lasted three years. These days, apprenticeships at La Côte d'Or were designed for only six months. Hard as Larry Knez worked, Bernard toiled even harder, with fewer legal guarantees. By law, apprentices today can work only eight hours in a single shift and must receive twelve hours of time off between shifts. At Troisgros, Bernard slaved from eight in the morning until after midnight. Every morning, he was responsible for lugging black coal from the backyard and lighting the old oven. It took two hours to warm up. For the rest of the day, he peeled potatoes or cut carrots.

"How can you give somebody twelve hours off when you finish at midnight and you have to begin at eight in the morning the next day?" asked Pierre Troisgros. "You can't, and that's the reason the old apprenticeship system is breaking down."

In three years at Troisgros, Bernard suffered endless jokes. Whenever trouble brewed in the kitchen, the other apprentices retreated. Not Bernard. "Bernard was the enfant terrible, the kitchen clown," recalled fellow apprentice Guy Savoy, now a leading Paris restaurateur. "If something went wrong, it had to be his fault."

One summer evening the Troisgros brothers started screaming at the apprentices about the poor quality of their potato peeling. All of the apprentices turned away in an attempt to avoid their anger—except Bernard. He strode right up to Jean Troisgros and said, "It's my fault." "He was the only one of us who would open up his mouth," said Bernard Chirent, another apprentice.

After months of hard work, Bernard finally was allowed to stop cutting and peeling and use the oven. By mistake, he responded by throwing a shovelful of coal, meant to fire the stove, into a skillet simmering with the famous Troisgros salmon with sorrel. The more severe of the Troisgros brothers, Jean, snarled: "If this kid becomes a cook, I'll be an archbishop!"

The situation became so bad that Bernard considered quitting—or at least made a great show of leaving. He picked up his kitchen equipment (apprentices supply their own knives and other utensils) and headed for the door. The Troisgros dog, a cocker spaniel named Ted, followed him. As one of Bernard's punishments, the Troisgros brothers had ordered him to fix their dog's meals.

By this time, Bernard had graduated from his bicycle to become the proud owner of a moped. He revved up the two-cylinder engine, preparing to return to Clermont-Ferrand. Ted, his face drooping, looked up at him. "It was like a Chaplin film," Bernard remembered, his eyes twinkling. "Everyone kept telling me I was terrible, that I was good at nothing. I was ready to return home until I took one look at Ted. I said, 'You like what I cook.'" He returned to his room above the restaurant—with a permanent reputation among his fellow chefs as the "world's best cook for dogs."

In one area, Bernard achieved success during his Troisgros years: playing *boule*. Boule is a simple game that can be played almost anywhere, on gravel, dirt, mud, or grass, and that a beginner can enjoy from the first throw. A small wooden ball, the *cochonnet,* is placed on the ground. Each player has three steel balls called boules, identified by different patterns etched into the metal, and at the end of the round, the closest to the cochonnet is the winner.

During their afternoon time off and after the evening service, until three each morning under the streetlights, many of the apprentis, commis, and sous chefs congregated in front of the Roanne town hall. The Roanne rules, particularly in the evening, were strict. First, to play, you needed a drink, preferably alcoholic. Second, cheating was permitted. Third, the stakes were much of an apprentice's monthly pay.

Bernard practiced hard. He wanted to be, in his words, the *best!*

Boule is a game of strategy, not athletic ability. A throw is made and play stops while the next to throw strolls up for a closer look and tries to decide whether to try to knock away an opponent's ball or to attempt a gentle delivery to approach the cochonnet. Bernard studied every nuance like a doctoral candidate. Gérard Naudo, one of the best players in France, taught him. Instead of paying for lessons, Bernard cooked Troisgros-like meals for Naudo and his wife. Naudo said Bernard snitched food from the Troisgros kitchen for the feasts, a charge Bernard adamantly denied.

Among his fellow workers, Bernard emerged as the best player, able to toss the ball straight and provide it with just the proper amount of backspin. On the court, Bernard had style, a way of grunting and encouraging his ball, no matter whether he was practicing the low, rolling throw that skittered along the ground or the high-trajectory shot aimed to knock the opponent's boule off the court.

"He always wanted to play against me, he wanted to beat the best," Naudo recalled. "He lost, of course, but he never gave up."

"I didn't lose *every* match," Bernard insisted. "I beat him a few times."

From his boule matches, Bernard took away an important lesson: an irreverence, even at the risk of appearing a fool, for the powers that be. Years later when President Mitterrand came to La Côte d'Or, Bernard arrived at the table to take the order. He recommended a plate of frog legs to the president, forgetting that the satirical television puppet show *La Bébette* caricatured Mitterrand as a frog.

"Are you serious, Loiseau?" roared the president. "Or are you being satirical?"

Bernard broke into a big smile—and the president ordered his frog legs.

"Thank God it wasn't the bicentennial of the French Revolution," he joked afterward. "Or I would have been worried about my head."

★ ★ ★

After leaving Troisgros in 1971, Bernard was drafted into the army. All young Frenchmen have to serve their country for one year. The more privileged devise schemes to avoid the army or find a cushy posting. For an aspiring chef, the ideal is to serve the year on the brigade of the presidential Elysée Palace. Bernard did not have the necessary connections. He was dispatched to the east of France, to the garrison city of Phalsbourg. There he was installed at the ovens of the First Regiment. In the army, no one was aware that Bernard was a failed apprentice. They only knew that this young Troisgros-trained draftee could cook. Bernard soon commanded twenty-two chefs. "The army was a miserable experience but a necessary one," he said. "It taught me that no one gives you a gift in life."

Discharged, Bernard returned home to Clermont-Ferrand and began looking for a job. He applied to the three-star restaurant in Alsace run by the Haeberlin brothers. Their Auberge de l'Ill is one of the most idyllic, romantic restaurants in France, its dining room overlooking a stream that flows by a garden full of willow trees. Unlike other great establishments located in the countryside, the Haeberlins enjoyed a steady supply of wealthy clients living nearby, thanks to their location close to the border with Germany. Because the Auberge de l'Ill was almost always full, the Haeberlins had assured Bernard of a job. He sent an application, expecting to be hired right away.

But the Haeberlins never replied. Bernard was too proud and frightened to telephone and ask for a straight answer. Instead, he found work in the kitchen of the Frantel Hotel, the French equivalent of Holiday Inn. He tried out his Troisgros dishes. After eight days, he was fired. "You're spending too much on food," the boss told him.

By chance, the following day Bernard ran into fellow Troisgros alumnus Bernard Chirent in the streets of Clermont-Ferrand. Chirent had been working in Paris for a restaurateur named Claude Verger. He told Bernard that Verger was looking for a chef. Verger had made a fortune selling kitchen equipment to cooks. Every day, Verger had lunch in the restaurants he sold to, and every day, no matter how good the cooking, he said he went away feeling that there was a brick in his stomach. "Archaic cooking, full of cream and butter," he said. "I thought that ninety-nine percent of all the food I ate was lousy. With that percentage of bad restaurants, there was no way I could fail."

A businessman and entrepreneur, not a cook, Verger soon owned six restaurants in Paris. In his search for potential star chefs, the Troisgros restaurant was one of his main recruiting grounds: he hired Chirent and Guy Savoy as well as Bernard. Verger took these Troisgros-trained minor leaguers and transformed them into major leaguers.

Bernard took over at Verger's La Barrière de Clichy. "I opened the door and here was this country bumpkin standing before me. He had never been to Paris and looked completely out of place," Verger remembered. "The first thing Bernard said to me was, 'I want three stars.'" La Barrière de Clichy was just over the Paris city line, within sight of the belt highway, in a working-class suburb. But it was a restaurant, and at the tender age of twenty-two, Bernard was the chef.

Soon Bernard was making his mark with a style of cooking that Verger favored: fresh, unusual, and light, tied to the rhythm of the seasons. "If anyone taught Bernard cooking, it was Verger," said Eric Rousseau. "The man was a tyrant, impossible, but with a great nose."

Much as they liked each other, Verger and Bernard formed a tumultuous team, like a father with his favorite, spoiled child. The child-chef wanted control over the menu. The father-owner refused to give it to him, fearing, among other things, that Bernard's determination to obtain the finest natural ingredients would drive up costs and ruin his business.

In a fit of adolescent rebellion, Bernard left to work at a two-star Michelin establishment, Hôtel de la Poste, in a small Burgundy town called Avallon. His departure lasted three weeks. Bernard demanded that his new employers let him work the grill. Anyone can peel potatoes or even learn to arrange plates like a painter, he said. Foul-ups, after all, can be corrected later. Real responsibility, the real test of a cook's manhood, comes when he cooks meat and fish. Overcooked food is wasted food. When Bernard asked to run the grill, his boss fired him.

Verger then made Bernard an offer: to return to Paris and become chef at his new flagship, La Barrière Poquelin. The restaurant was squeezed onto a narrow street near the Opéra.

It had only a dozen tables and a cramped galley of a kitchen. The staff consisted of three chefs and two waiters. There were no apprentices, few of the trappings of haute cuisine. But despite its modesty, the restaurant had a relaxed, easy-going charm. The decor—soft wood beams, a light shag rug, and comfortable, modern chairs—hinted at elegance without stiff formality. In the galaxy of Parisian restaurants, La Barrière Poquelin was the perfect place for a young, ambitious, and talented chef to practice his trade and prepare for the big time.

Verger taught Bernard about two groups of people essential to success in the restaurant business: influential journalists and pretty women. In addition to his gift for spotting good chefs, Verger knew how to get publicity. He invited the media to his restaurant for sumptuous meals. "The house policy was, all journalists ate free, even if they didn't write about food," Verger proclaimed. "Only the press could fill your restaurant."

Although nearing sixty and married, Verger liked to chase women. For many of his adventures, he brought along Bernard. Nothing at his all-boys Catholic high school or the all-boys kitchen at Troisgros had prepared Bernard for jet set Paris nightlife. French writer Fanny Deschamps describes chefs as a compassionate, warmhearted breed, obsessed with seduction; every time they send a dish out of the kitchen, it is an act of seduction. Used to putting their hands on nature's beautiful produce, they can't help but compare a luscious female to a ripe peach ready for picking. In almost all conversations between chefs, the subject of pretty women seems to come up like a regular part of the menu, like the cheese dish or the dessert. Women may not be welcome inside the kitchen. But outside they are pursued with a hearty appetite.

Young Bernard was hungry, and Verger helped him navigate the social waters of the sex-charged city. Once, the two met up with two gorgeous "fillies" who worked as television announcers at Channel One. No danger, the women thought, mistaking elderly Verger and youthful Bernard for a homosexual couple. The four went out for a drink at a fancy bar and ended up sprawled in the act over couches at the journalists' apartment.

"Bernard was my favorite colt in the stable," Verger said. "None of the others had his passion."

Bernard flourished in Paris. With Verger's help, he soon made friends with show biz stars, politicians, and business leaders. His cooking also had improved. *Tout* Paris began flocking to La Barrière Poquelin to discover Bernard's talent. In 1974, critics Gault-Millau awarded the restaurant 15 out of 20. They spotted Bernard as an up-and-comer, calling him "a remarkable chef." For a high school dropout who had managed only 7 out of 20 in his classes, Bernard had come a long way.

CHAPTER 3

★ ★ ★

# Falling to Earth

*Papa Dumaine*

IN 1975, VERGER heard that La Côte d'Or in Saulieu was for sale. A dark, drafty place with mediocre cuisine, its burial seemed complete when a Total gas station was built across the street. What Parisian would want to drive two and half hours for a meal and eat across the street from a gas station? If nothing was done, Philistines would bulldoze the restaurant within a few years in favor of a supermarket, drive-in bank, or—horror of horrors—a fast-food joint.

In public, Verger said it was in the national interest to stop such a desecration. In private, he sensed a bargain. Despite its decline, La Côte d'Or still had two Michelin stars and a historic facade. Its shadowy salons, its murals, and its hand-crafted woodwork, mellowed and darkened with age, gave off the aura of a grand old monument. "It had fifteen bedrooms and a reputation," Verger said with a chuckle.

Saulieu has long lived off its gastronomic reputation. In August 1677, the foremost fashion and food writer of the age, Madame de Sévigné, stopped for a feast at the Auberge Dauphin. She recorded fish in *meurette* sauce, and she drank so much good wine that she became tipsy for the first time in her life. Contrite, she donated a statue to Saulieu's basilica.

The town's strong gastronomic foundations are the result of location. In Roman times, Saulieu stood at the middle of the Agrippa Way, which led from Boulogne south through Marseilles. This central position made Saulieu a prime battleground. All French children learn how 250,000 Gauls commanded by Vercingetorix fought for six long weeks in 52 B.C. before succumbing to Julius Caesar's legions. The main battle took place around the hill of Alésia, just a few miles from Saulieu. Later, Napoleon's armies passed through the town en route to conquering Italy, obtaining a tardy revenge against Caesar.

Throughout the era of horseback transportation, Saulieu profited as a pleasant rest stop, right on the main artery from Paris to Lyons. During the nineteenth century, the town became a commercial center. Wine, fish, grain, and wood were exchanged at frequent fairs. When their business was done, merchants restored themselves with heavy portions of ham and andouillette sausages. In the 1860s, the industrial revolution arrived. Tile factories and tanneries crowded the town. But in the twentieth century, Saulieu was blighted by rural depopulation—until the arrival of the automobile, which re-created Burgundy's role as a major north-south communications axis linking the North Sea with the Mediterranean.

Saulieu was right on the Nationale 6, built over the old Roman road. La Six is celebrated in French folklore through songs and stories as the main route from the cold, rainy north to the warm, sunny south. Along the entire length of La Six stand inns and posthouses, monuments to the old days of leisurely travel.

La Côte d'Or was originally built in 1875 as a stucco-faced posthouse. By World War I, it had achieved a measure of fame under a chef named Budin. Newspaper clippings of the time recount how he produced a spectacular version of the local specialty, *jambon à la crème,* ham in a cream sauce infused with red wine. But Budin must not have been too talented. None of the reports mention his first name, and neither Bernard nor Dominique knew it.

Budin's successor really put the place on the map. His name was Alexandre Dumaine, and under his long reign, La Côte d'Or soared into gastronomic history. Dumaine was born in 1895, not far from Saulieu, in the modest city of Digoin. At the age of twelve, he started out as an apprentice in a simple local restaurant, working his way up in the profession to *grande toque*—head chef—at such famous establishments as the Hôtel Carlton, in the spa city of Vichy, and the Elysée Palace, not the presidential home but an elegant restaurant located right on the Champs-Elysées, in Paris.

During the first days of World War I, Dumaine enlisted in the artillery battalion and won a medal praising "his good humor and willingness to take on the most difficult tasks." One day, his colonel summoned him and told him President Georges Clemenceau would be arriving with the entire army general staff to inspect the front.

"Can you arrange the lunch?" the colonel asked.

Dumaine accepted, wondering how he would obtain supplies. He needn't have worried. The president and the generals were so satisfied that they asked him to become their regular chef. Dumaine refused and stayed in the trenches for the rest of the war. "I don't want to turn my back on my men," he said, showing a pride and stubbornness that later would serve him well.

Discharged, Dumaine embarked on another adventure, directing the kitchens of the three luxury hotels of the Transatlantic chain in Algeria. After nine years in the North African desert, Dumaine became nostalgic for France and, in particular, for his native Burgundy. "I was born Burgundian," he said, "and as sincere people, the Burgundians only accept robust and true things." When a friend from Dijon told him that La Côte d'Or was for sale, the chef immediately decided to buy.

Dumaine arrived in Saulieu in 1932. It proved a propitious time. Despite the deepening depression and the dark clouds of fascism and Nazism spreading across the Continent, a new epoch was dawning in French gastronomy. In 1933, Michelin awarded three stars to Fernand Point's restaurant, La Pyramide, in Vienne. The next year, the guide did the same for Pic, in Valence, and a year later it promoted Dumaine and his La Côte d'Or. Henry Clos Jouve, president of the Association of Gastronomic Chroniclers, dubbed them "Fernand Point the Marvellous, André

Pic the Debonaire, and Alexandre the Magnificent—in short, the Holy Trinity."

At the time, it was a three-day journey by car from Paris to the Côte d'Azur. Princes and gastronomes alike would leave the capital in the morning and arrive in the evening at La Côte d'Or in Saulieu. Sophisticated travelers stopped the second night at La Pyramide, in Vienne, and if they were addicted, the third night at Restaurant Pic, in Valence. They arrived, sated, for their holiday on the Mediterranean coast. The writer Yves Gandon used to say that the signposts leaving the capital should read "Paris-Dumaine, 260 kilometers."

Traditionally, "palaces"—big, luxurious hotels in the city—produced France's best cooking. Auguste Escoffier, the great nineteenth-century cook, had toiled at the Ritz in Paris and the Carlton in London, and his imprint still influenced all the critics, including Michelin. Escoffier was a man of the previous century; he cooked by rote, his recipes written in scientific terms. The master laid down ideal proportions for mandatory ingredients; *sole meunière* or veal Orloff was cooked one way, and one way only. Under Escoffier's influence, French cuisine became graven in marble, still delicious, but haughty and complicated.

Point, Pic, and Dumaine were pioneers who brought French cooking into the twentieth century and showed that provincial food could be as good as food in Paris, if not better. "Dumaine was able to get beyond his early experience of palace cooking, and adapt to the new, improvised cooking," said his student Jean-Pierre Billoux. He grafted regional tradition onto haute cuisine skills, reducing the elaborate menu of the palaces to a few daily specialties, which changed according to the seasons.

On La Côte d'Or's door, the following message was posted: "When you cross our doorstep, you are always assured of an excellent meal, even if you are very, very rushed. But beware, give us the time to feed you properly.

You will find daily specialties that vary according to the seasons. Do not arrive too late to taste them." Billoux said that the great chef's respect for his clients was matched by his demands on them. "If they reserved a table for twelve-thirty, it wasn't for twelve-fifty."

In 1935, Dumaine offered a lunch of elegant simplicity. The meal started with a variety of hors d'oeuvres, followed by a peasant omelette, little French peas, roast chicken, green salad, cheese, desserts, and fruit, all for the worldly sum of eighteen francs. For two more francs the guest could add a *feuilleté* of crayfish tails between the omelette and the roast chicken. For twelve more francs, a poached trout was also included in the nourishing feast. The trout came from the river Cure, just a few miles away, and the fowl from the famous Bresse district. The butter was fresh from the nearby Deux-Sèvres county, the eggs and lettuce from local peasants. It was flawless produce cooked exactly right by a genius, leading one critic to call Dumaine the Mozart of the ovens.

Saulieu also offered abundant choices for the less rich and sophisticated. In 1936, across the street from Dumaine's august establishment, a chef from Lucas-Carton in Paris achieved two Michelin stars for Hôtel de la Poste. Next door, Le Petit Marguery merited a single star. Six Michelin stars were squeezed into a town of fewer than three thousand people!

But Dumaine was Saulieu's celebrity. In both demeanor and appearance, he resembled a bear. His figure was rotund, his face round, and his growl legendary. He liked to be called the Burgundian prince of chefs and didn't care for anyone who pulled rank. When Alphonse Daudet's journalist son, Léon, author of the book *Drinking and Eating,* smothered his beef with half a pot of Dijon mustard, Dumaine snatched his plate away from under his nose with the devastating comment "I imagined Monsieur Daudet to be a gastronome. He is merely a heavy eater."

Dumaine always remained provincial, narrow-minded, and nationalistic. Writing about a trip to the United States, all he noticed was his fellow Frenchmen at the head of the fanciest restaurants. "To sum up my impressions of the trip," he wrote, "I came away with the feeling that our country possesses all the manners of perfection."

Once, the actor Gary Cooper dared lecture the master of Saulieu about the glories of American cooking.

"Monsieur, do not talk to me about your cooking," Dumaine replied. "When I returned from New York, American cooking kept me in my bed for two months with jaundice."

In contrast to the gruff, uneducated chef, his wife, Jeanne, was smooth and sophisticated. A Parisian-born correspondent for *Harper's Bazaar,* she was a woman of great beauty, fluent in both German and English, well connected in the circles of power, with an instinctive nose for public relations. Chef Dumaine insulted many of his highborn clients; Jeanne charmed them. Pictures of the couple always show her standing, a bit stiff and straight, to the right of her husband. Over the years, she began to look more and more like an English schoolteacher.

Jeanne Dumaine attracted everyone from Aga Khan and the sultan of Morocco to the Spanish king Alfonso XIII, and the artist Salvador Dalí. "Make me eat like my king," the Spanish artist commanded. At Madame Dumaine's encouragement, France's most prestigious gourmet society, the Club des Cents, a group of a hundred food lovers who met every Thursday for lunch in Paris, hired a private bus to take them to La Côte d'Or. Dumaine prepared a pâté of snipe, warbler, quail, partridge, chicken livers, and brandy—baked in a piecrust and served hot. The dish took four days to make, and naturally it was pronounced a triumph.

Dumaine, above all, was a perfectionist. "My research has for its goal nothing less than perfection," he said. Toward the end of his life, the great chef was ill and suffered fits of delirium. In his moments of lucidity, he would talk of nothing but cooking.

"I think I now know how to make a good *coq au vin,*" he told his wife.

"But you've been making it for thirty years," Jeanne Dumaine replied.

"I was just practicing," the aging chef answered.

★ ★ ★

Saulieu's golden days lasted from the 1930s to the 1960s, interrupted only by the war. The decline came with a bang. In 1970, the four-lane superhighway south, the Highway A6, from Paris to Lyons, was completed. Known as the Highway du Soleil, it bypassed Saulieu by fifteen miles.

Everyone agreed that the new expressway was needed. So many trucks clogged the old Nationale 6 that formerly leisurely trips became exhausting as well as time-consuming. When planning first began, in 1955, engineers traced the route for the new highway near the old Nationale 6. In a move of collective hari-kari, Saulieu's residents fought the proposal, and in 1964 the Ministry of Transport moved the road far to the east. It would take six years to build the four-lane expressway to Lyons and six more years to complete the last stretch, to Marseilles.

When the new highway opened, one of the most fertile oases of French tourism overnight became a desert. Parisians in search of sunshine no longer stopped in Saulieu to gorge themselves. They zoomed down the highway, filling themselves with steak-frites served up at gas station cafeterias. "We were stupid," said Saulieu's mayor Philippe Lavault regretfully. "We saw the highway as a source of noise and disturbance rather than riches."

Saulieu's gastronomic reputation plummeted. Although today the town still boasts some thirteen hotels and restaurants, most offer cheap menus and unappealing food. Almost all are close to bankruptcy, living off past prosperity and unable to invest in the future. They struggle by on a summer season of tourists.

Verger took over La Côte d'Or on March 1, 1975. Dumaine's successor, François Minot, called the Michelin Guide directors and told them he was leaving. When the new guide came out two weeks later, La Côte d'Or had lost both of its precious stars.

"Minot screwed me," Verger complained.

"I went to Saulieu because I was told to," Bernard remembered. "I just took my suitcase and came. When I arrived, I didn't know who Dumaine was. I was twenty-four years old and alone. If I had thought about the move, I probably would have been too frightened to come."

After his exhilarating life in Paris, Bernard fell to the ground in Saulieu. Pierre Troisgros took a popular French song called "Open the Birdcage" and transformed it into a satirical ditty entitled "Loiseau in His Cage."

As an escape, Bernard tried to interest some of the staff in boule. He organized some matches in the square across the street from the post office. Nobody was interested. Roanne considered itself part of the south and had picked up the Mediterranean pastime. Saulieu was set in the cold north. The idea of drinking a pastis, tossing a heavy steel ball at a little cochonnet, and then arguing over the results did not appeal to Burgundians.

Saulieu didn't even have a disco. The closest was twenty miles away, in Semur-en-Auxois, a small room on the second floor above a rustic café. It was called Chez Bob after its owner, Robert. On Friday or Saturday, the busiest nights at the restaurant, Bernard would lead the bachelor kitchen staff out after service to go drinking and dancing. Often, they got back in the early hours of the morning, just in time to grab a coffee and a croissant and return to the kitchen.

In Saulieu, Bernard graduated from his moped to a Renault Cinq. It was a little box of a car sold in the United States as a gadget, Le Car. One night, coming back from Bob's disco, Bernard fell asleep at the wheel and crashed into a tree. He was in a coma for three days. When he woke up, Verger was furious. The night before, the restaurant had a special event for a hundred customers and Verger himself had to direct the kitchen.

"After that, I lived like a priest," Bernard said with a sigh. "No girls, no action. I devoted myself to bringing La Côte d'Or back to the top."

This meant marrying and settling down. One of the first things that friends told Bernard when he came to Saulieu was that Michelin would never give him a third star unless he had a wife running the front of the house. In the restaurant trade, women are scorned, but so are unmarried chefs. Michelin prizes stability and figures that a happy family man is much more likely to keep his restaurant on an even keel than an excitable bachelor.

Poor Bernard. He grabbed the first woman he could find and married her. Chantal was ten years older than he, divorced from a car mechanic, and the mother of two young children. She met Bernard on her rounds as a vacuum cleaner saleswoman. She dreamed of a gracious and easy life of fame and fortune in a luxury restaurant.

Chantal encouraged Bernard to buy La Côte d'Or from Verger, who was ready to retire. In 1980, the young couple borrowed millions of francs from the banks and paid Verger twice what he had spent to acquire La Côte d'Or. Chantal had never worked in a hotel. She knew nothing about running a restaurant and soon became bored by the minutiae of keeping accounts, ordering food, and charming clients.

The newlyweds began pumping even more money into the property. Their first project was to turn the small hotel bedrooms into large, comfortable, and expensive ones, including three duplexes. The budget was $500,000. Chantal directed the work. The result was a staggering final cost of $1.1 million.

At the beginning, the renovation provided the couple with a common sense of destiny and in particular gave Chantal a role at the restaurant. By 1985, when the new bedrooms were completed, Bernard's marriage was in shambles. Chantal's children caused more tension. Once, they stole money from Hubert, the maître d'hôtel, and went out drinking. The police eventually returned the runaways to the restaurant, but the scandal soon made the rounds in Saulieu.

"Those children are ruining my reputation," Bernard yelled.

"All you care about is your reputation," Chantal screamed back.

"I was impossible," Bernard said later. "All I talked about was my work and the three stars. I forgot about everything else, including her."

In 1987, Chantal took up with one of the waiters. The affair almost sank the restaurant, both financially and emotionally. Bernard's cooking deteriorated along with his moods. Customers felt the tension and stayed away. Even unflappable Hubert thought about quitting.

"It became like war," Hubert recalled. "All of the rest of us would keep our heads down and hide in the corner while they went at it."

In his youthful naïveté, Bernard had given Chantal a 50 percent stake in La Côte d'Or. "I warned him that this was a recipe for disaster," his accountant, Bernard Fabre, said. "He just wouldn't listen. For love, he was ready to do anything."

When Chantal ran away with the waiter, the bankers became nervous and threatened to call in their loans. Bernard was lucky enough to have Fabre on his side. The thirty-nine-year-old Marseilles native spoke with a thick Provençal accent and had a wily, streetwise demeanor. When Bernard first called him, Fabre said he had too much work to take on any more clients. But Bernard insisted, and Fabre agreed to come for lunch.

He arrived, wearing a loud purple jacket and tie.

"May I please see Monsieur Loiseau?" he asked.

Bernard strode up and introduced himself.

"I am the accountant, Fabre," Fabre said.

"No, you cannot be an accountant," Bernard responded. "You are not bald, fat, and old."

For lunch, Bernard served him wild asparagus. By the end of the meal, Fabre had signed on and Bernard was addressing his new accountant as a close friend.

Bernard always felt uncomfortable when dealing with numbers. More than anyone else in the world, he listened to and trusted Fabre. "When I wake up in the morning, the first thing I do is call my accountant." After his marriage exploded, the shrewd Fabre warned Chantal that she was half responsible for the millions of francs of debts. Chantal wouldn't listen. Fabre persuaded the bankers to block her account. A month-long standoff ensued. Chantal succumbed and gave up her 50 percent. "Otherwise, she soon would have had nothing to eat," Fabre said. The divorce was finalized in 1988. Chantal received alimony for two years and never returned to Saulieu.

★ ★ ★

Not long afterward, Bernard met Dominique Brunet at a conference at the elegant Thermal Hotel, in Vichy. All during the lectures he kept staring at her until she noticed him. She had never heard of the flapping Bird with his big dreams in Burgundy and mistook Bernard for another balding chef, three-star Michelin winner Alain Chapel. The lectures ended without Bernard daring to say a word to her. When she asked for him the next day, he already had gone back to Saulieu, for Bernard could never spend more than a night away from his restaurant without feeling sick and guilty.

The two were formally introduced at another professional meeting, this time in Paris. Sophisticated, reserved Dominique could not have been more different from earthy, working-class Chantal. She was a university-trained biochemist with a doctoral degree in nutrition. Unlike Bernard, she spoke both English and German, a legacy of her upbringing in the eastern border region of Alsace, where the local patois is a bastardized German. After receiving her doctorate, she was offered a post as a biochemistry professor at the university in the dreary northern city of Lille. She preferred to stay in Paris and took a position teaching nutrition at a university. Finding academia sterile, she soon moved on to a successful career in journalism.

In her free time, Dominique consulted for Club Mediterranée around the world, everywhere from Malaysia and Bermuda to Israel. She set the nutritional guidelines for the club restaurants and made sure that their kitchen hygiene was up to snuff. Bernard, in contrast, had never traveled outside France.

Yet Bernard's infectious enthusiasm touched Dominique. He forced her to drop a bit of her natural reserve, managing to get behind her cool charm and allowing her to express her emotions. The romance was buttressed by practical concerns. Dominique, the ultraprofessional woman, wanted a family before it was too late.

Within a few months, the couple had married in a small, private ceremony, held in Dominique's hometown, in Alsace. Bernard was careful not to repeat his past error. He kept 100 percent ownership of the restaurant in his own name. Dominique became an employee of La Côte d'Or, with vague responsibilities.

"You're the *patronne* now," Bernard assured her.

Unfortunately, he didn't help her assert her authority or define her role. "Bernard told me to start taking care of the hotel, including all purchases of bedroom necessities," she said. "But he didn't even give me a budget." In some ways, Bernard treated Dominique like a weapon in his battle for success, proof to both himself and the Michelin judges that he was settling down. Dominique's obvious unhappiness left him perplexed. He didn't know how to help. So he retreated. He started spending more time in the kitchen. Dominique decided she had to make a bigger effort to integrate herself at La Côte d'Or. Otherwise, she feared, she would lose her husband.

She began reorganizing the hotel reception and welcoming the clients to the dining room. As hard as she tried, as much as she craved acceptance, she was not popular. Bernard and Hubert had been together for nearly a decade. Hubert had come to Saulieu when Bernard had only one star and was still rough around the edges. Where Bernard was impulsive, Hubert was calm and composed. From his childhood on a farm near Lyons, Hubert knew food. From his education at hotel school, he knew how to run a restaurant and hotel. He spoke good English, thanks to an internship in London. With his ever-ready smile and sweet demeanor, Hubert became Bernard's alter ego, the steady assistant who permitted his master to shoot for the stars.

Bernard trusted his maître d'hôtel more than his wife. In many ways, his real family was La Côte d'Or. Dominique didn't help with her domineering manner. One day Hubert was leading a team of waiters folding napkins in the dining room. Dominique came in for lunch and asked, "Why is my table not ready yet? Set my table immediately."

Hubert stared at her in disgust.

The receptionists also resented Dominique. Marie-France and Carmen didn't appreciate her suggestions, particularly because, in their opinion, they often were not phrased as suggestions but as orders. They considered Dominique an amateur. After all, they had worked in a restaurant for years. Dominique never had.

"Dominique never asked, 'How about this and how about that?'" Carmen complained. "She was always saying, 'Do this, do that!'"

"It was painful," Dominique admitted. "Letters they wrote were not even in proper French. They had to be corrected."

To their faces, Bernard's mentors and friends wished the couple well. Behind their backs, they snickered about their pretensions to gastronomic glory. Pierre Troisgros noted that the Gauls defeated the Romans at Gergovie, right near Bernard's birthplace, in Clermont-Ferrand. Caesar later conquered the Gauls at Alésia, close to Saulieu. "Let's hope that Bernard has not won the battle of Gergovie," Pierre Troisgros said, "only to arrive at his Alésia." Jean Troisgros was more brutal: Bernard's restaurant in Saulieu, he said, would be "a good little stop for truck drivers."

*At work*

CHAPTER 4

★ ★ ★

# *Slow Civilization*

*Bernard*

A COUPLE OF MINUTES before nine on a cool, cloudless Wednesday morning in mid October, Bernard put his rifle into the trunk of his black turbo-charged BMW 325. The car, almost a decade old, was one of his few luxuries. He often traveled to Paris for meetings with lawyers, bankers, journalists, and fellow chefs. In his BMW, he made the 150-mile trip in less than an hour and a half. Sometimes he drove to Paris in the morning, returned to work the evening dinner service, slept three hours, and then set off again at five in the morning for another meeting in the capital.

But today, in the still-soft early morning light, the high-speed chef would try to slow down. He was in a bad mood. The night before, La Côte d'Or had done a "zero"—not a single diner. Bernard had already passed by the hotel to check his fax messages. There were none. No journalists had called asking for interviews. No movie star or top-ranking politician had signaled his imminent arrival. For any ambitious French chef, and particularly Bernard, being admired and appreciated is terribly important. Like an actor, the chef approaches each meal as if he is going out onstage. If someone looks unhappy out in the dining room, the chef suffers. He doesn't just want to hear that the meal was good. He wants to hear that it was better than anywhere else. An empty dining room is terrible not because of the economic consequences, but above all because of the emotional toll. When Bernard found himself frustrated and fearful, only one medicine would calm him: a good hunt.

On many autumn weekends, the countryside around Saulieu sounds like a battle zone. Almost every red-blooded male resident takes his gun and his dog in search of sport.

Confiscate a Burgundian's driving permit and he will accept the punishment. Take away his hunting permit and you have declared war. With Roman Catholicism in decline, hunting has become a true religion. Along with a license, each hunter receives a little green book outlining the penalties if he sins and breaks any of the rules. Many a Burgundian worships Saint Hubert, the patron saint of hunters.

Under the Ancien Régime, the king and his nobles forbade anyone else from hunting. The aristocracy could trespass on anyone's land and kill any animal they came across. If an unauthorized peasant hunter was caught, he faced hanging. When the revolutionaries overthrew the old order, one of their first priorities was to abolish this archaic restriction. Three weeks after the storming of the Bastille, on July 14, 1789, all citizens were granted the right to *la chasse*. To this day, many nonhunters often take out a permit; they consider it a sign of their rights as free men won in the Revolution.

But with the growth of cities over the last generation, opposition to hunting has mounted. Most of the two million French hunters are from the country. City dwellers show little understanding or sympathy for them; polls reveal that a majority of the population of fifty-five million would like to see restrictions placed on hunting. Brigitte Bardot has launched a crusade to restrict hunting rights. The former beauty railed in particular against hunters who track thousands of pigeons as they try to cross France on their way south. She said that the shoot is barbarous. The hunters retorted that their sport is traditional. Bardot said that the persecution and killing of witches was also traditional throughout the Middle Ages. "If Brigitte Bardot knew what I do," Bernard often said, "she would shoot me."

At the main hunting store in Saulieu, gunsmith Roland Randus offered a complete range of artillery, sixty to seventy models. "We have a rifle for every occasion," he explained, "to kill anything and everything." There was the Verney Caron Grand, which would stop the largest, fastest moose or even a leopard, if one happened to run wild in Burgundy. There was even a Ruger .44 Magnum with an electronic sight that could kill an animal from more than half a mile away.

Gun mania is only the beginning. When a Frenchman takes up hunting, or for that matter any other sport, he wants to look good. Forget the American checkered jacket and cheap hunting cap. French hunting fashion contains everything a man needs for confronting beasts in the forests—and then heading straight to a cocktail party. There are jackets with zippered pockets and game pouches, easily washable to remove bloodstains. There also are forage caps and commando trousers big enough to hold survival rations. "I look more like an advertisement for country living than a hunter," Bernard joked to friends. For today's hunt, he wore a British-made green Barbour jacket, a stylish country garment favored by Prince Charles. A cashmere beret covered his balding pate.

Bernard adored being invited by the Elysée Palace to the Château de Chambord, the former hunting grounds of King Louis XIV. Politicians, diplomats, business leaders, and show business celebrities (with the exception of Brigitte Bardot) gather for the presidential hunt. A giant pack of dogs leads the way. Formally dressed aides-de-camp carry the guns for their privileged shooters. Flocks of pheasant are released into the air.

*Bang. Bang. Bang.*

The aides reload, hand the rifles to their masters, and another flock of pheasants is released.

*Bang!*

"It's not real hunting," Bernard admitted to his friends. "It's a shooting gallery."

In autumn, Bernard and a group of buddies often tracked birds together in the vineyards above Beaune. They packed a *casse-croûte* picnic lunch of baguette, pâté, cheese, and wine, not water, in the canteen and spent the entire day in the forests and fields, returning home with a dinner slung over their shoulder. The eating and drinking continued well into the night and were as important, if not more important, than the shoot.

But today Bernard was going on a solitary hunt, without any celebrities and without even a dog. Only a single nonpaying guest from the hotel joined him for company. Instead of hobnobbing with the rich and famous, Bernard wanted to relax and rediscover the roots of his inspiration in the deepest parts of the French countryside. Slowly, at about twenty miles an hour, he wheeled his BMW over Saulieu's narrow, cobbled streets. He passed the Basilica St. Andoche, with its squat belfry, and left the town's small stucco houses behind. Through the fine mist and early morning light, the small town looked like a medieval apparition rendered in perfect detail. Within a few minutes, he entered an almost virgin forest of birch, beech, and oak trees broken only by scattered single homes and clear blue lakes.

This part of Burgundy is called the Morvan, a place of brooding beauty and unremitting poverty. Here are no rich, busy winegrowing villages as in the Côte d'Or between Dijon and Beaune. There are no fertile, rolling wheat-growing plains as around Auxerre. There are no polychrome yellow-and-red tiled roofs, no romantic, dilapidated châteaux, and only few auberges. The Morvan's biggest industries are growing Christmas trees and producing nannies for export to Paris. When talking about the Morvannais, other Burgundians have a saying: "Neither good people nor good wind."

Although the real Morvan may not have pretty postcard villages with quaint shops and cafes in its isolated stone hamlets, its rhythms are tied to nature. Like Bernard in his BMW, most of modern France travels like a high-speed train. Writer Henri Vincenot once described Burgundy as a *civilisation lente*—a slow civilization. In Vincenot's writing, one rule is uppermost: never sacrifice pleasure for speed. Burgundy's regional symbol is the snail, a modest, sensitive animal that shows its horns from time to time but mostly goes about its business in silence. Snails are carved onto church capitals and decorate Dijonnais town houses, as well as resting on one's plate. Like the snail, Burgundians say, they are happy in their shell. In one of Vincenot's best-known books a snail breeder is described who fattens up his largest snail and ceremoniously eats it on the family feast day.

Bernard opened his car window and breathed in the cool, crisp air of this *civilisation lente*. The slow D-road ran through a thick forest, broken only by a farm with a grazing herd of sturdy white Charolais cows. Above, birds chirped. Autumn was in full bloom. A few miles from Saulieu, with not a single house visible, he pulled his BMW off the road, stepped out, opened the trunk, took his rifle out, and slung it over his shoulder. A small dirt path led him deep into the forest. Bernard took a dozen steps, then suddenly stopped. He peered into the moss and the light undergrowth around the roots of a soaring oak tree. He turned sideways toward the tree, advanced his boot-clad leg—and jumped.

"Look," he shouted to his lone companion. "*Des champignons.*"

During the long family walks in the forest, Pierre Loiseau had taught his children the secrets of mushroom picking.

Bernard soon located *girolles,* trumpet-shaped fungus with a flaring cap of deep egg yellow, looking and smelling nothing like the bland white mushrooms sold in supermarkets. They gave off a golden, apricot aura; in contrast, morels found in springtime are dark brown, pitted with thick, lunarlike honeycomb cavities.

Bernard put the mushrooms up to his nose and breathed in what he called the essence of *le terroir,* the land. The smell mingled earthy, rich, slightly nutty sensations. When combined with a poached egg, this mushroom would make palates quiver.

Bernard jumped again. His quick hand thrust forward, and up he came with a new species. These were *trompettes de la mort,* horns of death, dark brown and shaped like an elongated horn. But they are delicious, not poisonous. In autumn, the mushrooms taste the strongest; the summer variety are a bit sugary.

Another jump and another cluster of mushrooms, this time darker, larger than the first batch: cèpes, destined to find their way onto a plate with wild boar or venison. The finest cèpes can also be eaten raw in salad, cut into thin slices. Intrepid mushroom hunters showed up almost every day in autumn at La Côte d'Or. Bernard paid them as much as ten dollars a pound wholesale for the finest specimens with the largest, most bulbous stalks.

At the beginning of October, La Côte d'Or featured a special all-mushroom menu. Bernard offered a five-dish gastronomic feast, involving asparagus tips, onions, parsley, truffles, applesauce, local cheeses, apple sherbet, and baked apples—and, of course, *girolles,* cèpes, and many other types of mushrooms ranging in color from blue-black to rust and violent orange.

Having captured his mushrooms, Bernard was ready to hunt in earnest. He found a perfect staging point in the middle of the forest. His quarry was pigeons, not the parasitic gray creatures that congregate around city fountains begging for bread, but the plump, juicy wild variety that he served at his restaurant. He loaded his rifle and stood still.

Before him the ground dipped; flocks of birds nestled on the other side of the small valley. If he waited long enough, they would fly over his position, exposed, perfect targets. Suddenly the air stirred and the leaves rippled. A flock of pigeons passed overhead. Bernard raised his rifle and fired a volley.

All the birds flew off—except one. Bernard ran forward and scooped it up. He twisted the bird's neck to finish it off. A trickle of blood ran from its limp body.

"I told you," Bernard exulted. "Ever since I was a kid, I have been a straight shooter. I throw boules straight and I shoot straight."

Bernard wrapped his pigeon in paper and returned to his BMW. It was about noon. Even though he had almost no customers waiting for him, he did not want to miss the lunch service. The BMW roared off at high speed down the D-road back toward Saulieu.

On the outskirts of Saulieu, the road dipped and plunged under a train track—the track for the first Train à Grande Vitesse line from Paris to Lyons. Here, at the edges of the Morvan, next to Bernard's hunting ground, the superfast train reaches its top speed of close to two hundred miles an hour, cutting travel time between the capital and France's second city from six hours to two. Diners can whiz from Paris to Paul Bocuse's restaurant in Lyons for lunch and be home by dinner.

But no TGV stop is located near La Côte d'Or.

The train company directors said not enough people lived in Saulieu to warrant a station. To Bernard's horror, hordes of potential, hungry customers came hurtling through his part of the world—without any hope that they could stop for a meal. In this way, his fast France never met Burgundy's slow France.

"Why did I ever come to this village?" Bernard asked himself again. "Am I really crazy?"

*An array of sweets*

CHAPTER 5

★ ★ ★

# *The Michelin Mystique*

*Two chefs*

IN THE SUMMER OF 1990, a Michelin *inspecteur* ate lunch at La Côte d'Or. A Michelin man makes his reservations anonymously and reveals himself only after paying for his meal. But Franck Juenin, the number-two maître d'hôtel, thought something was "funny." Franck considered himself a bit of a Michelin counterspy. He had once met a Michelin man while working in Corsica. The inspecteur later showed up in Saulieu.

"He pretended not to see me," Franck recalled. "His daughter recognized me, but the father was as cold as could be. Incredible. Not a word. I just walked away feeling I was an idiot."

The inspecteur took a table in the corner of the main dining room and ate by himself. "When somebody is alone, he usually picks up the menu quickly and then closes it," Franck said. "This guy took notes, he really studied the offerings. He did the same with the wine list. He really studied it." After the meal, the inspecteur came up to the front desk and flashed his company card.

"May I please see Monsieur Loiseau?" he asked.

Bernard came running.

"How was the meal?" he asked him, with trepidation.

The inspecteur responded that the fish portions were on the small side. He offered neither further criticism nor praise. Bernard snapped his fingers and asked for "the plans." A receptionist rushed to get the architect's drawings for La Côte d'Or's renovation. Bernard unfolded all the plans on a table. The inspecteur said nothing, not a single word.

Michelin is famous for its discretion, and its criteria for ratings are the subject of vigorous debate. What distinguishes a two-star restaurant from a three-star? At both establishments, diners eat fantastic food. All Michelin Guide director Bernard Naegellen would say was "Three stars represent perfection, and two stars represent near perfection."

Because a bad Michelin judgment seems cryptic and arbitrary, it can be the cause for tragedy. "It's Waterloo," wept one chef at Laperouse, a great traditional restaurant in Paris that lost its third star back in the 1960s. When Alain Zick, chef of the fashionable Paris restaurant Relais des Porquerolles, learned that he had been demoted from one star to none in 1966, he blew his brains out. Zick reportedly was having personal problems at the time, and Naegellen insisted that the press exaggerated the link between its stars and the chef's fate. All the same, the tragedy added to the Michelin mystique.

At the heart of this mystique is the simple rule of anonymity. The Michelin inspecteur eats and pays his bill. Among French restaurant critics, this is almost unique. Except for Michelin, most have not paid for a meal since they started writing. They enter a restaurant and before they can even get to a table, the chef is cooing, the sommelier is uncorking the best wines, and the maître d'hôtel is unveiling the most expensive dishes. In return for a mention in their guide, magazine, or newspaper, some writers even ask for a small donation, usually in the form of advertising. Not Michelin. It carries no ads. Once a particular inspecteur has revealed his identity, he doesn't return for seven or eight years, so the secret matters little.

To Bernard's mentor Verger, the food was all that counted. Any money spent upgrading La Côte d'Or was a bad investment. Verger's penchant for seduction and free meals did not go over well with the Michelin inspectors, and predictably, none of his Paris restaurants ever won any stars.

Decor and family status matter. Historian Pascal Ory describes Michelin as a citadel of "catholic, paternalistic" values. In his opinion, Michelin is "a type of culinary Vatican" with "secret, absolutist decision making." Almost alone among the world's great modern corporations, it is still directed by a family inner circle. In 1940, during the German occupation of France, the Wehrmacht asked to visit the factories to see how to utilize them in the war effort. Michelin made tires for the Germans, but it refused to let any German soldiers inside. When the SS insisted, they were allowed a perfunctory tour. Later General de Gaulle was barred from most of the factory. Secretive? "We prefer to say discreet," said company spokesman Alain Arnaud.

In compiling its guide, the twenty or so Michelin inspecteurs crisscross France for an entire year, alternating two-week spells on the road with two weeks back in headquarters writing up reports. After a decade, they have covered the entire country. Then they begin again. Most are graduates of hotel schools, a unique mixture of gourmand and ascetic. They travel incognito, driving ordinary, moderately-priced cars, and dressing in conservative gray suits. Some call them the monks of gastronomy. Others compare them to KGB or CIA agents. Whenever Bernard saw a single male enter a restaurant and take a table, he looked him over and, if he fit the profile, said, "Aha, a Michelin man."

He said "man" because most Michelin inspecteurs are men. Although the first "nun" reportedly joined their ranks in 1986, the guide's chauvinistic spokesmen emphasize the feat of eating up to fourteen restaurant meals a week and say it's a man's job. Professional eaters express envy—imagine being able to eat in that many good restaurants—but those involved stress how hard they work. Yes, there are many good restaurants in France. But Michelin men eat many bad meals as well. "Contrary to what many imagine, this job is not easy," said Naegellen. "All year, you are on the road, eating alone, and changing hotels every night. I remember times when there was so much fog that I kept asking where I was, and times when I was scared to be on the road, even with our great Michelin tires."

An Englishman, Robert William Thomson, invented the pneumatic tire in 1845. But brothers André and Edouard Michelin were the first to produce a tire with an inner tube that could be easily taken off and put back on the rim without hours of messy gluing. In 1888 they set up their company in their hometown of Clermont-Ferrand. Michelin was soon manufacturing tires for bicycles and carriages and, almost immediately afterward, for the infant automobile.

For the Michelins, publishing, no matter how successful, has always remained a sideline to the main business of producing tires, a public relations device to promote motoring rather than reap profits. When the company was launched, André Michelin hired two dozen poster artists. One of them, a certain Monsieur O'Galop, came up with the famous Michelin Man. The rotund figure made of tires called Bibendum has become, with Mickey Mouse, one of the world's best-known and most successful corporate symbols.

The Red Tourist Guide was first published at the beginning of the century. Until then, the railroad reigned supreme; travelers were restricted by timetables and train stations. André Michelin guessed that liberated motorists would appreciate a brief catalogue of establishments where they could eat, sleep, and have their car repaired. His first edition, published at Easter 1900, was a little red book measuring ten by fifteen centimeters, bright red, and numbering 399 pages. Michelin gave it away free.

The guide listed French towns from A to Z with hotels of interest to the motorist. It opened with a fifty-eight-page lecture, on everything from suggested itineraries to directions on how to pump up a tire, fix a flat, or check a leaky valve. At the time, there were no garages: grocers sold gas, and saddlers and cobblers repaired tires. Emphasis was placed on cities within seventy-five miles of Paris, the limit of the primitive car's endurance. The guide was an immediate success. Its first print run was thirty-five thousand, the second fifty thousand. "The original guides never used the word *gastronomic,*" said former guide director André Trichot. "They were dedicated to the automobile and contained little about hotels and restaurants. The change in emphasis corresponded to the increasing ease of travel."

Over the years, the Michelin publications have grown in number and scope. In 1901, André Michelin introduced the company's first map, of Clermont-Ferrand and its environs. Michelin now publishes 118 maps of various locations around the globe. Like the guides, Michelin maps are distinguished by their attention to detail. As the automobile revolution spread across Europe, Michelin followed with its Green Guides, not describing restaurants, but conventional tourist curiosities such as cathedrals and museums.

In 1920, Michelin began charging for its publications. The decision to sell the Red and Green Guides, along with the maps, reportedly came after André Michelin visited a provincial garage and spotted a copy jammed under the leg of a table. "If that's the way they treat my guides," he said, "then they are going to have to pay for them." At the same time, Michelin banned advertising. The first Red Guides were filled with ads; their removal eliminated any suspicion that good reviews could be bought.

The guide's directors initiated the star system in 1926. Before then, Michelin didn't judge the quality of cuisine. At first it awarded only one star. A second was added in 1931, and the ultimate, third in 1933.

The two world wars interrupted publication from 1915 to 1918 and from 1940 to 1944. Historian John Sweets has documented how Michelin negotiated with German authorities during World War II for contracts to receive artificial rubber. When Allied bombers struck the company's main factory in March 1944, German orders accounted for 80 percent of Michelin's production. After the war, the enterprise was fined for collaboration.

But although Michelin collaborated, its collaboration was limited to economics and excluded politics. Company officials later could argue that by keeping their factory open, they helped their employees avoid deportation and forced internment in German labor camps. Many of the Michelins themselves were patriots. At this time Marcel Michelin was running the company. Three of his sons joined Gaullist units in North Africa, his wife was arrested, and he and a son of André's, Jacques, were deported by the Germans.

When the Allies were preparing to invade France, the U.S. Army issued a facsimile of the 1939 guide, marked top secret, to frontline officers; it was considered to have the clearest and most thorough coverage of the country. After the war, travel became easier, cars had greater reliability, and drivers enjoyed more time for leisure. The guide expanded and adapted to the changing times. "With the arrival of American culture, we began to single out hotels that had toilets and showers in their rooms," Trichot said. "Today, we list hotels that are accessible to the physically handicapped."

Michelin now is the world's largest tire company, with almost one hundred thousand employees in Europe, Africa, and North and South America. The tourism division accounts for only about a thousand people. In recent years, Michelin officials have admitted that sales of more than six hundred thousand Red Guides, at about twenty-five dollars a copy, are not enough to make up for the expense of paying all those hotel and restaurant bills. But the losses reportedly are balanced by profits on the maps and Green Guides. As it does on many other subjects, the ultrasecret company refuses to give exact details.

Even as it has spread across the globe, Michelin has kept its roots in the small city of Clermont-Ferrand. Its headquarters are there, and so are its main factories, their belching smokestacks visible from Bernard Loiseau's childhood apartment. The guide itself, however, is located not in Clermont-

Ferrand, but in Paris, on Avenue de Breteuil, behind the Invalides in the exclusive seventh district, in an art deco building that dates from the 1920s.

Guests are ushered into a stuffy, windowless, and barren conference room. The decor is resolutely out of fashion, a simple table and wooden chairs. It could pass for a school classroom or, at worst, a waiting room in a prison. Silver-haired Bernard Naegellen, not a pound overweight, has been the guide's director since 1985. Before then, the director's name was not revealed. Nowadays, Naegellen will talk with the press, but only on the condition that his photo not be published. Once, in a moment of great magnanimity, he permitted his picture to be taken from the back. Interviewing him is not easy.

How many inspecteurs are there?

"A certain number," Naegellen responded.

The fiftyish Naegellen wouldn't even give his exact age.

"Write about the Michelin Guide," he advised, "not Bernard Naegellen."

Naegellen explained that the Michelin clock moves in slow motion. In almost all cases, it takes at least a decade to go from no stars to three stars. "We begin with a star, and then we see," Naegellen said. Can the chef uphold the standards? If he does and improves, more visits take place, and several years pass before the second star follows. Michelin returns and continues tasting. "At any establishment under consideration for three stars, we eat five, six times, to test the consistency," Naegellen explained. He had his inspecteurs eat at one three-star candidate eighteen times. "We are patient, because everything has to be perfect," he said.

Once a year, chefs are allowed to visit Naegellen at the Paris headquarters. Naegellen enters the conference room and drops a bulging folder onto the table. Inside it are letters from clients, satisfied, less satisfied, and least satisfied. Michelin watches its mail with care. It receives about twenty-five thousand letters a year from readers, describing their experiences in restaurants. All this voluminous correspondence is filed. Like a defendant at a criminal trial, the chef is allowed to read the accusations. But he has no lawyer to defend him. "All the Michelin people do is show you the letters," Bernard said. "They never say anything."

This discretion has helped create Michelin's invincible reputation for integrity, but it also makes the guide cryptic. In the 1990 edition, there were 1,279 pages, focusing on 4,586 localities (614 with city maps), and within them, 6,604 hotels and 3,801 restaurants. There was no explanatory text, only a list of the number of rooms, days open, prices charged, and perhaps one or two recommendations for culinary specialties. Grades were expressed in symbols. One to five forks were used to show "the degree of comfort" offered by a restaurant. A red fork designated particularly "pleasant" restaurants. In addition to stars, less elaborate, moderately priced menus offering good regional cooking were listed in red. When making a reservation at a restaurant, the Michelin reader knew little about the cooking, atmosphere, or personality of the establishment.

Nothing in the history of cookery correspondence compares with this cold, severe anonymity. The first restaurant reviews probably were itineraries mapped out for the use of medieval pilgrims. They commented, often with considerable grace and eloquence, on the amenities of monasteries along the route. In the early nineteenth century, a new class emerged, the gastronomes. Jean-Anthelme Brillat-Savarin, in his *Physiology of Taste,* asserted that cooking was a true science, equal to chemistry, physics, medicine, and anatomy. He enjoyed describing food more than eating. In contrast, another early gastronomic writer, Alexandre Balthasar Laurent Grimod de la Reynière, regularly gorged himself. Beginning in 1804, he produced the annual *Almanach des Gourmands,* an anecdotal and practical guide to Paris that proved successful and controversial. Appropriately, he died on Christmas Eve, 1837, in his country home, during a midnight feast.

Until the eighteenth century, the best food was served in privately owned châteaux, prepared by the aristocrat's own chef. For those obliged to travel, various inns and post-houses were located at strategic towns, such as Saulieu, along the main roads. The modern restaurant was born in Paris only in 1765. A man reportedly named Boulanger—his identity is a subject of debate—set up a few tables down the street from the Louvre and began offering soup, chicken, and various egg dishes. He put a sign outside his establishment, in Latin, promising to "restore" empty stomachs to proper health.

The French bourgeoisie, profiting from the massive rebuilding of Paris during the glittering Restoration and Second Empire, adored eating out. In contrast, the English aristocracy continued to entertain at home, so while the restaurant became king in Paris, such establishments remained rare in London, one explanation for the failure of vastly richer Victorian England to develop as sophisticated or varied a style of cooking as France. Numerous gastronomic societies sprang up, many of which remain in existence, including one dubbed Le Club des Grands Estomacs, the Big Stomach Club. Composed of wealthy Parisians, the group met every Saturday at six in the evening at a restaurant called Pascal and ate for eighteen hours straight. The menu took up several pages. Suffice it to say that there were three servings of six hours apiece, each running from appetizer to dessert, and that over the course of the feast each diner downed six bottles of Burgundy wine.

Throughout the nineteenth century, the increasing popularity of restaurants boosted the sales of culinary guides. But food writing boomed only at the turn of the century, with the development of the automobile and tourism. Maurice

Edmond Sailland, also known as Curnonsky, a man of enormous size and weight, toured France by car and wrote thirty-two volumes of *La France Gastronomique* over as many years. He created the Academy of Gastronomes to set culinary standards, and in 1927, in a national ballot organized by a newspaper, he was elected Prince of Gastronomes. In contrast to the Michelin inspecteur, when the Prince of Gastronomes Curnonsky appeared at the front door of a restaurant, only a foolish receptionist or chef would not have known him by sight.

Gastronomy was still not considered a subject as worthy of a cultivated man's time as law, science, or theology. Right-wing journalists dominated the profession, attracted by the culture of style and the values of tradition and *terroir.* Left-wingers stayed away, a reflection of their skepticism about the good life. When a liberal American historian named Nancy Green once went to buy cheese in Paris, the *fromager* told her, "Madame, you may vote on the left, but you certainly eat on the right."

La Côte d'Or and Dumaine tended the wealthy, right-wing bourgeoisie. The Hôtel de la Poste was considered the communist hotel because its owner, Guy Virlouvet, was a relative of longtime Communist party leader Maurice Thorez. During the war, Marshal Pétain stopped in Saulieu on his way north from Vichy to Paris. Naturally, he ate and slept at La Côte d'Or. Rationing meant that Dumaine had trouble finding fresh ingredients. Nonetheless, he offered the marshal a vegetable soup, a mushroom omelette soufflé with potato croquettes, a country salad, some cheese, and a dessert of simple fruit. Because he didn't have enough eggs, Dumaine cheated by beating the egg whites to create the mirage of abundance. The wines for what the chef called this "sad meal" were, of course, "quite ordinary."

If Dumaine's collaboration was mild, other wartime gastronomes leaned further right, often falling over the line into extremism. For five decades, Robert Courtine was one of France's most esteemed French gastronomic critics, writing for the prestigious daily *Le Monde*. But in 1993, his byline suddenly disappeared. Courtine's retirement came after a few of his colleagues at *Le Monde* stumbled across uncomfortable evidence showing that during World War II, the food writer had published virulent anti-Semitic articles in a fascist newspaper called *Je Suis Partout*. Digging deeper, the investigators discovered that after the war, Courtine was convicted for collaboration and served time in prison. *Le Monde*'s founder, Hubert Beuve-Meury, had hired him after his release, in 1953. "The editors at *Le Monde* knew about his past but didn't think it was a problem," said Pascal Ory, the history professor. "After all, he wasn't going to be writing about anything political."

Today, a new generation of gastronomic critics, too young to have much experience with either Nazism or wartime rationing, has emerged. These critics came of age during the so-called thirty glorious years, France's three decades of unparalleled postwar growth and prosperity. In this modern, booming France, the values of pleasure spread across former sharp political, social, and religious divides. When a prominent Jewish socialist critic named Gilles Pudlowski published paeans of praise for his native Alsatian cooking, the values of pure pleasure had triumphed. "All the taboos of the past are gone," Pudlowski said. "I tell my readers that you can be Jewish and love France and that you can be liberal and love food."

The new personal, emotional, and apolitical school of criticism was led by Henri Gault and Christian Millau, both too young to have been associated with World War II's far-right extremism. Although Gault and Millau leaned toward conservatism in their politics, Ory argues that "their only real religion was hedonism." Neither Gault nor Millau had formal training in famous kitchens or hotels. Gault, the son of a Normandy physician, was studying medicine in Paris when his parents died in 1952; he dropped out because he could no longer afford the tuition or muster the energy needed to continue. In 1954, he joined a tennis magazine as a salesman, slipping onto the reporting side when he discovered that he could write. This talent took him to the flashy evening newspaper *Paris Presse,* where he received a cushy assignment: covering the world of tennis, golf, and polo. Bored by his beat, he started consoling himself with long meals and strolls around Paris, searching out choice charcuteries and unusual food shops. When Gault's editor and friend Christian Millau found out about his gastronomic sideline, he asked him if he would write up the results for the paper.

Millau's path to *Paris Presse* had been smoother. Scion of an old, established family of parfumeurs, he studied international relations at Paris's Institut des Sciences Politiques, then spent five years reading law at the Sorbonne. Unsure of what to do next, he chose journalism. By the time he was thirty, he was deputy editor in chief, responsible for the features page. Editor Millau gave his reporter Gault free rein. The results ran on a groundbreaking Friday leisure page and became an immediate sensation. So many readers lined up outside the first restaurant Gault praised that the owner threatened to sue: the mob, he complained, made it impossible to serve his regular customers.

In 1961, the publishing house, Julliard, offered the two young journalists an advance of $2,000 to produce a new restaurant guide for Paris. Within a year, the pair had sampled 350 eating places. Beyond the restaurants, hotels, cafés, and bistros were other finds: butchers, bakers, snail vendors, oil and wine merchants, and even antique dealers. The book became one of the year's best sellers, and Gault-Millau's reputation was launched.

In contrast to the drab, provincial Michelin inspecteurs, both Gault and Millau were pure products of Paris. They possessed flair and sophistication. Both dressed well, in the latest fashions, and once they became well known, the gossip pages recounted their comings and goings. In their youth, both kept trim despite eating out almost every night. Both were heavy smokers, in spite of the presumable damage to their palates. Of the tandem, Gault had the sharper pen and wit, while Millau had a shrewder eye for business.

The combination proved fruitful, and a mini-Gault-Millau empire soon emerged. In 1968, under their own corporate banner, they borrowed $50,000 and brought out a monthly magazine, *Le Nouveau Guide*. Within a few years, it had a circulation of 150,000. They also began producing guidebooks, one for Paris, one for France, and one for French wine. Eventually, the guides expanded abroad, scrutinizing cities as far afield as New York and countries as exotic as Tunisia and Turkey. Gault-Millau even licensed a series of products. The company created a "gourmet club" that selected wines and champagnes for its members, who were drawn from the subscription lists of the Gault-Millau magazine.

In their heyday, the pair generated gross annual revenues of more than $6 million. Both lived the high life. Gault bought a giant apartment just opposite the Elysée Palace. He took vacations with his wife and children at a large country house near the old Huguenot city of La Rochelle, on the Atlantic coast. Millau furnished an elegant town house in the capital's chic sixteenth arrondissement and used his vacations for culinary explorations around the globe. He published the results in his magazine.

Gault-Millau's reviews were personal and punchy. Restaurants were awarded from one to four toques and rated on a scale of 1 to 20. Ratings of 10, 11, and 12 were considered restaurants "of a respectable level" but received no toques; 13 and 14 obtained one toque; 15 and 16, two; 17 and 18, three; and 19 four. Each listing was followed by a witty, irreverent, street-smart text describing the establishment. While Michelin evaluates only the notable establishments and reserves judgment for as long as three years, Gault-Millau added ratings for inexpensive and little-known restaurants.

Their reputation rose in tandem with the acerbity of their reviews and their impressive list of plantiffs charging libel. Of one establishment, they wrote: "The fish soup was watery, the lobster brochette insipid." The offending Marseilles restaurant—appropriately named Le New York—lost not only customers but a subsequent libel suit as well. "We established the principle that journalists have a right to criticize restaurants by name just as movie critics and theater reviewers do with film and plays," Millau gloated in a 1980 interview for a *Time* magazine cover story.

Gault and Millau tweaked the French food establishment and, above all, debunked sacred culinary canons. They published features in their magazine that judged Israeli foie gras to be only "slightly inferior" to the French product. They graded Chinese, Indian, Indonesian, and Vietnamese food, dashing the chauvinistic notion that the only cuisine in the world was French. They even revealed that a tasting panel of famous chefs noticed no difference when fed a meal in which butter had been replaced by margarine in all the cooking.

When Dominique Versini opened her restaurant named Olympe, in Paris, spawning hopes and fears of a female invasion of haute cuisine, Gault-Millau offered three toques and lavish praise. "We do not hesitate to make her the first woman in the guide to be crowned with three toques," they wrote. "The exclusive domain of this little woman has never been so delicious and creative." With more than a touch of male condescension, they praised the restaurant's "elegant atmosphere where beautiful women are more beautiful yet."

Gault and Millau also broke oenological convention. They condoned serving red wine with fish and touted the virtues of American wine. In one celebrated test, the critics subjected cases of good Bordeaux to freezing and heating, even bouncing them around Paris in a car. Heat and light, they found, could destroy wine, but the cold and bouncing affected only those with a heavy sediment. In another test, they assembled 330 wines from thirty-three countries for a tasting by sixty-two experts from ten nations. In one test, four California reds and a Yugoslav red placed above a 1950 Premier Cru Château Latour.

As they went about their research, the pair began to calculate the metabolic costs of their work. During the first decade, they consumed between them roughly 7,760 quarts of wine and champagne, 45 quarts of liquor and aperitifs, 4,000 quarts of coffee, 1,500 pounds of beef, 220 pounds of foie gras, 35 pounds of caviar, 25 pounds of truffles, 55 pints of cream, 1,000 pounds of butter, 22,000 eggs, and nearly 15,000 oysters. They were eating more than 500 restaurant meals a year and developing formidable bellies. They wondered whether they could survive many more seasons of heavy sauces and butter-slathered dishes that "assassinated" the taste of good food and masked that of bad.

The diet was frightening, and the duo responded by championing a new form of cooking. It used less butter and cream and combined with shorter cooking times for meat, fish, and vegetables. After a visit to a health spa in the summer of 1973, Gault came away convinced that it was possible to eat well without eating too much. His born-again testimony appeared in the October magazine under the breathless headline "VIVE LA NOUVELLE CUISINE FRANÇAISE." Thus was born the famous phrase *la nouvelle cuisine*.

CHAPTER 6

★ ★ ★

# Nouvelle Cuisine

*Hubert Couilloud, maître d'hôtel*

THE FRENCH have actually been touting "new cooking" for centuries. As early as 1739, François Marin championed "modern cuisine" with "less pomp and impediment." Marin was horrified by the bloated, baroque tradition of overeating that reached its apotheosis at Versailles under Louis XIV. The Sun King employed more than fifty cooks in his palace and could eat a meal consisting of four different soups, an entire pheasant, a partridge, a large plate of salad, mutton served in its juices and spiced with garlic, two good pieces of ham, and an array of cakes, fruits, and jams.

The feasts were serious business. In 1671, a maître d'hôtel, Fritz Karl Vatel, was entrusted with organizing a banquet in the king's honor. The celebration began on a Thursday evening, and in the course of the supper Vatel discovered that several tables were without roast meat because a number of unexpected guests turned up. Learning at dawn on the following day that only two loads of the fresh fish ordered for the day had arrived, Vatel gave in to despair, declaring, "I shall not survive the disgrace." He proceeded to shut himself in his room and run his sword through his body.

Ever since, each generation of French chefs has watched his colleagues and concluded that only perfection was enough to save him from a disastrous fate. To reach the top of the trade, a distinguishing style was needed, something to set one's cooking off from that of his peers, something new. Bernard understood this lesson well. He worked hard to develop a daring, inventive, and personal approach to cooking. In Saulieu, he lived and worked in the shadow of twentieth-century culinary history. Dumaine's cooking was a romantic reaction to stuffy city cooking, and Bernard followed him in reorchestrating the classics of French cuisine, refashioning them for today's world. "We want to remind people of veal stew that their grandmothers made, to give them the old tastes," he said. "But we have to do it in a modern way."

Bernard's recipe for snails was a good example of how he updated a classic Burgundy specialty. Traditionally, snails were removed from their shells, covered with salt to make them give up their slime, and then washed. They were cooked for almost an hour in a *court-bouillon* before being put back in their shells with lashings of garlic butter, heated in the oven until the butter bubbled, and served piping hot. The first recipe for these *escargots à la bourguignonne* dates from 1825 and remained pretty much unchanged through Dumaine's day.

Bernard hated the idea of drowning the snails in butter and garlic and believed that cooking them with salt dried them out. During his forest jaunts as a child, he observed snails among nettles. Why not mix the snails with nettles? he thought. And why not cook the snails while they are still in their shells, removing them only at the last moment? That way, their flavor is conserved. Bernard served his steaming-hot snails, wrapped in green nettles, as a succulent appetizer. "I take all the fat and cream out of the dish, but keep the strong taste," he said.

For every innovation, Bernard paid attention to tradition. He called one of his specialties *poularde Alexandre Dumaine*. In the old days, Dumaine made a stuffed, cream-sauce chicken from the nearby Bresse region. Bresse chickens are free-range white Beny poultry reared just south of Dijon, around the city of Bourg-en-Bresse. Their flesh is yellow and flavorful and has long been highly esteemed. When Henri IV conquered Bresse in 1601 he remarked on the delicacy of the chicken. Brillat-Savarin's verdict was "Queen of poultry, poultry of kings."

Bernard's update was still a Bresse chicken, stuffed with leeks, carrots, and chicken liver, with a few black truffle slices placed under the skin. The bird was steamed over a combination of chicken stock, beef stock, port, and brandy. It came to the table in a steaming pot, with thick towels wrapped around the lid. With great ceremony, the waiter undid the toweling, lifted the lid, and served two plates of the simple, subtle poached bird.

To some critics, the *poularde* was rarefied boiled chicken in the pot, a simple grandmother's dish. To Bernard's supporters, it was a sublime blend of the modern and the traditional. Without doubt, the recipe showed how Bernard played up his restaurant's history, celebrating Dumaine's greatness while displaying his own virtuosity.

In Bernard's quest for a perfect cooking style, his training at Troisgros proved indispensable. The Troisgros brothers were Dumaine's successors, the next generation that pushed the master's innovations to their logical conclusions. On a technical level, the Troisgros spurned heavy sauces that masked the taste of the meat. They avoided flour and other starches as well and returned to a lighter, purer style, using the best raw materials and cooking them quickly—almost in a Chinese manner—in their own juices.

Pierre Troisgros's invention of *saumon à l'oseille* typifies what Gault and Millau called nouvelle cuisine. Until Troisgros, the accepted way of cooking fish was to take thick chunks and coat them in flour and bake in butter. Troisgros threw out the coating, cut the fish in thin scallopini, and cooked them in white wine until they were just rosé. In his garden, sorrel sprouted, so he threw it over the fish. Troisgros's cooking required the best-quality produce, for no longer could inferior ingredients be disguised in rich sauces. Bernard said his first epiphany in the kitchen was while making the sorrel sauce for Troisgros's famous salmon. "I was so nervous I could hardly stir," he recalled. He never forgot the idea of using the freshest products and cooking them just enough to bring out their sharpest flavor.

Troisgros eliminated the formal, garnished banquet platters of Escoffier, which themselves were simplifications of the grand sculptures inherited from nineteenth-century practitioners who had labored for noble houses or bourgeois restaurant patrons in love with pomp and circumstance. In Dumaine's posthumous autobiography, *Ma Cuisine,* published in 1968, the food is simple enough, but his culinary universe still revolves around the banquet. Platters of pâtés, suckling pig, or whole tarts are presented to a table of people or a large family assembled for a dramatic occasion.

By the time the Troisgros brothers published their *Cuisiniers à Roanne* in 1977, gastronomic writer Raymond Sokolov noted that they selected photos with food arranged on individual plates like paintings. The plates included designs of sliced vegetables in circular or other geometric patterns. They flowed from the evolution in thinking about food started by Dumaine and drew dramatically on the Japanese aesthetic.

Another important aspect of nouvelle cuisine's revolutionary cooking style was its emphasis on the chef-owner. Dumaine, Point, and Pic showed that chefs could own the places where they cooked and that the maître d'hôtel worked for them. At the time, they were exceptional. Their students generalized the phenomenon in a way that British writer John Ardagh has called "the revolt of the serfs." Point's protégés were led by the Troisgros brothers and a young chef named Paul Bocuse, whose family owned a modest auberge beside the Saône just north of Lyons. Most critics agree that Bocuse never was the greatest of the new cooks; the Troisgros certainly surpassed him in brilliant creativity. But Bocuse's magnetic personality and the powers of his leadership rallied the new generation to apply and disseminate the Holy Trinity's philosophy. More than any other single figure, Bocuse turned the three-star Michelin chef into a celebrity.

After completing his apprenticeship *chez* Point, Bocuse returned to Lyons and transformed his family auberge into a luxury showpiece for his new cooking. In 1961, Michelin awarded him his first star. By 1965, he had the third star, the fastest rise in Michelin history until Michel Guérard made it between 1974 and 1977, at Eugénie-les-Bains. When Bocuse reached the top, he already was his own master. All around him, however, he saw that the best restaurants were not in the hands of the cooks, but of businessmen who often knew little about cooking. The chef was a mere employee, forced to cook as he was told. Bocuse encouraged the master chefs to open their own restaurants where they could practice their art.

Bocuse relied on an immense talent for showmanship to promote his cause. He was a Rabelaisian figure, full of paradoxes, who made the backroom job of chef look glamorous. His father's restaurant was called Auberge du Pont de Collonges. When Bocuse took over, he put up a giant PAUL BOCUSE sign that stood forth majestically in huge letters at the entrance. He got himself invited as the guest of honor at the Elysée Palace, to prepare and eat a special meal with the president, an event that secured front-page play in all the major newspapers. He acted the role of provocateur to perfection. While traveling the world as an ambassador for French cooking, he still would arrange schoolboy pranks on his friends, such as importing striptease girls to a Paris party or sending a gift of flowers wrapped around the rotting carcass of a hare.

Today, almost all three-star Michelin restaurants are owned by chefs, as against a mere handful in the previous generation. Bocuse himself has become a tourist attraction. His commercial interests span the globe, from a restaurant at the Epcot Center, in Florida, to a cooking school in Japan, to a line of canned foods. Many said that his restaurant's quality suffered from his absences and his diversification. In recent years, as he edged well over the sixty mark, the jolly Bocuse became a moody figure, on one day, off the next.

Still, Bocuse's influence inspired Bernard, who considered him his spiritual father. In a conscious echo of the master, one of the first moves that Bernard made after he bought La Côte d'Or was to put up a sign on the facade in big, bold, black letters: BERNARD LOISEAU. Below it, in small letters, of secondary importance, "La Côte d'Or" was inscribed. "Bocuse taught us that we no longer are servants," Bernard said. "The cook used to be hidden in the basement. Now he goes into the dining room and Rothschilds call him up to ask favors."

Bocuse and Troisgros had nouvelle cuisine. Bernard knew that he couldn't simply play on Dumaine's reputation and update traditional recipes. He needed a manifesto and a slogan. So he thought long and hard and came up with something called *cuisine à l'eau*—water cooking.

A typical Loiseau feast began with a soft, sweet artichoke mousse, followed by pike floating in a bed of moist shallots and snapper soaring in sea urchin. Nothing was hidden behind deceptive cream sauces. Bernard used the plumpest and freshest scallops, the thickest fillets of perch, sweet and cloudlike, the freshest sole bathed in a remarkable vinaigrette.

"*Paf!*"

Bernard wanted a forkful of his cooking to explode in the mouth. In an attempt to strengthen his flavors, he banished butter, cream, and egg yolks, the usual stocks of French cooking, from his kitchen. He said they were bad for health in this cholesterol-obsessed era, and worse yet, they hid the pure taste of the true ingredients. Bernard even refused the elemental trick of deglazing a pan with wine or liquor. Red wine should add flavor to the meat or fish, but all too often it ended up hiding and distorting the ingredient's flavor. Bernard's solution was to reduce ten bottles of wine to one—and then, instead of using cream, to thicken the sauce with a puree of carrot. For a white wine sauce, he thickened with pureed onions. The technique concentrated flavors, letting his fresh perch in red wine float onto the diner's palate.

He employed a nonstick pan and even then he patted the food dry with a paper towel. When grilling fresh red mullet, for example, he cooked on the skin side with a touch of virgin olive oil for two minutes—not a second more and not a second less—and wiped the cooking oil off the finished fish. He slipped the fillet onto a hot plate, uncooked side down, and then passed the dish to his left. Another cook added a garnish of steamed zucchini flowers and sauced the fish with a puree of red wine or, more recently, sea urchins. When the food reached the diner, the heat from the serving plate had cooked the other side. "The fat and oil are left at the bottom of the pan," Bernard claimed. "You know what you're eating, you get the full taste of the red mullet in your mouth. "*Paf!*"

Cuisine à l'eau was controversial. For many lovers of rich, classical cuisine, minimalist, birdlike "water cooking" lacked flavor and substance. Critics such as Patricia Wells called it "tiddlywinks cuisine," lots of dull things cut in little shapes and bits. The vicious derided it as Maoist cooking for its extremist austerity. In addition to avoiding cream and butter, Bernard banned salt from the table. Using musical terms, the writer Rudolph Chelminski describes Bocuse as Beethoven and Bernard as "Stravinsky, Schoenberg, or perhaps even Stockhausen." Some loved the modern melody. Others found it jarring.

Part of Bernard's intention was to draw attention to himself. He succeeded, without a doubt. His inventions created a great and acrimonious debate within French gastronomic circles. No less than his good friend Bocuse came up with the definitive wisecrack when he was strolling along the banks of the river Saône. "What a pity," Bocuse said. "If only Bernard could see all that sauce going to waste."

These days, Bernard said he hated the label cuisine à l'eau. He claimed the term was misunderstood, and he preferred to call his cooking *cuisine de jus,* the cuisine of essences. Over the years, he toned down his battle against butter and cream and now accepted limited amounts of them in his cooking. A little butter, he acknowledged, is needed to blend the sauce and the meat. "For a long while I experimented with cooking without fat," he said. His goal, he has realized, should not be to avoid all "bad" ingredients. It should be good taste. "You need a minimum amount of oil or butter to bind the ingredients," he admitted.

Unlike the creators of nouvelle cuisine, Bernard consciously modernized traditional dishes. His recipe for frog leg is a good example. For centuries, the legs were deep-fried in butter and garlic and covered with parsley leaves. The recipe is tasty, but so full of fat that, Bernard said, "it made me sick to my stomach." Bernard lightened the dish by simmering fresh garlic cloves for half an hour—and then changing the water ten times to eliminate their overpowering taste. Hc blended the garlic with milk to the consistency of mashed potatoes. Then he made a thick green parsley purée. The frog legs were fried, and at the last possible moment all the elements were put on the plate. "You have the garlic taste without the force, you have the natural juice of parsley without the butter," Bernard explained. "Each element is put together at the last moment, when it adds to the other. Not too many different elements, either, just two or three. You can't have too many tastes in the mouth at the same time."

Bernard was an intuitive creator. He dreamed up new recipes in the solitude of the forest. When he returned to the kitchen, he explained his ideas to Patrick. Patrick cooked a sample. He, Hubert, and Bernard tasted. If they liked the result, they put it on the menu.

Another controversial aspect of Bernard's philosophy was his approach to luxury ingredients such as caviar, foie gras, and truffles. Nouvelle cuisine created dishes to play up these delicacies. Bernard believed they are earthy foods, and he was almost alone in attempting to restore them, as he said, "to their country roots," mixing them with such lowly foods as oxtail aspic and even potatoes.

Potatoes? In Bernard's mind, even the humble potato was worthy of reverence. In wintertime, for $70, he offered an all-potato feast called *Pommes en fête.* It started with baby leeks and potatoes soaked in a potato vinaigrette, followed by a *croustillant* of potato with dwarf vegetables and mashed potatoes, swimming in oxtail broth and studded with truffles. The culinary curiosity concluded with green apple sherbet and a shortbread of apples, caramel, and nuts. In the summer, the quirky Loiseau expressed the opposite side of his all-potato menu in La Côte d'Or's all-vegetable menu. Strictly speaking, it was not vegetarian, because meat and fish broths were used. All the same, diners paid $85 to eat dishes filled with little other than leeks and asparagus.

To most of the French culinary establishment, these theme menus were evidence of Bernard's flakiness. But Henri Gault defended him. As far back as 1974, when Bernard was still at La Barrière Poquelin, Gault praised Bernard the Bird as "a remarkable chef ready to take off." Later, Gault touted Bernard on French radio as "perhaps the best cook in the world."

The praise didn't help as much as Bernard hoped. But by the mid 1980s, Gault-Millau had fallen into desperate decline. They had taken a craft that always had its roots in peasant traditions, with generous portions, and created a new fad. Thanks to their jobs, both Gault and Millau were encouraged to eat two sophisticated French meals a day. No human being can take too much food, too much cream, too much butter, and too much wine. After a few days of such feasting, the stomach becomes bloated. Little wonder that these two professional eaters turned to salvation in the light, picture-perfect portions of nouvelle cuisine and cuisine à l'eau.

But the general public, respected by Michelin, doesn't eat in great restaurants every day. For such occasional visitors, a trip to a great restaurant is supposed to be a festive occasion, and a feast is supposed to emphasize rich foods. Middle-aged food critics, like many middle-aged people, suffer weight problems and hypertension when they eat and drink too much. No high-paid specialist was needed to diagnose the illness: the old spark had vanished. Gault and Millau, the former revolutionaries hungry for change, had lost their appetite. "These days they are more interested in the coat check girl's smile than they are in the food," some chefs said, in private. Admittedly, few still dared to be quoted by name when talking about Gault and Millau.

As they lost their spark, the founders fought over almost everything. One insider compared the situation to that of the Beatles before their breakup. Of the two men, Gault had the better nose for good food, while Millau had the more forceful personality and the more ravenous business ambition. Millau soon emerged as the stronger figure, and to Bernard's misfortune, he took a liking to the cooking of Marc Meneau, in Vézelay. In order to clear the playing field for his friend, Millau refused to give any other chef in Burgundy the top grade. Millau's indifference to journalistic objectivity led him to hire an advertising company to put together special regional reports; later it became clear that the publicists were telling restaurants that if they bought an ad, they could get a favorable article. Although the advertisers were fired, the damage was done. In contrast to Michelin,

Gault-Millau obtained a reputation for cronyism and grade inflation.

By the late 1980s, the guide was giving away many high grades, 18s and 19s. It even created the impossibly high notation of 19.5. "Since we were trying to get away from the Michelin style of gastronomic criticism—cold, impartial, and anonymous—our guide was personal and partial, and we became friends with many of the people we dealt with," Gault acknowledged. "Once you're best friends with someone, how can you lower their rating or take away a toque?"

The answer was that you can't. In 1985, Gault finally managed to get La Côte d'Or four toques and a 19.5 rating. Bernard was delighted. He hoped the promotion would give him 30 to 40 percent more customers, just like a third Michelin star. He went to the bankers and asked for loans to complete his giant renovation. But business didn't pick up. "It was then that I realized how hopeless we had become," Gault said. "Bernard is the nicest, most naive, enthusiastic guy and we couldn't do anything for him."

Not long afterward, Gault split with Millau. A big media conglomerate, the L'Express group, took over the guide. In a 1992 palace coup, the new owners deposed Millau, leaving him with only an honorary title and a monthly column in the magazine. Gault went to work as a freelance writer out of a small office near the Arc de Triomphe. He spent most of his time writing books for rich Japanese sponsors. Gault and Millau once staged a reunion, hugging and kissing for the cameras. But they never managed to overcome their differences and work together again. As a result, Gault-Millau's circulation kept plummeting.

The battle of the guidebooks was over. Gault-Millau, with their sprightly prose and their preference for innovative nouvelle cuisine, were the losers. Many still love to hate Michelin. It is haughty. It is impersonal and boring. It is traditional and passé in its cooking preferences. Some voices in the French gastronomic world even say that many three-star restaurants are beyond their prime. Although historical monuments such as La Tour d'Argent, in Paris, no longer are at the cutting edge of culinary excellence, they remain at the top of the Michelin pantheon anyhow.

Bernard was not the only rising chef frustrated in his Michelin dream. Other innovators, such as Michel Rostang in Paris and Michel Bras in Auvergne, had labored for years without obtaining the third star. But with Gault-Millau's demise, no one has been able to challenge the Red Guide's supremacy.

*A chocolate dessert*

CHAPTER 7

★ ★ ★

# *Grand Ambitions*

*Dominique*

ONCE BERNARD discovered that praise from Gault-Millau and other lesser critics wouldn't allow him to achieve his goals, he redoubled his Michelin efforts. He observed how other chefs won the precious three stars and recognized that it wasn't only food that counted. Down the road in southern Burgundy, in a small village called Vonnas, a chef-entrepreneur named Georges Blanc had gained Michelin's top ranking in 1980 by transforming a simple eight-room country inn called La Mère Blanc into a sumptuous hotel-restaurant with a swimming pool, tennis court, and even a helicopter landing pad.

Clients poured in. Up went a Georges Blanc boutique selling Georges Blanc foodstuffs and kitchenware. Across the village square Blanc built a less expensive hotel and bistro. La Côte d'Or's maître d'hôtel, Hubert Couilloud, joked that Vonnas, population 2,413, had become Georges Blanc City.

In culinary matters, Blanc had little to teach Bernard. In perfecting the art of "restoration," however, there was an important lesson. "Cooking alone isn't enough anymore," Bernard realized. "You need something more, to give the clients peace and calm for the weekend. They want to wake up to see trees and grass. They want to relax. They want to dream. Blanc understood all this. That's why he is my model."

In Burgundy, Marc Meneau was the first to upgrade his facilities. At the beginning of the 1980s, he knocked down the walls of his old restaurant and erected a shimmering glass veranda at his L'Espérance, in Saint-Pere-sous-Vézelay. Diners relaxed while looking out onto a garden reminiscent of a Monet painting, with the hilltop medieval village lingering in the background. In 1983, Meneau won the magical third Michelin star.

Chefs all over France soon were turning simple country auberges into elaborate châteaux. The Lorains in the small northern Burgundy village of Joigny even constructed a tunnel under the road between their main dining room and their riverside annex. Critics derided the edifice, which began as a family-style auberge, as an ostentatious palace. In 1986, Michelin awarded a third star to the Lorains.

Many chefs took similar gambles with both their financial futures and artistic reputations in their own frenzy of monument building. Great chefs seem to have awful taste in anything other than food. In the far reaches of the remote Auvergne countryside, a rising young chef named Michel Bras won two Michelin stars and then decided to shoot for the third. He built a supermodern outpost on a mountain perch. One writer compared the new restaurant and hotel to "Noah's Ark on Mount Ararat, transformed into an ocean liner."

The unfortunate Jean-Pierre Amat hired the preeminent practitioner of French high-tech architecture, Jean Nouvel, to redo his Hôtel Jardins de Hauterive and Restaurant St. James, just across the river from Bordeaux. Nouvel pictured the structure as a modern imitation of a local tobacco warehouse. The rough metal structure won numerous avant-garde design awards. But for many clients, it simply was too modern. They complained that it looked like a twenty-first-century spaceship ready to take off from a conservative nineteenth-century landscape. Amat's business fizzled away, and he was forced to declare bankruptcy.

Other talented Burgundy chefs faced a similar dangerous spiral. In 1981, not far from Saulieu, Jean-Pierre Silva opened a cozy family spot called Auberge du Vieux Moulin. Soon, he obtained a Michelin star. Business was good and the young chef was happy. Local clientele poured in. Then came a second star.

"Oomph," Silva said with a sigh. "We weren't ready. Foreigners started coming. They had high expectations and found only this simple family place."

Silva thought about going to Michelin and asking for a demotion. Instead, against his better judgment, he doubled his kitchen staff, from ten to twenty, and launched a giant building program. He installed an indoor swimming pool and constructed a glass-covered dining room. His country inn became a luxury resort, and the modest, unassuming Silva was left struggling to make ends meet.

"I certainly don't want three stars," he said. "We would have to have three maître d'hôtels, three sommeliers, too many employees. We could no longer be young, friendly, informal, and wear polo shirts."

Bernard was different. He was still ready to gamble millions on renovating La Côte d'Or, without any assurance of Michelin's approval. He planned to rebuild his kitchen, redecorate his salons, and add new dining rooms, complete with timbered ceilings, patinated walls, and large sliding windows. Instead of having to listen to the trucks roar by on the Nationale, as in Dumaine's day, he wanted his guests to contemplate a tranquil garden.

Normally cautious, Dominique supported him. She saw the renovation as her chance to carve out a role for herself. But Bernard had definite ideas about what he wanted. The chairman of the jewelry firm Cartier invited Bernard to lunch with Nouvel, thinking that the two artists, both bald and outspoken, would hit it off. Instead, Bernard launched into a diatribe against modern architecture. "No one who comes to Loiseau wants to eat in a Sputnik taking off for Mars," he said.

From her experience as a journalist in Paris, Dominique knew most of the builders who specialized in the field. When Bernard asked her for the name of an architect, she recommended Guy Catonné.

The fifty-year-old Catonné was small and stocky, with a white beard and a chirpy voice that made him look and sound like a squirrel. He ran a small architecture office in Paris. To all visitors, he made a point of mentioning that his office was originally built as a bordello. His specialty was renovating thematic restaurants. His major achievement was the makeover of Au Pied de Cochon, a classic bistro specializing in pig's feet, open twenty-four hours a day in the heart of the former market district Les Halles.

None of Catonné's projects had won architectural awards. But they all came in on time and on budget. Au Pied de Cochon was redone in five short weeks. "It was like a war, but we did it," Catonné said. For a chef, such efficiency is crucial. Every day closed is a day of revenue lost. "Dominique didn't want a dreamer," Catonné said. "She knew my previous work and told me that it was *serieux*."

When asked whether La Côte d'Or's building would have any specific architectural distinction, Catonné raised his voice and replied, "*None!*" Bernard did not want an architect who would overshadow him. Catonné agreed. "I don't want clients to say they are going to eat at Catonné," he said. "I want them to say they are going to eat at Loiseau." He returned a few weeks after their first meeting with preliminary plans. They required closing the restaurant for several months. "I'm not satisfied," Catonné admitted. He suggested making an offer for Le Petit Marguery next door.

"Let's go," Bernard said. He and the architect went to see Robert Pianetti, owner of Le Petit Marguery.

"I am buying you out," Bernard announced. "I don't care what price you ask."

Fabre, the accountant, did. He took three months to negotiate the sale. Every day Bernard called and asked, "Is it done?"

When Fabre told him no, he exploded.

"Finish it, finish it," he yelled.

"Bernard drove me crazy," Fabre said. But in the end, the accountant managed to knock about $200,000 off the initial price.

Bernard felt his responsibility was the big picture. He let Fabre deal with financial details and Dominique with decorating details. When Dominique decided that the restaurant needed new tableware, he agreed. La Côte d'Or used plain white plates. Dominique wanted something more sophisticated. Bocuse and other big-name chefs had their own, personalized place settings and china. Dominique organized a contest. France's best-known porcelain makers were invited to compete. During several months, designers visited Saulieu and presented their ideas to Dominique. Many made repeat trips. Dominique spent hours briefing them about her desires. "I want something functional, a thick porcelain," she told them. "But it also must be elegant."

The contest finals were scheduled for a Tuesday morning in early November. The salesmen and designers arrived around ten. They laid out their proposals in the main dining room. One was floral, another pastel, another modern abstract.

"That looks too cheap," Dominique judged, putting down one dish.

She explained how she wanted something modern and yet rustic, a difficult combination. When Bernard saw the samples—and heard the prices—he began to have second thoughts.

"What counts is what is on the plate," Bernard announced, storming off to the kitchen.

Ever-calm Hubert intervened.

"I like this," he said, pointing to a plate featuring a BL logo in brown on white. "It's modern and yet not too modern, rustic and yet not too rustic. The letters are framed like wood beams, and that's the spirit of the place."

"Do you think we need something a little more festive, perhaps something in gold rather than brown?" Dominique asked. "How about some gold leaf?"

"No, no, this is festive," the salesman said. "Otherwise, you'll make it too gaudy."

Dominique insisted, and the salesman agreed to add some gold leaf. Bernard, a bit calmer, returned from the kitchen. He seconded the choice, without giving it much thought. It was time for an aperitif. The winning and losing designers all sat down to a complimentary lunch.

Bernard and Dominique had another, more important lunch date, with Catonné, Fabre, and the banker Claude Schneider. French bankers have a bad reputation. As an old Burgundian saying goes, "When it's sunny, the banker will lend you an umbrella, and when it's rainy, he wants it back."

Some cautious chefs such as Pierre Troisgros had avoided the banks, opting instead for a slow, measured expansion financed by profits. Until a few years ago, Troisgros even kept his old neighborhood café for his clients. Only as more and more jet-setters flocked to Roanne did he finally decide to create a three-star bar. "We don't want to have a snobby Parisian place, with chauffeurs and formal wear," he said. "But our classy clients didn't like mingling with the locals."

Bernard didn't think much about the locals. He was more interested in attracting well-heeled clients from Lyons, Geneva, and Paris, who were willing to drive hours for a meal. That meant giving them luxurious surroundings and, despite his horror of financial matters, dealing with bankers. Two banks refused his renovation proposal; they demanded $3 million in collateral before lending $1 million.

Then Bernard met Claude Schneider from Crédit Foncier, in Dijon. Schneider liked good food and wine. When the Château de Puligny, in the celebrated wine village of Puligny-Montrachet, was put up for sale, and the Japanese giant Suntory offered to buy it, Schneider and Crédit Foncier came to the rescue. The bank paid more than $6 million for the privilege. Suntory reportedly was prepared to pay $2 million more, but the Ministry of Agriculture vetoed the purchase of the national monument by a foreigner. Under Schneider's direction, Crédit Foncier modernized and expanded both the château and its wine cellars, installing the latest wine-making technology. As a business proposition, the investment made little sense. As a public relations move, however, it was brilliant. The glamorous brand name added luster to Schneider's otherwise ponderous banking and property conglomerate.

Schneider, wearing a gray suit, announced that he had been dieting for the past month and had lost forty pounds. His wife, a handsome blond matron dressed in an elegant pink suit, came with him. She recently had been put in charge of the Château de Puligny. The couple exuded cosmopolitan self-confidence, an air of busy, successful executives.

Everyone went upstairs to one of La Côte d'Or's private dining rooms. Catonné was dressed in a beige sweater without a suit jacket. Next to him sat his assistant Christophe Daguin, looking like an eager student in a black turtleneck. Fabre wore his loud purple suit. Dominique, in a trim black suit, exuded her usual elegance. Bernard wore his white chef's uniform and rushed back to the kitchen to oversee the meal.

Over lunch, the group talked about politics, the arts, everything except the loan. They discussed France's alarming unemployment figures. They blasted the country's reliance on high interest rates to combat inflation. And they dissected the country's social order, concluding that no serious Frenchman would ever want to show off his wealth. On one serious point, everyone agreed: the French economy was turning sour. The luxury restaurant business was heading for tough times.

Lyonel served a prodigious amount of wine, starting with a golden Puligny-Montrachet donated by Schneider's château and moving on to a robust, inspiring Volnay before finishing with a sweet Banyuls Vieilles Vignes. The food surpassed the drink: sea urchins, followed by Bernard's classic perch in a red wine sauce and wild pigeon in foie gras, then a dab of creamy Epoisses, and, finally, succulent pastry swirls floating on layers of caramelized apples.

When coffee was served, the conversation finally turned to business. "After a meal like that," Schneider pronounced, "I'm ready to talk about anything." Catonné snapped his fingers and his assistant Daguin took out the drawings. Schneider lit a cigar. He knew he was in a position of power. Fabre outlined the restaurant's projected cash flow.

Schneider nodded and took a long pull on his cigar.

"I'm worried," he announced.

A long pause followed.

"My boss is going to ask me, 'Why the hell are you investing in Saulieu, in the middle of nowhere?'" Schneider said. "'Who's going to go there?'"

Bernard burst into the room.

"Coffee? More coffee? Coffee?"

"No, no, no."

"Mineral water?"

They accepted. Dominique turned to Schneider's wife and suggested a walk outside. The two women left. Fabre took out his calculator. Catonné conferred with his assistant. They suggested some modifications to bring down the price. The new garage would be covered with a cheap zinc roof, and instead of antique tiles for the floor, they would install smaller, modern ones.

"You won't be able to tell the difference," Catonné assured Fabre.

Bernard burst into the room again.

"A digestive?" he asked.

They declined.

For an eternity, Schneider chomped on his cigar, listening. Finally, he was ready to make a pronouncement.

"I'm going to be very American about this," he said.

Everyone understood. A French banker, in his eternal bureaucratic caution, would turn down the financing. But an American banker might take the risk.

"The American always takes the individual into account," Schneider said. "We French never do."

"If Bernard Loiseau was not here, this could be the worst investment I could ever make," he continued. "But with Bernard Loiseau in the kitchen, I believe in it."

For collateral, he insisted Bernard travel to Paris for a complete physical checkup so he could take out life insurance.

"If I give you the money and Bernard Loiseau has a heart attack, I will lose everything," Schneider said. "Once you have life insurance, everything will be fine."

The banker knew what he was talking about. Not long before, three-star chef Alain Chapel had dropped dead. Chapel was only in his early fifties and was as thin as a rail. By common consent, Restaurant Alain Chapel, outside of Lyons, remained as good as ever. Chapel's widow was still present in the dining room, and a chef who had worked with the master for years took over in the kitchen. But business was down, and his widow feared that Michelin might take away the third star. Once the founder was gone, no critic could ever again feel sure of the future. Alain Chapel would never have picked up and moved. But his talented replacement chef might.

"The cooking at Chapel's is certainly three stars," Hubert said. "But the business will still suffer."

Back in the kitchen, Catonné told Bernard his cooking had won the battle with the banks.

"What a feast," he sighed, with pleasure. "Now let's get on with the war."

Fabre was more cautious.

"Bernard, watch yourself," he warned. "Don't give away too many free meals. We have to have the account books looking good these days."

The work started in the summer of 1990. While diners feasted out front, construction workers busied themselves out back. In place of the neighboring café, the Bistro de Morvan, they erected a sparkling new kitchen, with dozens of ovens and stoves and modern refrigerators. The outlines of three new dining rooms stood under an ornamental tower built in the style of a Burgundy farmhouse.

When diners got up from the table at the end of their meal, Bernard would grab them and take them charging through Dumaine's cramped antique of a kitchen, which had been compared to a rabbit warren and once even to the galley of a Panamanian cargo ship. It featured two antique coal-burning ovens and a basement cubbyhole for the pastry chef. If Bernard knew the client well, he would show him where chewing gum remained from Dumaine's days. Down a set of steep stairs the chef went in his immaculate white uniform, right into the middle of the messy, mud-filled construction site.

"Look at this jungle," Bernard would say, helping his elegantly dressed visitors tiptoe among the overgrown weeds and toolsheds, soon to be torn down. "It will become a beautiful garden."

The more he talked, the more he smiled.

"Here," he added, "will be a new salon, with a gigantic, roaring fire, here aperitifs will be served, and here"—his voice rose to a climax—"you will feast as you have never feasted before."

Not surprisingly, some guests did not appreciate the grandiose vision, particularly during the construction. One night, a well-known Canadian singer named Roch Voisine came to La Côte d'Or. He had just finished two tiring performances in Dijon and hoped to recuperate for two tranquil nights in Saulieu. But early the next morning, a bulldozer made its way through Saulieu on the Nationale 6. No one paid much attention. In Saulieu, slow-moving tractors and trucks often hold up traffic and produce ear-shattering noise. When the bulldozer reached La Côte d'Or, it turned left onto Rue Jean Bertin—and smashed through the hotel's brick wall.

The noise jolted the singer and his lover out of bed. They called reception, furious. A waiter came running with a sumptuous breakfast, but the damage was done. Within half an hour, the star guest had checked out—and a furious Bernard was worrying whether his renovation would drive him into bankruptcy.

"Don't use your sledgehammer during breakfast or lunch," he told the workers.

"You can't make an omelette without breaking some eggs," replied assistant architect Christophe Daguin.

In financial terms, the renovation was risky. The total budget was $3 million. After it was completed, Bernard would have $45,000 per month to pay back to the banks—and not necessarily more clients. He began to have nightmares about whether he could make it through the next fiscal year. Money hung over the renovation like a migraine headache. At one point Fabre called Bernard.

"What's the problem?" Bernard asked.

"You have to cut the budget by another five hundred thousand dollars."

A planned fourth dining room was eliminated, and a less expensive wood staircase was substituted for one in stone. As they struggled to stay within budget, architect and client skirmished. Bernard was most concerned about the quality of the renovation. When he learned of the decision about the tiles, he was enraged. Catonné told him the new tiles would look just as good as the old ones. Fabre backed up the architect, saying he would not pay $300 a square foot for tiles.

"Remember, this cannot be a restaurant like any other," Bernard exploded. "It must be perfect. I want my clients to come in the front door and be surprised, to feel they are right in the countryside, with a beautiful garden, a big fireplace, everything warm and cozy."

A compromise finally was reached. Antique tiles were used for about half the floors and modern tiles for the other half.

The architect and client disagreed next over lighting. Catonné proposed a thin, supermodern light fixture. Bernard insisted it was wrong with the restaurant's traditional decor. "Bernard's adorable," Catonné said. "But sometimes you have to treat him like a child." The architect bought the futuristic lights and Bernard ended up happy with the choice. Afterward, he sometimes even suggested that the lights were his idea.

Lyonel the sommelier was less satisfied. He loved his new wine cellar, which held twice as many bottles as the old one; he liked the way it was arranged to let visitors descend for tastings; But the new fireplace was right in front of his bar, and the fire heated his digestives and other liquors. The heat also cracked the fresh plaster on the adjoining wall, leaving a large brown stain. Clients generously considered it a sign of age. Lyonel and the waiters worried that expensive repairs would soon be needed. "A disaster," Lyonel said.

Dominique invited some artist friends from Paris to show their paintings. Bernard treated them to five-course meals but didn't buy anything. His wife drank café au lait and ate meager portions of rice pudding. Before her second pregnancy began to slow her down, she dragged Bernard to all the local antique shops. Bernard would point to a dresser or bureau and say, "I want that."

"Calm down," Dominique would reply. "Let's first see how much it costs."

She started visiting the antique shops alone.

In a nearby town called Pontaubert, Dominique found a dealer who had a striking nineteenth-century hunt painting. In Saulieu, another dealer was offering a giant, brown-stained wooden chest for displaying tableware. She called Catonné and had the architect redesign the third dining room to incorporate it. In Beaune, Dominique even discovered a marble table from an old barbershop. Perfect for the ladies' bathroom, she thought, and at $4,000, it was a bargain. Catonné enlarged the bathroom so it would fit.

Dominique's purchases gave a well-heeled, homey, bourgeois feeling to the new restaurant. Her taste couldn't have been further from the nouveau riche marble excesses of the bedrooms designed by Bernard's first wife, Chantal. In addition, Dominique proved a tough bargainer. When she saw something she liked, she would knock 20 percent off the sticker price and make a take-it-or-leave it offer. Almost always, the dealer accepted the lower price. "It would have been easier to go to Paris and order new things," Dominique said. "But this way, I had a chance to make my mark."

By the beginning of December, La Côte d'Or had been transformed. The only room left alone was Dumaine's main dining room. Breakfast would be served there. Bernard restored the original color, even renovating the original 1930s chairs, so that the room became a sort of museum, with old menus, wine lists, and magazine clippings celebrating Papa Alexandre's glory. An oil painting of the great chef, arms folded, face serious, stared down over diners, a constant reminder that this restaurant had a long history with high standards to be upheld.

The restaurant's reopening was scheduled for December 22, 1990. The day before, Lyonel spent a full day wiping bottles and cleaning glasses. Hubert cut flowers in a sort of Japanese tatami design and placed a bouquet on each table and a giant bouquet at the head of the new main dining room. In his new kitchen, Patrick and the rest of the staff needed two full days to prepare a shellfish stock of clams, lobster, and crayfish. Michael Caines, the English chef de partie, spent an entire day cooking foie gras.

Bernard supervised the installation of a giant Christmas tree in the front hall. "No, no," he yelled at the workers when they tried to put gold paper around the tree. "That looks horrible." He forced them to redo the entire decoration.

Unexpectedly, France's most popular television host, Bernard Pivot, showed up at lunchtime with his two daughters. A rumpled, rather ordinary-looking man, Pivot hosted a talk show dedicated to books. For Christmas, he was heading home to Beaujolais. On his way, he decided to stop in Saulieu for lunch.

The TV star was standing in front of the darkened La Côte d'Or, holding his red Michelin Guide, when Bernard showed up. Not long before, Pivot's wife, Monique, had replaced Christian Millau as editor in chief of the Gault-Millau magazine. So the sight of Pivot standing with his guide pleased Bernard and confirmed the importance of the red bible.

"Imagine, he uses Michelin, not Gault-Millau," Bernard confided to Hubert.

"I thought you were open," Pivot said, disappointment showing on his face. "It says so here in the guide."

"I've been closed, exceptionally," Bernard replied.

"Oh," Pivot sighed.

"But," Bernard added, "don't worry. We'll take care of you."

A table was installed in the kitchen. The television star and his daughters sat down, wearing their winter coats. When dessert was served, big smiles swept over all three faces. They savored the delectable salted butter and caramel sauce filled with small, thin slices of apple.

"*Magnifique!*" Pivot enthused as he scooped up slices. "I've never tasted anything like this salted butter."

Bernard still had one final hurdle to overcome. That night, a giant snowstorm swept over Burgundy, depositing almost fifteen inches on Saulieu and blocking all traffic. The new chairs and tables for the dining rooms still had not arrived from the manufacturer. They finally showed up at ten-thirty in the morning.

Catonné, who had been staying across the street at the Hôtel de la Poste, rushed home to Paris to spend Christmas with his family. None of the staff at La Côte d'Or had time to celebrate. As the first clients arrived for a pre-holiday lunch, waiters still were washing the bay windows and installing tables in the octagonal main dining room and banquet hall.

Two days later, on Christmas Eve, Saulieu's Basilica St. Andoche was packed for Midnight Mass. The local curé, white-bearded Father Yves Hablezig, gave his usual simple homily. Dominique came early to the church and stood up front, with Bérangère. Bernard left before the end, rushing back through the knee-high drifts of snow to the restaurant. He needn't have bothered. When he arrived at La Côte d'Or, he faced a terrifying sight.

His sparkling new dining rooms were empty.

## CHAPTER 8

★ ★ ★

# Heavenly Nectar

*The wine cellars chez Bize*

THE HEAVY snowstorm had kept customers away for Christmas, a holiday almost all French mark anyway at home with the family, not at a restaurant. New Year's Eve was different. Bernard celebrated with a full house of 120 diners, each paying $200 for a memorable seven-course, truffle-studded, caviar-sprinkled feast.

When the guests arrived, Bernard took them to a balcony overlooking the new garden and the new dining rooms. At the snap of his fingers, a waiter came running with a bottle of champagne and Bernard's signature hors d'oeuvre, a delicate sliver of liver laid on top of a puff pastry filled with diced vegetables and garlic puree. Bernard raised his glass for a toast. Sipping, he smiled and said, almost not believing his own words, "This is mine, all mine!"

Architects were less impressed. Catonné's assistant Daguin later delivered a lecture on La Côte d'Or's renovation at the Charenton Architecture University, near Paris. The professors in the audience lambasted the project. They said the layout was not well organized. The main dining rooms lacked intimacy. The long hallways represented "wasted space." The fireplace was too big and too hot for diners to sit near. For $3 million, the architects said, Loiseau could have had a masterpiece if he had dared to be a little more Italian and modern.

"This is no Four Seasons," one professor said, describing the famous Manhattan restaurant designed by Ludwig Mies van der Rohe. "It's kitsch."

When he heard the criticism, Bernard lost his temper.

"Those fancy designers don't understand anything," he said. "We are in Burgundy, and that means tiles, warmth, the countryside."

Once the holiday festivities ended, the restaurant again emptied. Even strong Burgundian stomachs need a rest after feasts of foie gras, caviar, smoked salmon, and other delicacies. The hunting season was over, and Bernard could no longer find inner peace with his rifle in the forests. The winter menu, complete with the all-potato special, was printed. Bernard was bored, impatient, always worried about whether this would be the year for his third star.

A strange incident added to the tension. On the day after New Year's, a loud noise jolted Saulieu awake. Rifle shots seemed to be coming from the nearby parish house behind the Basilica St. Andoche. Later, a resident named Christophe Paris noticed that Mickey, his ten-month-old striped black tiger angora cat, was missing. He went to look for the stray animal. In front of the parish house, on Rue du Sabot, he found a white garbage sack. Inside was the unfortunate Mickey.

The next morning, he lodged a criminal complaint against Father Hablezig. When confronted, the priest confessed. He had shot the cat in cold blood. It wasn't the first time, either. Although the priest couldn't remember exactly, he admitted to burying two other cats in his garden. About sixty cats had disappeared under similar mysterious circumstances since the arrival of Father Hablezig in Saulieu five years before.

Father Hablezig loved pigeons. He kept fifty of them in his garden. They attracted the attention of his neighbors' cats, who would often climb over the fence and treat themselves to a pigeon feast. "After a cat tasted a pigeon, he would always return," the priest confessed. "I know that I was wrong, but I was so upset."

The affair shocked Saulieu. *Le Bien Public,* the local newspaper, printed a long front-page article. Almost everybody at La Côte d'Or took sides. Maître d'hôtel Hubert, perhaps the sweetest man on the staff, went to see the priest and expressed his support and understanding. "He's a good man," Hubert said. "Everything just built up in him and he exploded." But Hubert's children were much less understanding. They asked their mother to start preparing them "cat stew."

Everyone needed a break, so early on one crisp January morning, Hubert warmed up the restaurant's Renault Espace van for a day's expedition. Most of the Christmas snow had already melted, leaving only the slightest trace of white on the ground. A dense fog hid the hilltops.

It was time for wine tasting.

For the next few weeks, Bernard would accompany Lyonel and Hubert on daylong trips to the vineyards. Until Lyonel had joined the restaurant staff, Hubert had picked the restaurant's wines. These days, he delegated the responsibility to Lyonel. But he loved to keep in practice. Starting in the early morning, the Côte d'Or team would trundle through cellar after cellar, tasting wine after wine. When they finished in the evening, their mouths would be ruby red and their eyes glazed. The goal was to advance Bernard's quest for a third star, finding enough bottles to satisfy the inspecteurs without bankrupting the restaurant. Don't think we enjoyed ourselves, Lyonel and Hubert would tell their wives. This is hard work.

The France Inter newscast blared on the radio. The night before, Parliament had passed a law banning advertising for alcoholic beverages. France's drinking age is eighteen but almost never enforced. Wine, beer, and hard liquors are sold in almost all supermarkets. In the early 1950s, Prime Minister Pierre Mendès-France proposed milk as a substitute for wine. Everyone laughed.

Alcohol has long been a major French vice, even though few drunks stumble along the streets. French wine drinkers prefer the dull state of mild wine-induced inebriation to the blasted condition of the hard-liquor drunks of Northern Europe and the United States. In the nineteenth century, writers such as Emile Zola wrote such long, angry novels as *L'Assommoir* denouncing the evil effect of alcohol on the new urban working class. Peasants can still be seen early in the morning at the local café, downing *un petit coup* of red wine.

Since Mendès-France's day, a permanent High Commission has distributed anti-alcohol literature to schools. The commission doesn't advocate teetotalism. It only warns against excess. Many young people have turned away from their parents' style of heavy drinking; sales of Coca-Cola and other soft drinks have boomed. When they do drink, they consume little hard liquor and better-quality wine. By legislating an advertising ban, the socialists were continuing in the tradition of Mendès-France.

But to everyone at La Côte d'Or, the idea of alcohol as a problem was ludicrous. Unlike in Protestant countries, where drinking is often equated with sin, wine is part of daily life in France. It was ordained by Christ, and churchmen were the region's first oenological experts. In the opinion of Hubert, Lyonel, and Bernard, wine was responsible for the French characteristics they most appreciated: cordiality, frankness, good humor, a gift for conversation, and good taste.

The Renault van sped south from Saulieu along La Six. After the town of Arnay-le-Duc, it turned left, following the signs for Beaune. The first vineyards soon came into view. During winter, vintners prune the dormant vines. Workers, bundled against the raw cold, hunch over vines in the fields. They cut off much of the previous year's growth, tossing the excess canes and shoots into a wheelbarrow. When enough are collected, they are burnt. Careful pruning, particularly of Burgundy's pinot noir, limits the crop of grapes in the next harvest to fewer, top-quality clusters. Properly trimmed, the frigid, fruitless vines look naked; in fact, they are ready for their springtime bloom.

While the fields are at their most barren, the cellars below are at their richest. The vintners have time to talk, to describe the health and condition of the year's fruit, whether there was any rot and how much. Before January, the wine is still undergoing fermentation, and it is too early to judge how it will turn out. After the holidays, fermentation is almost over and, although the vintage is not yet ripe, it can be tasted. Buyers cannot wait much longer. If they do, the best wines will be sold out.

Hubert drove the van across the highway, took a sharp right and then the first left into Savigny-lès-Beaune. Despite the village's striking château—built first as a medieval fort and modified in seventeenth-century Renaissance style—the vintners' homes are modest and the streets narrow. Burgundy villages are squeezed into a tight knot, because no one wants to build on valuable vineyard lands. Few in this ingrown rural society dare to show off their wealth; conspicuous consumption and other signs of luxury attract unwanted attention from tax inspectors.

The result is that although Burgundy produces some of the world's most expensive wine, its wine villages do not seem rich. In Savigny and elsewhere, a whiff of claustrophobia hangs in the air. Windows are almost always shuttered, and metal gates, framed in giant archways, block entrances. Fierce Alsatian watchdogs prowl inside the big stone walls, guarding against intruders.

On one of the large gray-green metal doorways was posted a small sign that read DOMAINE SIMON BIZE. When the van pulled into the courtyard, it was only eight o'clock. The Bizes had been vintners for four generations, and with son Patrick's involvement, they could now claim five.

Patrick led the way down to the cellar. His father, Simon, was in his seventies and short, stocky, and strong. The forty-something son was lithe, with an arched brow and aquiline nose. His seriousness and a wry sense of humor made him a member of the emerging band of talented young wine makers in Burgundy. Neither he nor his father had any formal oenological training. They learned from doing, and they learned well.

In the cellar, the powerful aromas jolted the tasters out of their morning daze. Wines mingled with the smell of moist earth and rock and hints of the original fruit. Most of the cave was modern and spacious, but some of the older rooms had vaulted ceilings so low that Lyonel had to duck under the archways.

Patrick Bize started the tasting with the whites and moved on to the more elegant reds. He drew the wine out of barrels with his pipette, a long surgical-like instrument that squirted generous helpings into three waiting glasses. Carefully, all three tasters swirled the liquid, looking at it with intense concentration. Then in a single gulp, they threw the wine back into their mouths and rolled it around their lips, tasting the full flavor. When finished washing it around their palates, they spit the wine out onto the moist ground between the barrels.

The language used to describe the wine was a mixture of science and sex.

"Ahh, a good attack," said Lyonel the scientist. Wine, he explained, should "strike" the palate. Otherwise, it may have too little fruit. Spitting out the wine, he proceeded to the next step in his chemical test, evaluating the structure.

"This is big and full," he announced. It had lots of alcohol. A small wine lacks fermentation. A hollow wine lacks a satisfying middle flavor; something is missing between the first flavor and the last, often a result of vines producing too many grapes.

Lyonel emptied his mouth and gave his final judgment: a long finish. The aromas lingered well after tasting. The longer they last, the better the wine. Lyonel opened his notebook and marked down the points scored by Bize's Savigny-lès-Beaune. Michelin would approve.

"A classic," he concluded. "The wine is well balanced. It contains all the desirable elements of acid and alcohol."

Bernard took a different approach. He described what he tasted in terms of feminine beauty.

"This is round, oh so round," he said, tasting Bize's wine. It is "ripe, meaty, supple."

With a burst of orgasmic energy, he spit out the wine, produced a giant sigh, and pronounced his final verdict.

"Whooahh, that's it," he said. "Fireworks in the mouth."

★ ★ ★

When the tasters emerged from the chill of Bize's cellar, their fingers were almost as red as the wine. Hubert, wearing a thick leather jacket, rubbed his hands. Bernard, in his Barbour hunting jacket and cashmere cap, stamped his frost-numbed feet. Lyonel's breath produced a cold white cloud as he muttered: "Some people think this is romantic."

Simon Bize built a fire in the fireplace on the ground floor of the warehouse next to the tasting table. Madame Bize arrived with a platter of cold sausage made by the local butcher and some crusty baguettes. Simon brought out bottles of Savigny-lès-Beaune and told the men how his father started bottling in 1930. That made him one of the first Burgundy domains to label his own wine.

From the nineteenth century until after World War II, almost all Burgundy growers sold their juice to shippers, who blended, bottled, and sold it. Burgundy vineyards are small, and most vintners felt that they could not produce enough wine to warrant marketing the wine under their own labels. Merchants such as Bouchard and Patriarche bought young wine from the small producers, blending fermenting juices from the same districts. For a small grower, selling his young wine brought quick payment, with neither the expense nor the work of aging, bottling, and finding buyers for his small production.

But the result was a sharp deterioration in quality. Merchants couldn't buy enough from one producer to retain the wine's singular personality. Instead, they developed a "house style" that made it easy to recognize wines under a given label. This meant that the wine's appellation was obscured. A Gevrey-Chambertin should not taste like a Volnay. But many merchants' bottles did.

The practice of growers bottling their wine became commonplace in Burgundy only after World War II. Before then, no national wine legislation existed to protect the growers. A 1905 law required vintners to declare the amount of wine they had produced in a year and to state the place of origin. The law allowed bottles to be labeled Burgundy. But it did not recognize wines from specific villages. Comprehensive legislation came into effect only in 1935, following the Depression. This new system of Appellation d'Origine Contrôlée defined a wine's district and awarded the right to use the appellation only to those vineyards located within the given boundaries. The type of grape used in an area also was specified, as were the permissible amount of alcohol content for each wine and the maximum yield per acre.

Until the Appellation Contrôlée, it was common to find inferior grapes—gamay and Aligoté—planted in the elite first-growth vineyards, called in French grands crus. Afterward, only pinot noir and chardonnay could call themselves true Burgundies, while other grape varieties were denoted Bourgogne Passetoutgrains and Bourgogne Aligotés. To enforce the laws, the government established a division of the Ministry of Agriculture called the Institut National des Appellations d'Origine.

When the 1935 law was enacted, Simon Bize's father fought hard for Savigny-lès-Beaune to receive its own appellation instead of being placed in the generic Côtes de Beaune region. Much politicking was involved. Winegrowers from the Côte de Beaune accused winegrowers from the nearby

Côte de Nuits of breaking into town halls late at night and tampering with the list of appellations. Politicians from the Côte de Nuits did push harder than the politicians from the Côte de Beaune and had better connections and bigger pockets. As a result, the Côte de Beaune still has few grands crus.

Savigny-lès-Beaune was awarded no grands crus and became something of a Cinderella among Burgundies, finding it hard to convince connoisseurs that it was capable of producing serious wine. But it did obtain a village appellation, permitting Simon Bize's father to begin bottling his wine. These days, the attitude toward appellations is changing. Before, a winegrower's status depended on the land he possessed rather than on his wine-making ability. Now the estates that excite the most attention are those such as Bize, which make superlative wines from modest vineyard holdings.

"Half a century ago, Savigny meant nothing," Monsieur Bize explained. "The Appellation Contrôlée gave us a fighting chance."

A few courageous pioneers encouraged the growers to bottle. An American named Frank Schoonmaker began to import estate-bottled Burgundies. He later was joined by Alexis Lichine, an author, lecturer, retailer, importer, and, finally, producer of wine. In France, the key figure was Raymond Baudouin, the creator of the magazine *Revue du Vin de France* and the wine buyer for such great restaurants as Point's La Pyramide. When Simon Bize took over his domain from his father, he did not forget the lesson. With great pride, he listed the famous restaurants where his wine was served: Guy Savoy's, in Paris; Freddy Girardet's, in Switzerland; Georges Blanc's, in La Mère Blanc, in Vonnas; and, of course, Bernard's La Côte d'Or, in Saulieu. "We need great chefs such as you, Bernard," he said. "Your clientele are the connoisseurs, and my best publicity is when my wines are served in your restaurant."

"Many vintners are spoiled; they don't realize our importance," Bernard replied. "But you, Monsieur Bize, you are a class act."

Everyone in the group grabbed a last morsel of sausage. It already was ten o'clock and they were behind schedule.

Hubert drove into the heart of the Côte de Beaune. The road revealed the historic folds of the land, and Lyonel explained the intricacies of production. In flat, poorly drained vineyards at the foot of the Côte d'Or, the Gold Coast, ordinary Burgundy is produced. The quality of the wine improves as the land rises. Village wines come first, then premiers crus and finally grands crus. Another slice of village wines lie on the top of the hill, just below the woods and wasteland at the summit. The best wine is produced about two thirds of the way up the slope, where the land is best placed to catch the sun and drain excess water while still sheltered from the wind and frost.

Unlike Bordeaux, which enjoys a temperate climate, Burgundy can be one of the coldest places in France during the winter and one of the hottest at the height of summer. The region suffers from violent storms. During the spring, the vines are vulnerable to frost. During the summer, hail can strip leaves, buds, and even branches from the vines. In autumn, thunderstorms can ruin a ripening crop before vintage. Worse, the climate is unpredictable; it varies from year to year and, more than elsewhere, so does the quality of the wine.

Each Burgundy wine has a distinct character, being lighter, richer, or quicker-maturing than its neighbor. The soil matters. From the French point of view, the land gives a wine its particular voice. In Burgundy, the appropriate word is *terroir,* which suggests not only the chemical qualities of the terrain, but also precipitation, air, water drainage, elevation, sunlight, and temperature. A good vintner listens to the land and lets the grapes speak.

Burgundy vineyards are often handkerchief-size plots. A few acres of precious Burgundy grapevines may be owned by more than a dozen proprietors. This parceling produces a kaleidoscope range of styles—and a wide range of quality. Two vintners in the same village, with vineyards next to each other, often produce two completely different wines, one worth buying, the other worth flushing down the toilet. This inconsistency, both Lyonel and Hubert emphasized, is the bane of Burgundy.

Hubert, speeding at more than sixty miles an hour, soon arrived in the town of Nuits-St.-Georges, which divides the Côte d'Or into two districts, each about fifteen miles long. In the north, the Côte de Nuits is home to such famed wine villages as Gevrey-Chambertin, Chambolle-Musigny, and Vougeot. South lie the Côte de Beaune and villages such as Volnay, Meursault, and Puligny-Montrachet. Within each village, plots are identified by such additional names as Savigny-lès-Beaune Vergelesses, Chambolle-Musigny Les Amoureuses, or Volnay Clos des Chênes.

"There's a whole encyclopedia explaining the appellations," Lyonel said. "I'm studying it now for my competition."

In Vosne-Romanée, the van turned off the main road and pulled into the small parking lot in front of Domaine Pernin-Rossin. André Pernin-Rossin emerged from the cellar of what looked like a prefabricated home. A frizzy-haired man in his mid fifties, Pernin-Rossin was a third-generation vintner. His father produced wine for other growers. André started off that way, working fourteen years for grower Jean Grivot in Clos Vougeot and another fourteen years for the Hospices de Nuits. In 1964, he was given a parcel of Nuits-St.-Georges Premier Cru by his father and started off on his own.

Pernin-Rossin eventually built up his domain to twenty acres scattered all about the Côte de Nuits. If a vintner has only a small property, he finds it hard to blend a magnificent wine. Ownership of a small plot in one vineyard usually is not enough to support a living, so winegrowers often are forced to have a number of small, separate holdings.

Pernin-Rossin's big break came when actor Gérard Depardieu tasted his wine and liked it. With financing from Depardieu, Pernin-Rossin bought a few more acres of Burgundy property and planted sixty-two acres of vines in the Loire Valley.

Madame Pernin-Rossin brought in three giant tasting glasses. Bernard, impressed with the Depardieu connection, didn't pay much attention to the wine. In between tastes, he kept asking questions about the famous actor. Pernin-Rossin seemed delighted to have another budding celebrity, Bernard, in his cellar, and his wife took a picture of the chef and her husband.

Lyonel, the ever-serious sommelier, sneered. He didn't like to go tasting with Bernard, who considered the drinking expeditions pure pleasure, while Lyonel saw them as preparation for the tough job of wine buying.

"You can't study the bouquet with Bernard around," Lyonel muttered. "He distracts everyone with his show."

Hubert had a question. "What are your yields?" he asked.

"About three hundred seventy-five gallons an acre," the vintner announced.

Lyonel took down the figure and thought, *A little high*. In the 1980s, many vintners began using fertilizer and other tricks to extract greater quantities of valuable wine from the same amount of land. But quality suffered. Lyonel believed that a vintner shouldn't produce any more than 320 gallons an acre.

"How much sugar do you add?" Lyonel asked.

The vintner grimaced.

"A little," he answered, adding to Lyonel's suspicions.

Vintners add sugar to the fermenting juice when there is not enough natural sugar in the grape. Grapes with too little sugar cannot achieve the required levels of alcohol, and if the alcohol level is too low, a wine will taste weak and have little staying power. Cistercian monks, who first planted vines in Burgundy, used sugar to help their wines in poor years, and many of the world's cooler wine regions rely on the process, not only Burgundy, but also Alsace and Champagne. In moderation, adding sugar can improve the quality of a wine. But when too much sugar is artificially added, the character of the land vanishes and the wine loses its special, distinctive flavor. In the 1980s, abuses proliferated. Vintners pushed their vines for ever-greater production, using more and more sugar to make up for the missing natural alcohol. Just the year before, a French consumer magazine, *Que Choisir?*, provoked a scandal when it was able to prove, through nuclear magnetic resonance tests, that sugar had boosted the alcohol in some Beaujolais wines by as much as one third of the total, double the permitted level.

Pernin-Rossin explained that he added sugar and also fermented the wine at low temperatures. Most wine is warm when it ferments. But Pernin-Rossin argued that his technique imparted more taste and power to the wine.

Lyonel took another mouthful, swished it about, spit—and winced. The wine tasted strange, he thought, like a syrupy mixture of cassis and grapes.

By this time, Hubert and Lyonel couldn't wait to leave. But Bernard, still entranced by the Depardieu connection, continued his small talk. Finally they managed to push him out the door. In the van, the final judgment was severe.

"He is making money, not wine," Hubert said. "It tastes like . . ." Hubert was at a loss for words.

"He has great land and his wine could be like a Ferrari," Lyonel added. "Instead it's like a jalopy."

"OK," Bernard admitted. "He does have sort of a big head."

★ ★ ★

The three tasters were beginning to look a little red and puffy. They suffered from the taster's malaise, a mild cerebral high mixed with a dull muscle ache. Although they did not swallow wine when they tasted, the heady aromas of the alcohol seeped into their bodies, particularly in the cold cellars. Bernard the Bird was flying, his mouth spinning off in every direction. Hubert's eyes twinkled, and even sober Lyonel wore a large smile. It was noon—lunchtime.

"Where should we eat?" Hubert asked, sniffing the air.

"I want some man's food," Bernard said. "Nothing sissy."

The Renault van headed back to Beaune and parked in front of a bistro called La Ciboulette. The cheap plastic tiling on the floors, the Formica tables, and the simple wood chairs signaled a restaurant without pretensions. Even though La Ciboulette had been open for nine years, the Michelin Guide still did not list it. The *patronne* said she had received a recent visit from a Michelin inspecteur. He didn't bother to study the available choices and plat du jour. Instead he ordered a simple set menu and ate quickly. "I mistook him for a wine merchant," the patronne said. "We don't care too much about the guidebooks. We depend on word of mouth."

That simple marketing technique seemed to be working, because no table was available. But Bernard pulled the patronne into a corner for a few words in private, and she snapped her fingers. A waiter carried in a new table and placed it before the bar.

"We can't let Bernard Loiseau go hungry," she said.

"What did you say?" Hubert asked. "That you were in love with her?"

"No," Bernard responded. "That she was invited for a free meal at La Côte d'Or."

Bernard did not bother to pick up the menu. He ordered a *gras double,* a traditional hors d'oeuvre of grilled pig's intestines. For a main course, he commanded a juicy, thick steak, served blood rare. Hubert and Lyonel ordered the same, and Hubert selected a rich fifty-dollar Côte de Beaune. At lunchtime, no one spit out the wine.

"The meat is perfect," Bernard said, chewing a big chunk. "It *attacks* you."

A short discussion about Michelin's conservatism followed. Bernard asked how the supposedly thorough inspecteurs could overlook this wonderful bistro. No one had a good answer. Next, the conversation turned to a perennial subject: the high price of Burgundy wine. An economic boom beginning in the 1960s created middle-class Europeans and Americans with the money and desire to buy the best wines. The new highway to the south of France that so hurt Saulieu helped Burgundy's growers. It attracted new Danish, Dutch, German, and Swiss customers on their way to and from holidays.

As demand for Burgundy wine boomed, supply could not grow. The Côte d'Or is a narrow strip of about thirty miles. In contrast to the great Bordeaux châteaux, most of which are in the hands of big investors, Burgundy domains remain family-owned. The large Bordeaux region produces eight times more wine than Burgundy. A typical small Burgundy grower may own tiny pieces of half a dozen different vineyards and make five or six barrels of wine from each, for a total of 125 to 150 cases. Compare that with a Bordeaux first growth like Château Lafite-Rothschild, which in a typical year releases 25,000 to 30,000 cases.

In addition, Bordeaux achieves more consistent quality. Its cabernet grape yields a deep black currant color and firm tannin structure. The Burgundy pinot noir grape is chameleonlike, often weak, weedy, and pale, or too ponderous, pruny, and tannic, with an unpleasant flavor of cooked fruit. Nonetheless, from 1980 to 1989, prices for Burgundy bottles more than quadrupled.

"It's Texas out there," Hubert said. "The growers just pumped out the wine and commanded any price they wanted," Lyonel added.

Lyonel hoped prices had peaked. At the annual Trois Glorieuses auction in November, classic red vintages such as Auxey-Duresses and Volnay-Santenots were sold for the same price as the year before. Famous white Meursault, Puligny-Montrachet, and Chassagne-Montrachet had even fallen a bit. The Three Glorious Days are the commercial high point of the Burgundy wine season, a dizzy whirl that moves from tasting to luncheon to tasting to dinner, with buyers, connoisseurs, and tourists trooping through the cellars of the Hospices of Beaune.

The Hospices is one of France's great buildings, a mixture of Flemish-style fantasy and traditional French lines. Founded in 1443 by Nicolas Rolin, chancellor of Burgundy, as a hospital for the elderly and infirm, today it is a museum and Beaune's major tourist attraction. Almost from the Hospices' inception, it became the custom for Burgundians to donate parcels of vineyard land to finance its work. Since 1851, the wines have been sold at the annual November auction, providing funds to operate the Hospices.

The tradition continues, even though these days the state picks up almost all of the hospital's tab and Les Trois Glorieuses is most useful as a way of promoting tourism. Even for the most experienced wine professionals it is difficult to judge a wine that is scarcely six weeks old. Tasters make their way through seemingly endless cellars—proof that Beaune has as much construction belowground as above.

On the auction's second night, rock and jazz bands play in the streets. Free glasses of plonk, handed out in the marketplace, stimulate the party atmosphere. Connoisseurs meanwhile sate themselves on grands crus at a true

Rabelaisian six-course feast in the cellars of a restored Renaissance château known as Clos Vougeot, a magnificent Cistercian building set amid its own vineyards. Hosted by the Confrérie des Chevaliers du Tastevin, some six hundred guests in black tie cram the cellars around long refectory tables. The confrères come in red velvet robes and hats.

Hunting horns herald each course, and each dish is accompanied by a different wine. Flocks of serving ladies come and go at full tilt, offering cheese and filling glasses with an Echézeaux "of noble lineage." When dessert arrives, an ice cream cake in the shape of a snail, the waiters stride out into the dining room with such force that several guests are usually knocked down on their way to the bathroom. During the meal, the chevaliers entertain the guests with speeches and songs that range from the foolish to the amusing. The speeches mix Christian and pagan elements and educate "the honored guests" in the rituals of international bonhomie. By the end of the evening, the chevaliers and their guests are sozzled. Everybody has trouble finding his or her car. The auction itself is held the following afternoon across the street from the Hôtel-Dieu. Prices are high, particularly for wine not yet bottled—the sellers hope that the revelry causes a spurt in generosity.

Lyonel himself never attended Les Trois Glorieuses. He had too much work at the restaurant, and besides, the connoisseur in him scorned the occasion as public relations flimflam. Now he poured Hubert and Bernard another glass of red wine. Although prices had dropped at the previous year's auction, he still feared being priced out of the market for the bottles he wanted to buy.

"The good growers won't suffer; there never will be enough of their wine to go around," he said. "It's only the bad growers who are going to have problems."

The conclusion was clear: buying good wine would be as difficult as ever. Silence fell over the table at the thought. A waiter came and took away empty plates. It was time for cheese and dessert. Bernard chewed a thick morsel of Epoisses and then made everyone laugh by ordering a crème caramel.

"Make sure it really is swimming in the cream," he told the waiter. "Like two big tits."

"Stop talking like that," Hubert reproached him, in a rare prudish moment.

Bernard chuckled. When the dessert arrived, he gulped it down. A coffee arrived and he gulped that, too. Then, impatient as ever, he commanded: "Let's go."

He settled his account by offering the patronne a parting kiss.

★ ★ ★

Within a few minutes, the tasters arrived at their next stop, in Volnay: Domaine Lafarge. Like Bize, Lafarge was a classic Burgundy wine family. Michel Lafarge, the family's patriarch, had notebooks showing records of his great-grandfather's wine sales dating back to the late 1800s. His great-grandfather began selling wine in barrels to restaurants, and the family bottled its first wine in 1904, for personal use. Its first commercial bottles were sold in 1936. In their cellars, the Lafarges still guarded a few precious bottles of both those vintages.

Like many other Burgundy winegrowers, the Lafarges lived above their cellars, on Rue de la Combe, one of the narrow streets radiating from Volnay's small central square, Place de l'Eglise. In 1974, a new cellar was dug under the house and a freight elevator was installed to avoid the uncomfortable walk down treacherous stone steps full of dangling spiderwebs.

The new cellar connected to the old one, with low, rounded ceilings that date from the twelfth century. Outside, the stone facade was plain, with only a small plaque identifying DOMAINE LAFARGE.

"My rule," Lyonel said, "is the smaller the sign outside, the better the wine inside."

Hubert rang the doorbell, and Michel Lafarge answered. A rugged man with biting blue eyes and striking white hair, he emanated the self-confidence that comes with deep roots and a strong sense of mission. Behind him stood his eldest son, Frédéric, who had begun to work in the vineyards when he was nineteen. He was thin and bespectacled, a timid, younger version of his father. The other Lafarge children, two daughters and a son, had no plans to enter the wine trade. "There was only room for one child at the domain, and Frédéric was the most interested," the father explained.

Frédéric lived in a house next door to his parents' home, connected by a doorway. He was a graduate of an oenological university and had trained at a venerable Bordeaux château. From his behavior, no one could sense his knowledge. During the wine tasting, he opened the bottles but, except for a few words with Lyonel, not his mouth. In the Lafarge family, respect for tradition and seniority remained strong.

Frédéric began opening bottles. He started with the cheapest and youngest wines, the fruity white Aligoté, the simple Passetoutgrains (a blend of pinot noir and gamay), and moved on to the village Volnay before arriving at the top-of-the-line Volnay Clos des Chênes. For a moment, Lyonel forgot his scientific calculation and blurted out, "Wonderful, wonderful, wonderful."

"Monsieur Lafarge," Bernard pronounced in a solemn tone, putting down his glass. "You are the best of Burgundy."

A small smile, more a crease than a grin, crinkled over Michel Lafarge's weathered face.

The past five years, he explained, had produced terrific harvests, "as good as I can remember." This was a man with a memory, too. He remembered how hail destroyed 90 percent of the harvest in 1946 and how as late as 1983 he lost 50 percent. "The last five years are too good to be true," he told the group. "Truly exceptional."

For some Burgundy winegrowers, the austere nineties promised a true shock. Not for Michel Lafarge. He confirmed Lyonel's suspicions by telling the tasters that he still could charge the premium price of fifteen dollars for a simple village bottle. "Here we don't speak about money," he said. "We speak about whether it is good."

Venerable Burgundy domains and Bordeaux château used to have a monopoly on this quality, Michel Lafarge said. Now Australians and Chileans, not to mention the Californians, have begun exporting good wines. Some joke that even Canada soon may be planting vines. When the Lafarges visited the United States, they made a special visit to Oregon. About twenty years ago, growers in Oregon planted pinot noir and chardonnay, the noble grapes of Burgundy. Michel Lafarge, the Burgundy traditionalist, wanted to test the upstarts.

"How was Oregon wine?" Lyonel asked.

"Good," Michel Lafarge responded. "Very good."

He admired the efforts of his pinot noir cousins across the Atlantic to turn out a quality product. But he did not fear any competition. He was confident of his own abilities and his own wine.

As a parting gesture, Michel Lafarge took an unlabeled bottle down from a musty, cobwebbed section of the cellar.

"Guess what year this is," he said. "The only thing I will tell you is that it comes from after 1959."

Frédéric uncorked the bottle and poured a glass for everybody.

"To your health," Michel Lafarge said.

The vintage made an amber color in the glass, paler than the rich red of a young wine. Its aroma was more delicate than that of new bottles. Different tastes mingled on the lips.

"It's still relatively light and fruity," Lyonel guessed. "It's an 'eighty-three."

"No, a 'seventy-six," Hubert countered. "Not a great year, but one that grows on you."

"No, no," said Bernard, "It's a 'seventy-eight. I know it's a 'seventy-eight."

"All wrong," Lafarge announced, smiling. "It's a 'seventy-two, a year the critics said would be terrible, but one that ages surprisingly well."

In a moment of generosity, Lafarge promised to sell a few of his old vintages to La Côte d'Or. That made Lyonel happy. He always had trouble obtaining old bottles. But he knew that if he was to win at his upcoming contest, he could not make such grievous errors in dating.

"Wine," he sighed, on his way out of the Lafarge cellars. "It's a great lesson in humility."

★ ★ ★

The next stop was Daniel Chopin. For the past few years, Bernard had been buying Chopin's wine and labeling it Bernard Loiseau Bourgogne.

Chopin lived in Nuits-St.-Georges, south of the main part of the town. Here begins the long Burgundy plain that stretches to Lyons and Geneva. Chopin's modest house, a cramped, prefabricated rectangle no different from thousands of other postwar suburban constructions in France, had the Levittown look. As at the Lafarges', the house sat above the wine cellars. Chickens ran free in the courtyard. When the Renault Espace pulled in, it almost ran some of them over.

Madame Chopin, a stocky, smiling woman, stopped sweeping the front steps and went to look for her husband.

Monsieur Chopin soon arrived and led the group alone into the cellars. He was sixty-eight years old, a spare, rugged man of medium height, who had been producing wine for thirty-two years. His shoulders still were straight, and what was left of his curly hair was cropped short. Decades in the fields had left Chopin's face crinkled and his cheekbones sharp and angular. He wore baggy corduroys and a beat-up sweater, and he spoke with a thick country accent. As long as he could get up in the morning, he said, he would make wine. Lyonel called him, affectionately, "the Peasant."

Chopin's family had been involved in wine making for three generations—"Not long," he said. When he took over the family holdings from his father, in 1959, he harvested both wines and cereal crops. With his marriage in 1957 to a girl from Vougeot came some precious parcels in Chambolle-Musigny and Vougeot. Over time, he managed to assemble almost ten hectares of decent vines in the Côte de Nuits. He also had a long memory. The best vintage was in 1947. The next year, 1948, "was bad," he said, "very bad."

On most days, Chopin worked from about six in the morning until six in the evening, six days a week. After the harvest, he still took off his clothes and lowered himself into a vat, where he jumped for hours on a crust of crushed, fermented grapes until he was exhausted. This process is called *pigeage*, and Chopin was not the type to order a fancy vat with an automatic *pigeur* to crush the pips and electric pumps to bring the juices to the surface.

Chopin conserved his vines, because old vines give the best wine; the best grapes come from vines that are thirty to forty-five years old. He had some vines more than sixty-five years old that were still producing. He used only grafts from the vines in his own vineyards for new plantings, while many younger vintners used clones. Chopin did not want vines that produced bigger quantity. He wanted quality.

Most Burgundy vintners don't bother these days with wine contests. They don't need them to sell their wine. The proud Chopin always entered them—and usually won a prize.

Chopin began to uncork some bottles. The first cork was rotted. He refused to serve it and opened another bottle. Lyonel sniffed and tasted.

"Please, please, tell me what you think," Chopin asked.

"Round," Lyonel replied. "It has a good structure in the mouth."

For most of his long career, Chopin sold to the merchants, only to become more and more angered by the prices they paid. "One year it was good, the next year it was terrible," he complained. For the past seven years, he had bottled his entire production. Even in the heady eighties, he kept his prices reasonable, as low as $8 a bottle for Nuits-St.-Georges. A bottle of his Vougeot first growth, premier cru, cost only about $15. That was about half the cost of a top-flight Volnay from Domaine Lafarge.

"Many other growers were greedy," Chopin explained. "They will have problems. I prefer to keep my prices reasonable and not worry."

Lyonel almost never placed an order during a tasting. "You risk being carried away by impulse and making a foolish, expensive mistake."

From Chopin, however, Lyonel had bought large quantities ever since he joined La Côte d'Or.

"May I have a thousand bottles?" Lyonel asked.

Chopin looked as if he were about to collapse from a heart attack.

"A thousand bottles!" he repeated, astonished. "I don't have a thousand bottles. How about six hundred?"

"Eight hundred?"

"Seven hundred."

"Is that the best you can do?"

"Yes."

Out in the van, Lyonel explained, "Before we can buy more wine from Daniel Chopin, one of his other clients has to die."

★ ★ ★

In the immutable world of Burgundy wine, death is indeed just about the only way change seems to come about. Vineyards almost never come up for sale. Burgundians like to think of Bordeaux as belonging to foreign consortiums and tax-investment funds—and to an occasional Rothschild. Not many people besides Rothschilds can afford a Bordeaux château. From the Burgundy point of view, Bordeaux is in the agribusiness, anonymous and commercial, with little in common with the rustic wine making in Burgundy.

Everywhere else in France, children are fleeing the land. In Burgundy, many children stay. Almost all young winegrowers live on their parents' lands or their in-laws' lands. Christian Amiot went to work for his father-in-law, Jean Servelle, who owned five hectares in Chambolle-Musigny. It was 1980, and he was twenty-two years old. Then in 1989, his stepfather collapsed, victim of a heart attack.

Christian and his wife, Elisabeth, inherited the domain, renamed it Domaine Amiot-Servelle, and set out to make improvements. Elisabeth, an accountant by profession, modernized the commercial side of the business. In the vineyard, her husband's path was evolutionary, not revolutionary. He stuck with the fermentation techniques he learned from his father-in-law, aging the wines in old wooden barrels. But he changed little things here and there, and word soon was out: here was a comer.

Lyonel picked up the scent. He was always looking for promising young growers. Ambitious youngsters have drive, he said. Many are yuppies, attracted like investment bankers during the 1980s to an easy way of making a fortune, but the best want to improve, and they often make the most interesting wines. Christian Amiot possessed that burning desire for improvement. The Gault-Millau Wine Guide published an article in praise of Amiot. "Everything we ordered was delicious," it noted. "But the best of the best was signed Amiot-Servelle. It was true velvet."

Lyonel read the review and called for an appointment.

There is no Michelin Guide to wines, and winegrowers do not hold guidebooks in mortal fear like chefs. Most Burgundy vintners are able to sell their wine even with terrible reviews. But important wine critics can help. Robert Parker, the American editor of *The Wine Spectator,* is both despised and admired for his remarkable stamina; he tastes two hundred wines in a row and then scores them on a scale from 50 to 100. Most notable wine critics are Anglo-Saxon, thanks perhaps to their neutrality in the never-ending feud between Bordeaux and Burgundy growers. Although their rankings are not a life-or-death matter, critics make a difference, especially for relatively unknown young growers. "A good review is a good way to make a reputation," Amiot said.

Rotund and bearded, Amiot looked like the caricature of the fun-loving Burgundian who eats and drinks too much. Today, as he led lBernard, Lyonel, and Hubert down into his cellars, he seemed to be in a bad mood. He explained that after the upcoming harvest, he was going to lose his best parcel, in the village of Vougeot. Amiot rented most of his vines, and his landlord had decided to sell. To buy, Amiot needed about $100,000. He didn't have such a sum, and the bankers did not want to help.

Hubert and Lyonel paid little attention to his complaints. They sipped the wine, and even though their heads were whirling, they knew that what they tasted was superb. They asked Amiot some questions and were pleased with the responses. "He is not pissing the vines," Lyonel said later.

Just before leaving, Amiot pulled the same trick as Lafarge had. He picked a cobweb-covered bottle and opened it.

"What year?" he asked as he filled the waiting glasses.

Bernard said 1972. Hubert said 1962. Lyonel said 1964—"The year I was born."

"No," replied Amiot. "It is 1952."

Everyone laughed, even serious Lyonel, who felt the day had been fruitful in his quest for stocking a three-star wine cellar. In Dumaine's time, almost all the wine came from the merchants. Michelin didn't demand more, either. "Dumaine had a good cellar, but a narrow one," Lyonel said. When Bernard took over La Côte d'Or, the cellar contained only about 100 labels. After this year's tasting, Lyonel said, he would reach 660 labels and about 18,000 bottles. Impressive as that sounded, it remained small compared with cellars of certain Parisian establishments. The Tour d'Argent alone boasted 400,000 bottles.

Lyonel hoped to impress the inspecteurs not so much by the size of his cellar, but by its quality. Sometimes he was forced to buy from merchants because he could not find the vintages he wanted anywhere else. But overall he accused the merchants of betraying the Burgundy heritage by neglecting the individuality that the soil imparts to the wine. He thought a wine list worthy of three Michelin stars must be dominated by family producers such as the Bizes. Anybody could buy wine from merchants; it took time and care to search out and sift through the myriad of individual growers.

Lyonel was satisfied. In a single day, he had scored several important successes. Bize and Lafarge remained classics, and they would sell him the old vintages he needed to impress Michelin. "The Peasant" Chopin would provide enough inexpensive, quality wine to make it through the upcoming summer season. And in Amiot, he had spotted a talented up-and-comer.

On the drive back home, his mouth purple from all the tasting, Lyonel fell into a contented sleep.

★ ★ ★

A few days later, the annual Festival of Saint Vincent took place. Vincent, an obscure Spaniard martyred at Valence in 304, has become the patron saint of the winegrowers because of the *vin* in his name. Traditionally, the festival marks the beginning of the year's work in the fields.

For most of its history, the festival was celebrated by a simple Mass, followed by a visit to the cellars for a glass of wine and a splendid feast. Then, in January 1938, the Chevaliers du Tastevin organized the festival on a much grander scale. Ever since, a different village has hosted the event each year, and the date was changed to the third Saturday of January. The goal was simple: not to revive tradition but to promote tourism.

This year, Puligny-Montrachet hosted the festival. As the gray dawn broke, representatives from each community lined up at the village outskirts. It was a bitter-cold morning, with frost on the vines. Two saint bearers from each village shouldered little wooden stretchers that held wooden carvings of the saints. A third took charge of their village's own rich, embroidered banner. The procession made its way past colorful paper flowers and bows of blue and silver foil hanging along the streets and into Puligny's small church. A gigantic crowd watched, some clutching wineglasses, others wearing wine-tasting cups on silver chains, and others sporting curious caps, sashes, or badges of honor.

The band struck up a solemn drum roll. The procession pushed through the throng to the war memorial, where the mayor laid a wreath. Then the band erupted into the "Marseillaise." Inside the church, dignitaries filled the nave. After the line arrived, a group of priests and bishops entered. A priest gave a short speech of welcome. He referred to the ideals of solidarity and fraternity and, with sadness, to the war that had just erupted in the Persian Gulf. The reading was from the Gospel of Saint John, which recounts the miracle of Cana, when Jesus saved the wedding feast by turning water into wine. Children from the village carried bread and wine to be blessed at the altar. "Let us bless the Lord," sang the choir. "Amen."

The Mass over, everybody rushed for the doors, surging outside into the tiny village square. The procession slowly trooped out. The band began to play again. In a specially converted hangar, hunting horns called the chevaliers to attention. The commander offered a paean of praise for Puligny and inducted the oldest winegrowers of the village into the confrérie. Television cameras whirled, and journalists interviewed the honored ancients.

After the ceremony, there was a gigantic six-course meal: fish terrine with *sauce verte,* snails, lobster Florentine, chicken and morels, cheese, chocolate cake and ice cream. The wines, of course, were from Puligny, though all of mediocre quality. No vintner wanted to give away his best bottles. Still, everybody stayed at table until it was almost early evening.

Outside in the street, giddy tourists gulped down free wine offered by various cellars. Soon many were drunk. A cacophony of different languages—German, French, Spanish, and English—filled the air. Men urinated in courtyards against walls. Couples huddled for protection from the cold and the crowd. In three days of revelry, a total of seventy-five thousand merrymakers tramped through the narrow streets. Puligny was submerged under a mountain of broken glass, plastic cups, and paper wrappers.

By Monday morning, the festival was over and silence returned to the village streets. The winegrowers were back at work in the fields, ready to begin another year.

*Wine tasting*

# CHAPTER 9

★ ★ ★

# *Kitchen Drama*

*The chefs of La Côte d'Or*

THE DRAMA BEGAN with an *oeufs à la neige*—floating islands.

In the repertoire of French pastry, the combination of creamy egg custard topped with islands of whipped egg whites is a classic. When boiled in water and whisked with sugar, the egg whites become light and airy, like powdered snow. But oeufs à la neige is a delicate, difficult dish to make. Beat the egg whites too little and they never achieve the proper consistency; beat them too hard and the light, snowy whites become brittle.

One February day, Bernard decided to eat lunch in the dining room with Dominique. La Côte d'Or had only three reservations, so the dining room was quiet. For dessert, Bernard ordered oeufs à la neige.

They arrived—hard as rocks.

Bernard was already in a bad mood. Now he became furious. Business was down 30 percent from the previous February. France was beginning to fall into a recession, and luxury restaurants were among the first hit. And just before he had ordered the fateful dessert, receptionist Marie-Christine informed him that reservations for April and May were slow.

"If this continues," Bernard told her, "we'll all soon be dead."

In addition, Bernard's ego was bruised by a slight from Paris. President Mitterrand has just announced the Legion of Honor list. Mitterrand was a regular client at La Côte d'Or, and Bernard had hoped to win the award. Instead, the president had chosen to honor Bernard's colleague Joël Robuchon.

In contrast to the emotional, exuberant Bernard, Robuchon was a timid, soft-spoken person, a chef's chef, known for his perfectionism. While Bernard had come to the countryside, Robuchon remained behind in Paris, and his restaurant, Jamin, won three Michelin stars, which propelled it to a decade of unparalleled prosperity. Despite the most expensive prices in expensive expense-account Paris, Jamin had a three-month waiting list. As Dominique said, "When you can only get a reservation three months ahead, you earn a type of mystique."

Bernard considered Robuchon both a friend and an inspiration. When it comes to affection, a great chef is like a child. He doesn't just want to be loved; he wants to be preferred. His food cannot be just heavenly; it must be better than his colleague's. So while Bernard praised the "great Joël," he envied his success and fame. When Marie-Christine told him that Robuchon had called and invited him to a celebration lunch the following day in Paris, Bernard decided to attend. He wanted to be seen by his peers. But he was angered about not winning the award himself.

"I should have gotten it," he muttered. "Why does Robuchon have all the luck?"

When the overcooked oeufs à la neige arrived on his plate, Bernard roared into the kitchen in a rage.

"What went wrong?" he asked Thierry, the pastry chef.

Pastry chefs are notoriously temperamental, and Thierry De Meo was no exception. He lived by himself and almost never went out with his fellow chefs for the traditional after-service beer at the Café du Nord. At work, he said little and frequently wore a sneer on his face. Unlike the other members of the kitchen staff, who are organized in a strict hierarchy, pastry chefs enjoy autonomy. Thierry worked off in a corner, by himself, with the help of a few commis whom he commanded. The pastry chef is just about the only member of the staff who can talk back to the boss, and that's what Thierry did now.

"Your oeufs à la neige aren't the only thing I have to do today," he told Bernard.

Bernard blew up.

"We only have three covers and you tell me this isn't the only thing you have to do," he fumed. But Bernard felt powerless against the rebellious pastry chef, whom he could not replace easily. Someone else would have to suffer. He turned to Patrick Bertron, his kitchen lieutenant.

"I have a pastry chef that answers back to me," Bernard screamed. "We only have three covers. What are we going to do?"

He paused and answered the question himself.

"Get rid of someone," he said.

That evening, Larry the American stagaire was fired.

When the oeufs à la neige drama erupted, Larry was standing off to the side of the kitchen in the hors d'oeuvre section, making liver tarts. He heard the commotion and thought it had nothing to do with him. But after the evening service, Patrick called him to his office.

"Sunday is your last day," Patrick announced. "Monsieur Loiseau said we can't afford you. You've learned all you can. We don't need you anymore."

Larry couldn't leave on Sunday, because he had some clothes at the local laundry. He waited to pick them up on Wednesday. On that day, a group of three-star Michelin chefs showed up at La Côte d'Or: Paul Bocuse, Georges Blanc, Pierre Troisgros, Marc Meneau, Marc Haeberlin, and Emile Jung.

Larry spotted Bocuse as he was leaving the restaurant. To the American, Bocuse was a hero. When Larry was a seventh-grader at H. B. Thompson Junior High School, in Syosset, Long Island, he borrowed from the school library a copy of Bocuse's cookbook, *La Cuisine,* with its pictures of the famous French chef in his sparkling white uniform topped by his toque. Just as Bernard dreamed of equaling his master Troisgros and winning a third Michelin star, Larry hoped one day to capture a little bit of Bocuse's magic. To him, the star chef's toque looked like a king's crown. "I would dream of Bocuse at night," Larry told his fellow stagaires. "Everything about him, the food, the presentation, the uniforms, it all looked so spectacular."

When he saw his idol, Larry rushed to his room to get his camera and asked if he could have a picture taken with him. Bocuse assented. Larry handed his camera to Dominique and asked her to take the shot.

She was stunned at the request. She had never noticed Larry before in the kitchen and didn't even know that he was a stagaire or that he had just been fired.

But composed and controlled as ever, Dominique focused and snapped. By this time, the rest of the kitchen staff had stepped outside and was watching.

"Everyone was so embarrassed," Larry said afterward. "Here I was fired and out in the front row, taking some of the fame away from Bernard."

Bernard did not forget.

"Why was the American still here?" he yelled at Patrick the next day. "Why was he pushing himself to the front of the line to have his picture taken with Bocuse?"

"He has some laundry to pick up," Patrick answered.

Bernard was furious. Larry had braved his wrath to get a picture with Bocuse and hadn't even bothered to be photographed with anyone at La Côte d'Or.

"Oh boy, Bocuse still is better known than I am," Bernard said. "I really have my work cut out to overtake him."

Before Larry left later that day, he picked up a certificate of his internship. He hoped to find a job at another top-flight French restaurant, and the recommendation was crucial. When he arrived in the chef's office, Patrick had left for his afternoon break. The certificate was sitting on his desk. In it, Larry's last name was misspelled.

*How could they misspell my name?* Larry thought, incredulous. But he didn't want any more confrontations. He took the next train back to Paris, leaving with nothing more than a worthless piece of paper for his six months at La Côte d'Or.

★ ★ ★

Turnover was rapid in the kitchen. Bernard liked interns to stay six months, maximum. Any longer and they became frustrated with toiling for no pay. His favorite recruits were Japanese. When they decided to learn about a subject, they imitated the best. In cooking, that meant the French. Japanese interns had come to France ever since 1960, when an Ecole de Cuisine Française was established in Osaka. In the 1970s, a Japanese entrepreneur named Tsuji set up a hotel school outside of Lyons.

The Japanese fell in love with nouvelle cuisine and found Bernard's cuisine à l'eau, with its emphasis on fresh, unadorned presentation, particularly appealing. Burgundy as a whole exerts a strange hold on the Japanese. Mike Sata, a Japanese industrialist, spent twenty million dollars transforming the Renaissance Château de Chailly, not far from Saulieu, into a hotel. He also built a new golf course. One stubborn peasant refused to sell his land because Sata was Japanese. As a result, the golf course was built on flat land right next to the highway.

Sata tried to hire away Bernard's maître d'hôtel, Hubert, to run his giant hotel. Hubert thought hard about the offer before turning it down. He decided the château lacked soul, and anyway, he wanted to stay and shoot for stars with Bernard. Since the Château de Chailly opened, the Japanese have supplanted the Americans in Burgundian folklore. Villagers talk with awe of these exotic imperialists, arriving for lunch by helicopter, then sweeping off to examine vineyards in the Côte d'Or.

But the French have few insecurities about the Japanese when it comes to cuisine. Paul Bocuse once told Bernard about his experience of giving a cooking course in Osaka. He began by preparing a *boeuf bourguignon,* the traditional Burgundy stew. Bocuse invented as he went along, adding the beef and onions until he felt the dish was just right. Before he could finish, a student interrupted him.

"Master, that's not how it should be done," the student objected. "In his manual, Escoffier says that for one kilogram of beef, you need two hundred fifty grams of onions and a hundred milligrams of salt."

"I see you know more than me," the inimitable Bocuse responded. "Instead of showing you how to cook beef, you should show me how to paint a rose. I will distribute three tubes of paint to each of you, one red, one green, and one white. There are four hundred of you in the class. Do you think that you will paint four hundred identical roses?"

The students understood that cooking, however disciplined, remained an imprecise art, and Bocuse told Bernard that he never had any further problems teaching in Osaka. Bernard enjoyed a similarly ambivalent relationship with his Japanese staff. In most cases, he didn't even know their names. They spoke bad French, so little communication was possible. They didn't have much creativity, but they worked hard. Ask them to cut carrots or peel potatoes all day and they cut carrots and peeled potatoes all day. Above all, the Japanese were quiet—unlike the noisy, aggressive Americans. To Bernard's way of thinking, stagaires should keep their eyes open and their mouths shut. They must know how to take orders.

Just before Larry's forced departure, two new nonpaid interns arrived. One was a fresh-faced French girl, twenty-year-old Anaïs. She managed to obtain the position thanks to her father, who knew a journalist friend of Bernard's.

Anaïs was small, timid, and cute. She was a student in a vocational school in a distant corner of Brittany. Even though her father ran a hotel there, Anaïs had never cooked before or worked in a restaurant. She didn't even know about Michelin stars. When she started, Patrick and the other chefs thought that like other women, she would last no more than two weeks.

Dominique warned her to shut her mouth. Anaïs did. For whole days, she said not a word. She stood off to the side, cutting carrots and peeling potatoes. Eventually she was allowed to pluck ducks. From eight in the morning to midnight, she plucked and plucked. Never once did she complain. When anyone asked her how everything was going, she smiled and replied, "Just fine, just fine." Nothing more.

Anaïs became a great success story. She lasted her full six months at La Côte d'Or. When she left, she was as timid and fresh-faced as ever. But she had learned determination and grit. She vowed to finish her studies and continue in other kitchens. Later, she said, she would open her own restaurant.

"My place will be nothing like my father's hole-in-the-wall," she vowed. "I want to cook haute cuisine."

Another new intern was a tall, fair-haired, handsome American named Paul Lynn. Paul came from a well-to-do family outside of Washington, D.C. Unlike working-class, mustachioed Larry, Paul was the spitting image of the rugged American cowboy the French so love and admire in Hollywood films. Because of Paul's resemblance to Robert Redford and his boisterous temperament, his fellow staffers started calling him Sundance Kid.

Paul was a graduate of the prestigious San Francisco–based Culinary Institute of America. He already had worked in Michelin one- and three-star restaurants in Paris, and he had met a pretty French blonde named Patricia, who drove him to Saulieu in her Peugeot 205. When the couple pulled up in front of the restaurant, Paul recognized Bernard from pictures and rushed to greet him.

"*Bonjour,*" he said. "I am the new American."

Bernard slapped him on his shoulders with enthusiasm and turned to a guest.

"An American," he said. "You see, everybody comes to learn from Loiseau, the Americans, the Japanese, everybody."

Bernard went into the room at the back of the kitchen and handed Paul a white chef's uniform. He asked Patrick to show the American his grimy, grubby room upstairs. Paul put down his suitcase and changed into his work clothes. Within an hour, he was at his position in the new, sleek, stainless steel, space-age kitchen, picking parsley and dicing vegetables.

Paul made a good impression. For the first few weeks, he worked in the *garde-manger* section, preparing the small liver appetizer tarts. Then he was promoted to *dressage,* where he arranged servings on dishes. "If you show that you can do things, they let you do it," he said. "If you aren't capable, they see it and give you nothing."

Paul had started cooking as a child in suburban Gaithersburg, Maryland. His workaholic parents were so busy that he wouldn't have eaten unless he had learned to make his own meals. After high school, Paul went to community college and studied marketing. But he hated it. He went off to the California Culinary Institute, in San Francisco. One of his teachers there knew Philippe de Givenchy, the chef and owner of the Michelin one-star restaurant La Timonerie, right near Notre Dame in Paris.

La Timonerie was a tiny restaurant, with a dining room of only ten tables. Madame de Givenchy and one waiter served, while her husband ran the kitchen with only three other chefs. Paul was happy. The place was so small that he was allowed to do a bit of everything.

One evening, the waiter left, giving no notice. Desperate, the de Givenchys called a young French marketing student, a family friend. Patricia showed up that night to fill in. In her twenties, lithe and blond, she was the daughter of a wealthy family from Mulhouse, in eastern France. Her father ran a sausage factory with 450 employees and owned fifteen delicatessens. A month later, she and Paul moved in together. By this time, Paul had risen to chef de partie, responsible for all the meat dishes, at La Timonerie. Paul decided to stay a full three years in France.

His next stop was Lucas-Carton, one of Paris's oldest and most prestigious palaces. Chef Alain Senderens had recently achieved three stars. The brigade consisted of more than twenty chefs. Paul started out at the bottom of the bottom. Senderens didn't take many interns, but Philippe de Givenchy had managed to convince him that this American was better than the hundreds of others lining up in front of his doors.

Paul proved to be as good as his reputation. He soon was cooking Senderens's signature dish, duck in four spices.

Then Patricia finished her studies. Unable to find a job, she returned home to live with her parents. Paul could not afford to live alone in Paris. So he followed her and took a job working at the family sausage factory. For an ambitious chef, making sausages was not the most inspiring work. Paul wrote Bernard and other famous chefs, asking for an internship. Bernard was the first to say yes.

When Paul arrived in Saulieu, he was surprised by Bernard's openness and friendliness. Often, the chef would walk through the kitchen and pat him on the shoulder, saying, "You're doing a good job here," or would take him aside and confide, "God, we always need an American here." Bernard and Paul shared the same kind of voluble, expansive personality.

But Paul had one problem: a big mouth.

"If you blanched the garlic like this, it might be better," he told a fellow chef one day.

"Oh yeah, you think so," the chef sneered back, continuing to put the garlic in boiling water as before.

Paul persisted. When another chef didn't clean his part of the kitchen well, Paul told him, "That's not good enough."

"Shut up," the chef responded.

"No, I will not shut up," Paul said. "After all, doesn't this place want three stars?"

Paul continued to find his young colleagues boring and immature. On days off, many of them went to McDonald's in Dijon. Paul couldn't believe that Bernard's workers, masters of haute cuisine, liked nothing more than a Big Mac. Paul hated Big Macs.

The gregarious American also found the French too stiff and formal. Paul once spotted Patrick the chef and his wife in the local Maxi Mart supermarket. Before he could say hello, Patrick turned away.

"He ran away, can you believe that?" Paul said later. "I grabbed him and said we should say hello. I'm not going to hide."

The tense kitchen atmosphere grated on Paul's nerves. Even when he was doing a good job, his colleagues would shout at him, for no apparent reason, "You fucking whore, you fucking whore."

One day, Paul overheard Patrick talking to a fellow chef.

"What should I do with Paul?" Patrick asked. "Send him to the meat section?"

"Oh, no," Paul said to Patrick, interrupting. "There's a lot of screaming in the meat section. I want to stay in fish. We all get along here."

Later Paul explained, "The American way is to say, 'Let's work as a team.' In France, everything's authoritarian. You give orders. You take orders. I believe we must work together to achieve perfection. If a side dish is bad, the whole plate is not three stars."

In Paul's opinion, his fellow chefs were not "communicative."

"The French guys are too stupid to go and ask questions," he complained. "The lesson I have to learn in the kitchen is to watch and copy. Just watch and copy. I have to remind myself to listen to these jerks and take their lessons."

Staff meals were a final annoyance. Each week, one intern was appointed to cook for the entire staff. He was instructed to use the leftovers as he saw fit. When Paul was responsible, he spent hours dreaming up inventive preparations. Other interns were less creative. For one whole week the staff ate reheated duck confit, and Paul felt sick. Another week, he was served omelettes every day.

"If the intern tries, he can make excellent food for the staff." Paul said. "But all too often, these guys make no effort."

One day off, Paul could take no more. He decided to eat out. The only restaurant open that day in Saulieu was La Côte d'Or. He walked in and asked for a table. Marie-Christine thought he was joking. Staff members almost never ate at the restaurant. Paul asked again for a table and sat down. The maître d'hôtel Franck walked into the kitchen and announced, "Paul is in the dining room."

Everybody thought he meant Paul Bocuse.

"No," Franck replied. "Paul the American."

Paul ordered the *filet de boeuf*. It was wonderful. He finished off with a 1959 Armagnac. Lyonel tasted it with him.

"Wow," Paul said as he sipped the strong digestive. "This bites in the mouth."

By the time he finished, Paul was alone in the dining room. Nobody was left to take the bill. When he came back the next morning, to pay, Marie-Christine told him, "It's on the house."

"Boy, was I surprised," Paul said. "Bernard is really a great guy."

For Valentine's Day, Patricia visited and Bernard gave his American protégé the day off. Hubert and Lyonel helped set up some wine tastings for him, and Dominique offered the young lovers a three-hundred-franc room in the hotel at half price. Not long after Larry was fired, Patrick the chef approached Paul after lunch service.

"We want to keep you for the season," Patrick said, "and we can afford to pay you."

★ ★ ★

Michael Caines, the English chef de partie, was leaving for Robuchon's restaurant, Jamin, in Paris. Traditionally, on a chef's last shift at work, the crew throws a party: everyone vies to create the most disgusting concoction with leftovers from the kitchen. The favorite method at La Côte d'Or was to ferment broth from scallops for several days. Often the smell was so bad that members of the staff had to stop work and step out for a gulp of fresh air. In this food war, the garbage provided material for other popular weapons. By reputation, the English are the most vicious at this game; at home they have been known to add urine to the mixture.

Michael was prepared for the worst. Each night during his last week at work, his fellow chefs had given him previews of what was to come. On his last day, they lured him up into the office and filched his car keys. When Michael managed to get free, he found his car filled with logs. It took him a half hour to empty it. At ten-thirty in the evening, after the last dishes were served, mayhem broke out in the back room. Olivier, a sous chef, had created a thick puree of salmon bones in his blender. He grabbed Michael, pulled him into the back room, and poured the gook all over him. Michael was covered from head to foot. He retaliated by spraying cold water on Olivier. Back and forth they battled, like two children. Olivier was soon also soaking.

Bernard returned from the dining room.

"What's going on?" he asked.

"Michael's going-away party," Patrick answered.

Bernard nodded uh-huh, and then said with a smile: "Don't use my foie gras or caviar to get him."

Michael and Olivier finally declared a truce. They embraced each other. Both left to shower. Michael's girlfriend, Laurence, an attractive blonde, arrived with a change of clothes. The muck-covered work clothes were thrown into the laundry, and Michael and Olivier once again were presentable.

A waiter placed four bottles of champagne on the kitchen table. It was a time for memories. Patrick stood in one corner and reflected on how Michael had arrived a year and a half before, with two strikes against him, his color and his nationality.

"Who is this guy?" Bernard has asked.

"He's Michael Caines," Patrick responded.

"Who?" Bernard asked again.

"We all knew he meant, 'Who is this black guy?' " Patrick remembered. "I know Bernard isn't racist or anything like that, but he just doesn't know any other blacks."

Being English was another handicap for Michael. Although La Côte d'Or had used English stagaires before, they had not earned a strong reputation for their work, and there never had been an English chef de partie. An Englishman who actually cooked is almost unheard-of in three-star restaurants.

Eric and many other waiters at La Côte d'Or had worked in French restaurants in London, because they needed to perfect their English. But when they returned to France, they usually hadn't found much to admire in their Anglo-Saxon neighbors. Too cold, they thought; the English had no style, little feeling for the good things in life. When Michael first arrived, his colleagues ignored him. Patrick the chef was always telling him, "That piece of meat is overcooked, this one is undercooked."

"I was going crazy," Michael said. "They really gave me the runaround because I was English."

But Michael managed to carve out a good reputation. He finished up as chef de partie on the meat side and even created a lamb dish that went onto the menu. Bernard considered him the best English chef he had ever trained. At one point in his final weeks, when both Bernard and Patrick were out of the kitchen, Michael took over the final inspection of dishes. Patrick thought Michael had a special hunger for success that came from growing up impoverished; his parents were Jamaican, and he had been adopted by a white English couple as an adolescent.

"Michael, he's a winner," Patrick said. "He understands I can call him *vous* in the kitchen to give him orders and afterward go out and have a drink with him as a buddy."

"I felt I had a lot to prove, being English and black," Michael said. "I think I've shown that I can cook, and here all that matters is whether you can cook. No matter who you are, if you can cook, they end up liking you."

Now it was time for farewells. Olivier gave Michael a gift from the kitchen staff, a portable compact disc player and designer compact disc case. Everyone clinked their champagne glasses.

"I know you don't give gifts like this to everyone," Michael said, tears in his eyes.

He was proud of what he had accomplished. Not only had he proved that he could hold his own in a three-star kitchen, but he also had constructed a life for himself in this country town. He considered Olivier and Patrick his best friends in the world. He was in love with beautiful Laurence. Why not stay in Saulieu?

"It's too small," Michael answered. "I've learned all I can here, I've shown that the English can cook, and now I have to move on."

In a week, Michael would be starting as a chef de partie at Jamin. Bernard had written his buddy Joël and asked for a position for Michael. The answer came back, "He can start anytime he wants."

Tough as the atmosphere often was at La Côte d'Or, it could not approach the discipline at Jamin. Robuchon had a reputation for running the strictest kitchen in France. He watched over his chefs with a video camera. He never offered compliments, and no day went by without multiple outbursts of anger. At lunch one day, he started screaming at an apprentice waiter. The apprentice's fault? Robuchon had spotted a tuft of unshaven stubble on his chin.

The word was, if you work for Robuchon, never look him in the eye. He hates that. Why should Robuchon be so haughty? The intern told Michael that it was to increase his already formidable reputation for toughness. Hours were also supposed to be much longer with him than with Bernard. One intern at La Côte d'Or told Michael he had worked at Jamin for four months and that Robuchon had only spoken to him twice during that time, once to ask him to work late for a special party and the other time to say good-bye.

Michael still looked forward to the challenge. Perhaps he was a bit of a masochist. He wanted to work with the best, no matter the cost. He was going to be the first English chef de partie ever at Jamin, an accomplishment that made him proud. The joys of city living beckoned. "In Paris," he said, "there is more to do in life than cooking." He hoped his girlfriend, Laurence, would join him there. After a year or two of hell at Jamin, perhaps a year or two more at another three-star, Michael thought he would move back to Britain and open his own restaurant.

"I want to be the first English chef to have a three-star restaurant in Britain," he said.

Until now, all the three-star Michelin restaurants in England have been run by expatriate Frenchmen. Hubert and the others at La Côte d'Or, those who had worked in England, didn't think that any restaurant across the Channel warranted three real stars. But they recognized that Michael had special drive.

"You see hundreds of those guys go through the kitchen, spending one year here, another at Troisgros, a third at Blanc, and they come out with nothing," Hubert said. "Michael has talent."

Michael believed that cooking in England was improving fast. Fresh, fresh French products were available in the markets, he said. Some English products, he insisted, were the best in the world. Norfolk pigeons were "better than anything Bernard finds here in Burgundy." Scottish Angus beef was "much more consistent than the crazy Charolais."

When Michael first went to hotel school, in England, he said, no one knew what Michelin represented. That was no longer true. More and more English chefs were shooting for stars. Like their French counterparts, they were building bigger and better restaurants. Michael was convinced there was an English clientele for his style of haute cuisine. As a home-grown but French-trained English chef, he would, he thought, have an advantage over the imported French variety. He was ambitious, and he knew he had talent.

Once the champagne and toasts were over, it was time to dance and party. Patrick, Olivier, Paul, and the rest of the staff joined Michael on the hour-long ride to a disco in Dijon. The group didn't get back to Saulieu until five-thirty in the morning, even though many had to start work at seven-thirty. A day or two later, Michael was still beaming about his send-off. His experience at La Côte d'Or left him more confident than ever in his future.

★ ★ ★

Soccer fever swept Saulieu. The team in nearby Auxerre had reached the semifinals in the European Cup. Hubert, Lyonel, and a third member of the staff, Emmanuel, managed to get tickets to the match. All three were soccer fanatics, willing to pay upwards of fifty dollars a seat. The last time a French club played in a European Cup final, Hubert had traveled all the way to southern Italy to watch. One of his biggest regrets in life was that most Auxerre games were played on Saturday nights—the busiest time at La Côte d'Or. "If I could go to every match, that would be heaven," he said.

Auxerre's team meant a lot to the staff at La Côte d'Or, not just because it was a championship soccer team, but because it was a championship team put together with little money. In a city of only forty thousand people, with a stadium that could hold only twenty thousand spectators, Auxerre could never find the funds to pay players like the big clubs in Paris and Marseilles. It managed to make the most of its small resources, a little like La Côte d'Or made the most of its own built-in limitations.

The recipe behind Auxerre's success was created by a brilliant coach named Guy Roux. In the 1970s, Roux started out at Auxerre with almost no talent. He opened a soccer school and recruited some of France's best teenagers. He trained them and turned them into promising players. Slowly, Auxerre rose in the rankings, moving from the second division to the first.

As soon as a player became well known, Roux sold him to a bigger, richer club. Auxerre needed the cash to make ends meet. But Roux saw to it that enough young, talented players were left in the pipeline. Throughout the 1980s, the club stayed near the top of the rankings, though never winning the league championship.

Bernard loved to compare himself with Guy Roux. Both saw themselves first and foremost as trainers and teachers, encouraging and exhorting their teams to improve and strive for the top. Both made an advantage out of the poverty of their resources. Both valued teamwork over individual success. And both totally dominated their players. In his few moments of freedom, Bernard liked nothing better than to go to an Auxerre match. He was not a soccer fan as much as a Guy Roux fan.

"Guy Roux and me, we're both the same," he said. "We don't put the ball in the goal ourselves, but we're always number one in the championships."

This year, Auxerre was aiming beyond France to become number one in Europe. In the first round of the semifinals, against the German powerhouse Dortmund, the Burgundians had lost, 2–0. To advance to the finals, they needed to win the return match at home, in Auxerre, by at least three goals. In professional soccer, a three-goal margin is almost unknown. Newspapers loved the contrast between the teams, portraying the upcoming match as David of Auxerre against Goliath of Dortmund.

The day before the match, Guy Roux took his team into seclusion, as usual. The players practiced and rested at a small hotel deep in the Morvan forest near the Abbaye de la Pierre-Qui-Vire. During the Middle Ages, when Burgundy became a focal point of Christianity, it was home to some of the world's greatest abbeys. Bernard loved the image of the soccer players and the monks. In seeking his third star, he said, he often embraced celibacy. "The monks have no lessons on the subject to teach me," he said. Guy Roux obviously felt the same way with his team.

Hubert, Lyonel, and Emmanuel took the night off to attend the match, leaving Franck and Eric to struggle in the main dining room. Bernard wasn't there, either. He was doing a radio show on Europe 1 entitled "Cooking in the Year 2000."

The match was a humdinger. Auxerre notched two quick goals to tie the series score. In overtime, it had several good opportunities to score another goal and finish off the Germans. But the overtime ended in a tie. Penalty kicks would decide.

There cannot be a more unfair way to decide a championship than by penalty kicks. Hubert compared the process to rolling dice. Professional soccer players make 80 to 90 percent of their penalty kicks, when the ball is placed twelve yards from the center of the goal. The goalie cannot move until the ball is kicked, so he has almost no chance to block the shot.

The shoot-out began, with the teams alternating kicks. The Dortmund players shot five times and scored five times. The Auxerre players shot five times and scored five times. Then an Auxerre player missed, kicking the ball over the goal. The next Dortmund shooter put the ball in the net and won the series.

At La Côte d'Or, some of the diners asked Eric to find out what was happening. He went up to reception and watched the game on television. When it was over, he returned to the dining room, where most of the diners were engrossed in their desserts. The disappointing results gave a bitter taste to the sweet confections.

The next day, Emmanuel was still in the dumps. "What a match. The atmosphere in the stadium was incredible," he reported. He sighed and added, "I guess Auxerre just doesn't have it in them to get three stars."

CHAPTER 10

★ ★ ★

# The Most Pungent Cheese

*Colette Giraud and her goats*

THE RENDEZVOUS was fixed for seven in the morning.

Well before then, Eric Rousseau was out in front of La Côte d'Or, surrounded by a sea of swirling white mist. The biting winter cold did not bother him. Eric stood tall, trim and smiling. He was wearing sneakers, jeans, and a white T-shirt with the insignia BERNARD LOISEAU.

It was Tuesday, his day off, and he was going cheese hunting.

As the frail morning light fought with the mist, Eric drove the restaurant's Renault van north on the Nationale 6 out of Saulieu. On the radio, he heard about the latest farmers' demonstration in Paris. Hundreds of angry farmers had marched on the American embassy, near the Place de la Concorde. Some carried posters screaming, "Down with GATT, Down with American Imperialism." Others hoisted torn American flags on pitchforks. One even dragged a hay-filled effigy of Uncle Sam.

Helmeted riot police responded with tear gas. By the time the battle was over, as many as fifty-six policemen were injured and twelve farmers arrested. Throughout the winter, the farmers had been carrying on a guerrilla war against American pressure for cuts in European agricultural subsidies. In Clermont-Ferrand, they burned tires and haystacks in front of the local McDonald's. Even after the other Europeans agreed to a deal with Washington, France alone resisted.

"Oh, those Americans, they want to rule us," Eric muttered. "If Europe becomes too strong, it frightens them."

Deep down, Eric considered himself "a peasant." In French, the word does not carry the same connotation of backwardness or poverty as in English. It represents instead a proud, age-old way of life, an ideal that has always been the anchor, the keel, of the ship of France. Despite all the noise they make, French farmers are fatalistic. They know their old way of life is vanishing and admit they are fighting a rear-guard, losing battle. Hijacking trucks full of imported produce and attacking the police are their cry of despair.

Eric tried to ignore the news on the radio, without much success. GATT aside, he was angry with America because of a recent run-in with Paul Lynn, the intern. Eric considered himself the waiter who got along best with the kitchen staff. The other waiters kept their distance from the cooks. But Eric attempted to bridge the two worlds. After service, he often went out drinking with the chefs across the street from La Côte d'Or at the Café du Nord. During meals, he often walked into the back, to arrange his cheese tray. One evening, he had rushed into the kitchen and bumped into Paul, who was dressing a plate.

"Get the hell out of my way," Paul said.

"Get the hell out of *my* way," Eric shouted back.

Before the verbal blows could become physical, Bernard bellowed, "*Stop!*"

Later, Paul told Eric that no one should get in his way when he was working. "All good waiters know they should not walk across the kitchen in the middle of a service," Paul said.

*That arrogant American,* Eric thought. *I have been here for years. I have build La Côte d'Or. Then this intern comes along and tells me how to do my job.*

Paul should know his place. Interns should observe, not ask questions, and, above all, not get in the way of professionals like him. That's why the incident with Paul bothered him so much.

For Eric, being a waiter was a métier—a profession. "Lots of guys have a hundred thousand francs and say, 'Let's open a restaurant,'" Eric said. "They can't do it. You have to know what you are doing. You have to be a professional." When Eric was drafted into the army, he served as a bartender on the base. Once, he was asked to set up a dinner for 250 officers. Until then, the commanding general had always said restaurant work was not serious work. But after the sumptuous meal, as the 250 officers sipped their after-dinner digestives, the general came up to him and said, "What you do is a real métier."

For Paul, La Côte d'Or and Saulieu represented a single step in what he hoped would be a long, exciting career. For Eric, they composed his entire existence. "If I ever see that stupid American again," he vowed, "I'll crush him."

As Eric simmered behind the wheel, he passed virgin forests and sleepy villages. The countryside made him feel at home. During his childhood, his home village of Brazey-en-Morvan had a population of five hundred, two cafés, a hardware store, a bakery, and the grocery store his mother ran. Eric's parents, both born in the village, still lived there, in a new house they built across the street from the church.

A decade before, Eric's mother closed the grocery store. The last café shut a few years later. Today, Brazey's population does not exceed one hundred souls. Most of the strong stone farmhouses strung along the winding road through the village are boarded up, empty, not picturesque enough to warrant restoration. Like many rural communities, Brazey, in Eric's phrase, "has become a desert."

Eric moved full-time to Saulieu.

Although he could have built a house in Brazey, his wife, Claude, hated life in a small village. She worked as a secretary in the local Mavil factory, which produced plastic pieces. Their children soon would go to school. Their friends in villages were always driving back and forth to Saulieu, to bring the kids for dance and music lessons, to do shopping. Claude did not want to be tied to the car. If she lived in town, her children could walk to school and she would be free. Eric could walk to work and back home for his afternoon siesta. So the couple was building a new home, just on the outskirts of Saulieu.

"I would have loved to stay in Brazey," Eric said. "But it just wasn't practical."

★ ★ ★

When Eric came to the sign for Epoisses, he turned. The brooding beauty of the Morvan faded, replaced by the Auxois's generous and gentle rolling pastureland. Dark brown fields slept, ready to be planted in springtime. The region was once the granary of France, until grain prices and foreign competition reduced the amount of land under cultivation. Lazy white cows still grazed. Farmhouses stood guard over the fields.

At the edge of the village of Epoisses stands an impressive fifteenth-century château. It is a registered historical monument that originally served as a ducal residence. Madame de Sévigné and other guests crossed a drawbridge and moat to enter the *cour d'honneur.* Off to one side, a well is decorated with delicate ironwork produced in a nearby foundry. Medieval towers blend with Renaissance rose-colored roofs and the warm striped stone and vine-covered walls. The village itself is nestled in a small valley, just above the château. Sloping Burgundian roofs top worn stonework. Elaborate chimney pots and sculpted facades grace the seventeenth-century houses.

Epoisses, however, is not known so much for its architecture as for its cheese—a pungent cow's milk cheese with an orange rind. Of France's numerous cheeses, Epoisses is among the smelliest, so strong that it explodes in the mouth and opens clogged nostrils. The cheese resembles Langres, from the Champagne region, and its more famous Alsatian cousin, Munster. All three are creamy and leave a taste of cooked earth in the mouth. Couples are known to quarrel over Epoisses. One loves its taste. The other hates the fact that it can ruin a refrigerator full of fresh produce.

The most famous producer of Epoisses was the Fromagerie Berthaut. When Eric called for an appointment, the director of production, Michael Doret, told him to come at seven o'clock. Good cheese makers start at an early hour. That was when fresh milk arrived and was treated.

Just before seven, Eric parked the Renault van in the Berthaut courtyard. On the street, the builders had kept the seventeenth-century facade. Inside, they had knocked down an old stone farmhouse and replaced it with a modern factory. The walls were shiny, mustard-colored metal, which stood out against the soft traditional stone facades of the surrounding buildings.

Eric winced. He didn't like factories, or anything that seemed too modern. Doret, a stereotypical Burgundian with a broad frame and clipped mustache, asked Eric like a proud new homeowner, "What do you think of the new building?"

Eric turned the conversation to other subjects.

"How many workers do you have now?" he asked.

"Thirty-six," Doret answered. "We're large but not too large. Officials from the Historical Monuments Commission restricted what we could do. With them, every modification became a battle. This renovation cost us a lot more money than if we started new."

"It's better that way," Eric responded. "You need to keep some ties with tradition."

"Yes, you're right," Doret concluded. "That's what we try to do: ally tradition with the industrial age."

Monks developed the recipes for the best French cheeses, in part because the diet of many Catholic orders was restricted to fruit, vegetables, and dairy products, in part because only the monks had the time and inclination to test recipes. Similarly, monks long produced the best wines in

Burgundy. This common root helps explain why wine and cheese are closely linked in gastronomic literature.

During the French Revolution, most of Burgundy's monasteries were closed. When the Abbaye de Cîteaux, near Nuits-St.-Georges, in the Côte d'Or, reopened in the nineteenth century, it no longer owned its precious vines. The monks needed to find a means of supporting themselves. Cheese became their main source of income, and the Cîteaux monks began producing a creamy, pale salmon, disk-shaped cow's milk cheese. At another abbey, in the heart of the Morvan, Abbaye de la Pierre-Qui-Vire, monks make a similar smooth yellow cheese. Both have a mild, tangy taste, lacking the sharp power of Epoisses.

In his definitive work on French cheeses, Patrick Rance writes that forms of the creamy Chaource and pungent Epoisses were first produced in the Abbaye de Pontigny and the Abbaye de Fontenay. Later in the Middle Ages, a small group of Cistercians settled near the village Epoisses. They discovered that curdled raw milk from the local cows aged well when covered with the local eau de vie called marc. The alcohol turned the curd mass a deep orange and provided its unique flavor. At the end of the nineteenth century, more than three hundred farms in the region manufactured Epoisses. Records show that the town exported five hundred to a thousand rounds per week to Dijon, Autun, Lyons, and even Paris. But it then became more profitable to grow wheat and corn and raise Charolais beef, and the practice of making cheese faded. By 1950, only two farms in the Epoisses region still produced cheese.

One peasant farmer, named Robert Berthaut, discovered in his attic the molds that his grandmother had used to coagulate and age cheese. He started to experiment with the milk from his own cows. The result was popular. Old man Berthaut began selling some to friends, local restaurants, and grocery stores. Soon competitors from all over the country began turning out imitation Epoisses; a pale white Epoisses came from the Alps, a tangy, tart version from Provence. "Some people even colored yogurt orange and called it Epoisses," recalled Eric.

In the mid 1980s, Robert's son, Jean, took over the family fromagerie. He realized that a way had to be found to distinguish his true Epoisses from the generic variety flooding the market. Jean saw the success of his fellow winegrowers and decided to lobby for the distinction of calling his product Appellation Contrôlée. For ten years, Berthaut fought with the bureaucrats at the Institut National des Appellations d'Origine. Farmers from regions far away from Epoisses were demanding to be included in the Appellation Contrôlée. One producer from the Champagne region insisted his Epoisses was a real Epoisses, and to support his claim he got the help of his local deputy to the National Assembly.

Berthaut countered with his own lobbying effort. He enlisted Bernard, among others, to testify to his cheese's authenticity. Bernard helped draft the list of requirements to produce a true Burgundy Epoisses. Anything that promoted Burgundy and its gastronomic traditions, he figured, was good for La Côte d'Or.

Even after the bureaucrats agreed to deliver the special appellation, politicians continued to squabble over the territory delineated by the new Burgundy Epoisses label. Berthaut finally capitulated. He accepted the fact that his competitor from Champagne would be allowed to use the label. The appellation Burgundy Epoisses was born, not a moment too soon. With it, Paribas, the genteel Paris-based investment bank, took a 20 percent share in Fromagerie Berthaut and helped finance a modern new facility. Construction began soon afterward.

Eric was eager to see the factory. He wondered whether Berthaut really had recovered his old levels of excellence. Was Jean forgetting traditional quality and becoming too industrialized? What would the American writer Patricia Wells, who had already criticized Bernard's cheese tray, think? Should Eric continue serving Berthaut, or should he try to find a better Epoisses elsewhere?

"We're sticklers for hygiene," Doret explained as Eric put on a white laboratory coat, covered his hair with a plastic shower cap, and stepped into long plastic boots.

The "factory" certainly was sterile. Workers poured the fresh milk into a stainless steel vat and heated it to 30 degrees Centigrade (86 degrees Fahrenheit)—hot, but not hot enough to pasteurize the milk. Gourmets say there is no comparison between cheese made from raw, untreated milk and that made from pasteurized milk. The same bacteria that are destroyed by the heat of pasteurization give the cheese much of its powerful flavor and unctuous consistency. But pasteurized cheese costs much less to produce than the traditional raw-milk variety—and it lasts twice as long. A generation ago, no serious Frenchman would have dreamed of putting a pasteurized, factory-made cheese in his mouth. Today, bland industrial cheese, even mild Dutch Goudas, crowd French supermarket shelves.

Another, potentially mortal threat to the traditional raw-milk cheese comes from Brussels and the European Community. Under plans for the united market, single food standards will be put into place across the Continent. Almost every few months some bureaucrat suggests banning all nonpasteurized cheese on health grounds. Already, most raw-milk cheeses are outlawed in the United States. American law prohibits the sale of cheese made with unpasteurized milk unless it has been aged at least sixty days. Epoisses, and almost all other raw cheeses, are aged longer, for at least six weeks.

"It's ridiculous," Doret said. "I've never become ill eating our cheese."

"Americans eat sterile products anyway," Eric added. "But they're no healthier than we are."

In front of Eric, workers, dressed in hygienic white uniforms, poured rennet into huge stainless steel vats. The natural coagulant, drawn from the cow's stomach, separates the milk into curd, white lumps resembling soft custard. Doret explained that it takes 2 liters of milk to produce every 400 grams of curd, which then yields 270 to 290 grams of cheese. The new Berthaut factory could treat up to 16,000 liters of milk, turning out 32,000 rounds of cheese.

Production varies according to the season. During the cold winter, the cows are kept inside and must eat hay. They produce less milk. In dry summer, the cows are able to stay outside, but there is little grazing grass left. The best production times are during the cool spring and fall, when the fields are full and fresh. Consumers want cheese most in the winter.

"Meeting supply and demand is not easy," Doret complained. "We do twenty-five percent of our year's production in December and then hope the supply holds out through the winter."

In February, the factory was operating at 50 percent capacity. As Eric watched, workers drained off the whey and poured the curd into thick oval molds. The new cheese would spend the next two weeks in a refrigerated drying room. In the modern Fromagerie Berthaut, huge ventilators kept the temperature constant between 8 and 9 degrees Centigrade (46 and 48 degrees Fahrenheit). A little farther down the production line, workers flipped more mature cheese rounds and fed them under a giant pump of cold running water. The machine washed the rounds with a mixture of three-quarters salt water and one-quarter marc.

"It takes twenty minutes now to wash all of these rounds," Doret said. "By hand, the work used to take two days."

Eric's face revealed doubt. He was not convinced that a machine could take the same care as a pair of human hands.

"You mean a machine does this," he said. "Is that really the best way?"

"We've had problems," Doret admitted. "It takes time to get used to it."

After two weeks of initial aging, the skin of the cheese had lost its cream color and gave off a pale orange glow. The maturing round was no longer a baby; it was ready for a big night on the town. Workers poured a giant swig of Burgundy 100 proof eau de vie onto the thirsty round and wheeled it into another cellar. For five or six weeks, depending on the progress of the contents and on the demand, the rounds of cheese would be stored until they turned bright orange. Eric and his guide Doret opened the door to the cellar and walked in.

"Wow." Eric jumped. "It's freezing in here."

"We air-condition it," Doret explained. "The worst thing for the cheese is humidity, and the cold eliminates any humidity. If we keep it here at four degrees Centigrade [39 degrees Fahrenheit], then it stays free of unwanted bacteria."

Aging is a delicate process. Traditionally, individual farmers produce only one or two rounds of Epoisse a day by hand in small, dark farm cellars. Even if they sell their cheese, the process remains artisinal, no more than fifty rounds a day. The technology is variable and so are the results. One round would be good; the next would have to be thrown away.

"Our goal is to obtain a consistent product," Doret said. "That's what technology helps us do."

When the cheese was judged ready for shipping, workers placed it in a small wooden box. Just as wine takes on some of the flavor of its barrel—vintners argue over whether to use new wood or old wood barrels—cheese will be seasoned by its wooden packaging. The last step before the finished Epoisses left Berthaut's factory was to cover the wooden box with plastic wrap.

"We used to buy the cheese without the carton," Eric said, "But it came out dry."

"The carton lets the product breathe," Doret explained.

"Super." Eric nodded.

"This is a living organism," Doret continued. "We do everything possible here to guarantee a consistent quality, but you can never be sure. You have to treat each round like a child, with care."

Eric asked how long he should age the cheese in the restaurant.

"I wait two weeks," he said.

"What temperature do you use for storage?" Doret asked.

"Nine degrees."

"That's a good cruising speed."

"After I open it, I keep it out at room temperature during the day," Eric added. "At night I cover it with plastic wrap and put it in the refrigerator."

"Perfect," Doret approved.

The tour over, Eric stepped out of his white coat and headed for the office upstairs. Jean Berthaut greeted him with a firm handshake. He was a medium-size man of forty-five with a strong, rugged face revealing his rural roots. But this was no peasant. He wore a tie and jacket and looked the part of the efficient, modern manager. In publicity photos, his white-haired father, Robert, resembled a grandfatherly farmer, wearing a white gabardine and holding a small round of cheese. Jean stood behind him with a much larger round of cheese. He was dressed like a fashionable businessman, in a double-breasted brown suit and Hermès tie.

"Welcome," Jean said. "We love you guys from La Côte d'Or. Bernard's help was indispensable in us obtaining the Appellation Contrôlée."

"Bernard really believes in you," Eric responded. "He loves authenticity."

Jean Berthaut explained his strategy. Recalling his father's difficulties, he refused offers to sell to the giant supermarket chains. He wanted to retain an artisan image, even as he modernized production. He targeted the small luxury market. Demand for his cheese was growing, he said. Bigger competitors could produce cheese at lower costs. But the new Appellation Contrôlée prevented them from calling their cheese real Burgundy Epoisses. Before he left, Eric picked out a few rounds to take back to the restaurant for tasting.

"Authenticity is important," Berthaut reminded his visitor. "Otherwise, we'll end up like the Anglo-Saxons, with standardized, banal cheeses. Did you know that Denmark is Europe's largest producer of Greek feta? Scandalous! This is a north-south battle. We are fighting for the survival of our age-old traditions!"

Eric smiled, but he was not convinced. Recent deliveries of Berthaut's Epoisses had seemed inconsistent, too salty. To him, machines could not wash cheese with the same care as human hands. In addition, Berthaut recently had begun using colored paper instead of a real leaf to wrap his cheese. Eric wondered whether Jean Berthaut was becoming too much of a businessman and too little of a cheese maker. Could his new factory deliver the ripest, smelliest Epoisses?

"There are big question marks here," Eric thought. "I will have to look elsewhere."

★ ★ ★

Burgundy is not renowned for goat cheese. The big industrial producers are located in the Loire Valley, and that region claims to be France's true goat cheese region. But every part of France produces generic goat cheese. Goats adapt easily to almost all climates and are satisfied with almost any grazing grass. What counts is the love and care of individual producers. During the nineteenth century, goat cheese was considered the cheese of the poor. Nowadays, the humble goat—an adorable but impossible animal that eats almost anything in sight—has been raised to the status of a queen, and her cheese is considered a delicacy.

All winter, Eric went to market after market tasting the little white rounds. None was as fresh as he wanted or as aged as he desired. Then Bernard served on the jury of a regional goat cheese festival. Colette Giraud had entered her homemade goat cheese. Bernard tasted a round.

"This is for us," he said.

When Bernard returned to the restaurant, he told Eric to go and meet Madame Giraud.

"Once Bernard tastes something, he decides right away if he likes it or not," Eric said. "There's no reflection—his reaction is right from the gut."

Eric was more measured in his judgments. He wanted to check Colette out. Before leaving Epoisses, Eric asked Jean Berthaut for his opinion. Berthaut sold her goat cheese in his cheese shop out in front of the factory. Colette not only made the best goat cheeses in the region, he said. She was a character worth meeting.

Colette's farm was only a few miles from Epoisses—but she lived in another world and time, in the thick, forested Morvan, where the villages become progressively poorer. Eric drove past a lake, up a winding road, and down again into the hardscrabble hamlet of St. Germain de Modéon. It numbers fifty full-time residents and only three working farms. Next to the town hall, a small handwritten sign announced COLETTE GIRAUD, FROMAGES DE CHÈVRE.

When Colette came out to exchange kisses with Eric, she looked like an advertisement for peasant chic. She wore a blue workman's uniform set off by dark horn-rimmed glasses. The glasses sharpened her already angular face and gave it a funky look. Her house was primitive, two rooms full of bric-a-brac and hand-me-downs.

"Let me show you my fromagerie," she said. "I've just finished my morning production."

Colette led Eric to the side of the house, where she produced her goat cheese in a small room that resembled an amateur photographer's developing studio. The only light came from a small ultraviolet lamp, which kept bugs away from the maturing cheese. The room was warm, not hot.

To make her cheeses, Colette poured her fresh goat milk into small molds. A shot of rennet was injected to form natural curds. No alcohol was added. The quality of the milk and the care taken with aging determined the final results, not artificial ingredients. As the whey drained off, the cheese became firmer, and Colette added some salt. The time of maturation depended on the kind of cheese desired. A fresh, white goat cheese should be only a day or two old. It takes three weeks or more for a well-aged goat cheese to achieve a blue-green color and the stronger taste.

Colette's production averaged only 120 rounds per day, and her maximum was 150 rounds, sold at 50 cents each. With that, she was lucky to clear $1,000 a month—about the minimum wage. Money was not her motivation. Even when she was away, she left the door to her fromagerie open, with a note asking customers to pay for what they took. No one had ever stolen from her.

Colette was proud that she wasn't on the government dole. "You shouldn't have to live on subsidies," she said. "You have to adapt your production to the market."

Eric nodded.

"Colette," he said, "I think you are my kind of person."

Like the workers at Fromagerie Berthaut, Colette had risen before six in the morning. Unlike the makers of Epoisses, though, she alone was responsible for the entire cheese production. Her thirty-six goats lived out back in a tunnel constructed of plastic wrapping. When she arrived to milk them, the goats greeted her with a chorus of "*Baaah, baaah.*"

"I'm coming, I'm coming," Colette replied.

She patted each goat on its back, addressing each by name.

"Doucette, how are you?" she asked.

"*Baaah.*"

"Good, good.

"Super Nana, how beautiful you are," she said to an aging, humpbacked goat. "You're old, but so very, very good.

"Triquette, now come here," she yelled, taking out a stick and snapping it over the next goat's generous behind.

"Oooooh, Mamoutte—you're so fat.

"Ahhh, Kiki, you had problems with your milk yesterday," she said, moving on. "Let's see how you are today."

The milking took about an hour and a half. After she finished with each goat, she patted it on its behind and sent it out into the yard to graze. Then she ran an electric wire around the yard to keep the goats from running away and said good-bye: "*Voilà,* now enjoy yourselves, my girls."

Colette grew up in Lyons, where she received a university diploma in biology. After six months' trekking in Canada, she returned home and began working as a teacher in the laboratory of an agricultural high school. She married young and had a son but soon became bored with the life of a suburban mother. The ideals of the 1960s—free love and free life—attracted her. She divorced, sold her home, and moved south to the rough Lozère region. Her destination was a commune that made its living by producing goat cheese.

"We were children of the sixties," she said. "I had to get out and breathe fresh air."

The move was a disaster. Lozère is one of the most isolated places in France. It is dry and arid, a good climate for raising goats, but a bad one for finding customers for goat cheese. Colette's house there had no running water or electricity. In 1984, she answered an ad in a trade newspaper for "a worker on a goat cheese farm" and was hired by Monsieur Cavin, who owned a farm in St. Germain de Modéon. For the next few years, Colette lived on the Cavin farm—until the old-fashioned farmer went broke. She took out a loan for $2,000 and bought forty goats. The municipality rented her the shack that now served as her living and working quarters.

"Everybody said I was foolish," she said. "But poverty in the countryside doesn't mean the same thing as misery in the city."

Every morning, Colette's thirteen-year-old son Mattias boarded the bus for school in Saulieu. His passion was not goats, but computers. He spent his summers in England learning English. Colette's parents thought she was crazy. They wanted her to go back to teaching. As a single woman, forty years old, and living in the middle of nowhere, she raised eyebrows. Her open relationship with a younger farmer, Alexandre, only made her seem odder to her traditionalist neighbors. "They call me an old man," she joked, with more than a touch of bitterness.

Her big break came by chance, and thanks to another woman. One day, she went to Epoisses and asked the Berthauts to taste her cheese. Madame Berthaut suggested some improvements. Colette made them, and Berthaut began selling her cheeses in his store. A year later, Colette won the first prize in a local contest. Since then, she had won first prize in almost every other competition she entered. Local supermarkets and fromageries started carrying her cheese. Still, she did not dare to take her cheese to Bernard Loiseau's restaurant.

"I thought no one so famous could like my cheese," she told Eric.

Now Eric was ready to taste. He took a bite of the fresh, one-day-old cheese and then a bite of the oldest, bluest cheese. After each bite, he let out a soft sigh. No doubt about it, this spunky woman produced the region's best goat cheese.

"Can you deliver twice a week?" Eric asked. "Or even three times a week?"

"No problem," Colette said.

"We want the freshest fresh goat cheese you make and the oldest, most aged. Nothing in between. Bernard loves strong tastes."

"Of course."

★ ★ ★

The next step in redoing the cheese platter was painful. For years, Simone Porcheret in Dijon had supplied La Côte d'Or. Her fromagerie, located right near the city's central market, was the most renowned in all of Burgundy. From Simone, Eric bought fresh Reblochon, tangy Fourme d'Ambert blue, a creamy Brillat-Savarin, a smooth Beaufort, and a ripe St. Nectaire to round out the homegrown Epoisses and goat cheese.

But recently Eric had noticed "irregularity" in Simone's deliveries. Often her cheese was too dry, not aged properly. Eric felt loyal to Simone. She was, after all, a fellow Burgundian. But he knew that neither Michelin nor Patricia Wells would pardon an inconsistent cheese tray. So he asked Joël Robuchon, in Paris, who supplied his cheese. Roger Alléosse, he answered. Alléosse ran a store in Paris's seventeenth arrondissement. Eric called him, and he drove to Saulieu with samples. They were excellent.

So the decision was made to fire dear old Simone. Hubert gave her the news. Afterward, Eric was relieved. With Alléosse, the cheese arrived in perfect condition every time. "I loved Simone—she's a fine woman—but we need consistency," Eric said.

Consistency meant better Epoisses. Eric renewed his hunt for the perfect round. In the kitchen, he tasted samples from several other producers. All disappointed him. One looked and smelled like Kraft cream cheese. Others were either too hard or not well aged. Then, on Bernard's advice, he visited the bistro La Ciboulette, in Beaune. Their Epoisses was wonderful.

"Where does it come from?" Eric asked.

"From Brochon," a village near the famous winegrowing town of Gevrey-Chambertin, the waiter answered.

Eric already served a cheese at La Côte d'Or from Brochon's Fromagerie de la Côte, the famous Ami du Chambertin. The Ami comes from the same cheese family as Epoisses. It resembles Epoisses but is taller and thinner in shape, denser in consistency, and perhaps even stronger in taste. Eric hadn't known that the makers of the Ami also made Epoisses. The lead sounded promising.

A few weeks after his first cheese-tasting excursion, he made an appointment with Brochon's director, Jean Gaugry. This time he took his own car, a battered ten-year-old gold BMW 320. He drove an hour into the wine country and pulled up in front of a nondescript, two-story white stucco building that could have passed for a primary school. On the door, the words FROMAGERIE DE LA CÔTE were printed in tiny, old-fashioned lettering.

Monsieur Gaugry was a gangling, balding man, fifty-six years old, who measured every word and seemed to have little charisma or driving force. But once the subject turned to cheese, his face lit up. Gaugry's grandmother collected milk for a dairy. His father owned a cheese shop in the village and was friends with the winegrowers. He decided that the famous Gevrey-Chambertin wines needed a proper cheese to accompany them. So he created the Ami du Chambertin.

Son Jean enlarged the cheese shop into a full-fledged fromagerie, employing twenty workers and producing eighty tons of cheese a year. Two thirds of the production was the famed Ami du Chambertin. This was a family firm through and through. Jean worked with his two sons: Sylvan was the technical director and Olivier was the marketing director. Unlike Berthaut, the Gaugrys had no desire to create a business that could be quoted on the stock exchange.

For them, the first pleasure was still eating their own cheese. Gaugry described how he drank half a bottle of Gevrey-Chambertin every day accompanied by a ripe round. Local vintners sold him the bottles for only five dollars or so, off the books, of course.

"The combination is heavenly," he said, smacking his lips. "Just the right balance between wine and cheese."

The Gaugry Epoisses had a deeper, browner color than the bright Berthaut orange. It was denser and thicker and gave off a stronger smell than its competition. When placed in the mouth, it exploded—*pow*—opening up blocked nostrils.

"There should be nothing antiseptic about our cheese," Gaugry said, his hand thumping on the table. "We want a cheese that *smells!*"

"I like it here," Eric said on his way out. "It's more human, less mechanized than Berthaut." In the future, he would still buy a few rounds from Berthaut, "because Berthaut is a classic and you can't cut off all your ties with him." But most of his Epoisses would come from Gaugry.

★ ★ ★

Before he returned to Saulieu, Eric made one more stop, in his home village of Brazey—to buy some bread. Good French cheese requires not only good wine but also good bread. Although many haute cuisine restaurants go to the trouble of baking their own bread, Bernard did not. In his old kitchen, inherited from Dumaine, he didn't have space. Baking equipment is expensive, and he had not installed the necessary ovens in his new kitchen.

Flour, salt, water, and yeast are the only ingredients used in traditional French bread—a model of simplicity. Yet French bread is one of the supreme emblems of French gastronomy. Nothing seems more French than a crisp, fresh baguette. A French meal without bread is inconceivable. At the humblest café, a waiter brings bread to the diner with the menu. French housewives consider it normal to go out twice or even three times a day to get bread that is hot and freshly baked.

In recent years, though, industrial bakers have emerged producing a cruel parody of the genuine article. Horror: many people ate the stuff. Industrial bread soon captured about 15 percent of the market, particularly in the countryside, where one must drive long distances to the nearest boulangerie. Horror again: many traditional bakers grew lazy, preparing their dough the previous evening and deep-freezing it overnight, rather than starting work from scratch in the cold hours before dawn. Some bakers even resorted to buying ready-frozen dough from industrial bakers and then passing their baguettes off as homemade.

Small wonder Bernard was having trouble with his bread. For weeks, Hubert had worked with the local bakers, the Dechaumes, to produce acceptable rolls and country loaves, crisp but not to the point of being burnt. Every day, Hubert would visit the Dechaumes and give constructive criticism. "I would tell them to add a little yeast, or to cook just a smidgen longer," Hubert remembered. The results improved. Hubert even persuaded the Dechaumes to bake a delectable fig bread, which was a perfect accompaniment to Epoisses.

Then the Dechaumes retired. Their replacement had a hard time meeting La Côte d'Or's high standards. One afternoon, the new baker dispatched burnt loaves. Bernard grabbed the telephone.

"These loaves are burnt," he exploded.

"I had a problem with my ovens today," the baker said.

"I don't care about your problems," Bernard continued. "I cannot accept this bread."

Before long, the two men were screaming at each other. As he slammed the phone down, Bernard yelled the final words:

"You're fired!"

When Hubert returned from his vacation, he was shocked.

"A disaster always strikes when I leave," he moaned. "Bernard blows his top, and I have to pick up the pieces."

When Eric heard the story, he chuckled. He knew where to find the region's best bread—in Brazey. Just a few blocks from his father's house, a farmer baked soft and tender baguettes, unlike anything Eric had tasted elsewhere.

He reached his hometown in early evening. He passed the church and continued on to the far end of the village, where he pulled into the front yard of a farm. No sign announced a boulangerie. The only hint was a couple of German tourists pulling out of the driveway. The bakery was in the barn. Inside, the air was heavy with yeast and heat. A radio blared can-can music. A bare-chested man kneaded dough into long baguettes. He placed them on a long-handled wooden peel and thrust it into the oven. The baker had a broad frame, bulging stomach, white mane, and white mustache. His name was Pierre Michot—known to everybody by his childhood nickname, Pepette.

"Pepette, how is everything?" Eric asked.

"Just fine, just fine," the baker answered with a giant smile. Pepette usually smiled. In the village, he was considered the deputy mayor, not because he was officially elected to any position, but because if anybody had a problem, they called him.

Pepette, I need help with my kids, they implored. Within five minutes, Pepette was there to baby-sit. Pepette, my car ran out of gas. Pepette brought the refill. When Eric needed to know what was happening in his own village, he didn't ask his taciturn parents. He went to see Pepette.

"And how's Ginette?" Eric asked.

Ginette was Pepette's wife. While her husband always smiled, she always seemed to smirk. Pepette baked. Each afternoon, Ginette piled the bread into her small Renault minivan and made the rounds of the neighboring villages. That's why his boulangerie was known as Chez Ginette.

Pepette handed Eric a small roll to taste. It was still warm. When Eric tore it open, the dough gave way like a baby's soft skin.

"Mmmmmmm." Eric inhaled the pleasant odor.

"Yuuuuummmmmm," he said, placing it in his mouth. A satisfied smile spread over his face.

"This is real bread," Eric said. "The rest is imitation."

Pepette laughed. He was proud of his work but shrugged off compliments. His father was a baker, so he became a baker. His oven was installed in 1929, the year he was born. He pointed to the dark, encrusted inscription reading STRASBOURG, 1929.

"This oven and I grew old together," he said.

It was an old wood-burning oven, the kind almost no one used anymore. It required hours to heat up and round-the-clock care. A gas oven can be turned on and off at will. But the slow, soft-burning wood gave the bread a remarkable taste. To heat it, Pepette had to wake up at four in the morning. He didn't own an alarm clock.

"I have a natural alarm clock," he said. "I've never once overslept."

Pepette baked with natural wheat flour and used a minimum of yeast. The flour gave off a pale yellow glow. In the late 1960s, bleached American white flour was introduced in France. For farmers, the wheat required to produce this new flour took less time to grow. For bakers, it was cheaper than the traditional, untreated variety. It rose fast and gave baguettes a clear, chewy, chemical white interior, just like that of Wonder Bread. For some reason, traditional Burgundians loved the American-style bread, and for a while even the residents of Brazey began to buy their baguettes elsewhere. All the boulangeries soon switched to the easy-to-use white flour. Pepette refused.

"I'll bake bread like my father baked bread," he insisted. "Otherwise, I won't bake."

Pepette took to raising Charolais cattle instead and baked only for himself and a few friends. But recently, tastes had begun to change. Pepette had sold all his Charolais except one, which he milked for his own consumption, and resumed baking. White bread baguettes went stale overnight. Pepette's baguettes stayed fresh for several days. Most French bakers still prefer to use fast-rising flour and add a lot of yeast to shorten the baking time.

Eric paid 15 francs, or about $3, for his customary order of three baguettes, and Pepette added two small rolls.

"For your children," the baker said, waving off Eric's attempt to pay him extra, and then offered him an aperitif. There was no café left in Brazey, so Pepette's boulangerie was transformed into an informal substitute. In the winter, clients stood around in the bakery, warmed by the oven. In the summer, they sat out front around a picnic table and Pepette served them, free of charge.

"What do you drink?" he asked Eric. "A little pear?"

"No." Eric shook his head. The home-brewed pear brandy packed a 100 proof wallop of alcohol.

"Something lighter," Eric suggested.

"A beer?" Pepette asked.

"Yes." Eric nodded.

The baker disappeared into his farmhouse next door and returned with the beer. He handed Eric one. After a few gulps, Eric got down to business.

"Would you ever like to bake for Bernard at La Côte d'Or?" Eric asked.

Pepette broke into laughter.

"No way," he replied. "I can't bake on a restaurant schedule."

Pepette explained that his temperamental oven would not allow him to increase production. Already, he said, he had problems filling the demand. Now he baked only four days a week. To supply Bernard, he would have to work every day and take on an employee.

"I don't want the stress," he said, sipping his beer.

His refusal saddened Eric. He didn't like the idea that La Côte d'Or would be forced to make do with second-rate bread. Worse, he feared for the future. All of Pepette's brothers had moved to the cities. None was a baker. When Pepette stopped firing his wood-burning oven, no one in Burgundy would continue to bake such loving baguettes.

Pepette was proud of his bread, of his traditional way of producing the best possible product. Pepette was a Burgundy star without ambition. Baking bread the traditional way was not just a job for him, it was a way of life—and that way of life did not include ambitious chefs and fancy restaurants.

*Fresh out of Pepette's oven*

CHAPTER 11

★ ★ ★

# The Battle for Frogs

*Jean-François Vadot and his snails*

IN THE MIDDLE OF February, Bernard received a telephone call.

"I can supply you with frogs," the caller said. "Are you interested?"

Bernard was interested. One of his specialties was sautéed frog legs, served with a puree of garlic and parsley. If the typical British dish is roast beef and Americans are famous for their hamburgers, what could be more French than frog legs? The mere mention of frogs fills intolerant Anglo-Saxons with disgust and supplies them with a derisive nickname for the French.

The draining of marshlands in recent years has almost eliminated production in France. These days, most frogs are imported from Central Europe and the former Yugoslavia. They tend to be larger and have more meat than the local species. Frozen bullfrog legs are also imported from Cuba and the United States. They are almost as big as the legs of guinea fowl but have little flavor. Tender frog legs should taste like fine-grained chicken breast.

Most of Bernard's frog legs came from Greece. They arrived ready to cook, their legs skinned and strung along a stick. Bernard had no complaints with the quality of the frog legs from his Greek supplier. But he always preferred to use local produce. So when he was offered the opportunity to buy local frogs, he responded eagerly.

The caller said he farmed his frogs in a swamp near Dijon. Bernard smiled. He sensed the real thing. They would have a fresher, more powerful taste than his imported frog legs.

"OK," Bernard answered. "Bring me a batch of frogs as soon as you can."

The frog entrepreneur arrived the next day. He told Bernard, "I have the frogs right outside, in the car trunk."

Bernard ordered Paul, the American stagaire, and the other kitchen assistants out to the car to help carry the packages into the kitchen. The frog producer opened his trunk. When Paul saw what was inside, he let out a scream.

"They're alive!"

"Yup," Bernard said. "That's how they should be. Wriggling, fighting—alive."

Paul and the others brought them into the kitchen. The frogs jumped all over the kitchen. The staff scurried to and fro, trying to catch them. When they did manage to grab one, they placed it on a table and hit it on the head. *Thwack!* "I've got one," the chef announced. It took hours for the kitchen crew to skin and prepare all the frogs.

"What a mess," Paul moaned.

For him, the frogs brought back unpleasant memories from biology class. For Hubert, the incident showed once again how Bernard's natural generosity could get the best of him. "Fools walk through the door and say they have good products," he said. "We know it's a joke. Bernard takes them seriously." The local frogs were so small that twice as many were needed to make a plateful. "Yes, there are frogs all over the place," Bernard said. "But I wanted to give the guy a chance—to get live frogs from around here."

As he spoke, Paul batted another one dead.

"This one's for you, Bernard," he said.

*Whack!*

Bernard gave in.

"OK, we'll go back to the old supplier of frog legs," he said.

★ ★ ★

Bernard's defeat in the battle of the frogs did not mean the end of his war for local produce. Far from it. His unending search for the freshest possible ingredients represented a crucial part of his quest for the third star.

For French gourmets, it's not just wine and water that have the taste—the character—of where they come from.

Milk is distinguished by the breed of cows that produce it, and by the kind of grass the cows graze on, which in turn gets its character from the soil. There is no true Epoisses that does not come from the milk of cows grazing on the land around the village of Epoisses. And there is no true Charolais beef that does not come from around the city of Charolles. To the French chef, this attention to origin has deep metaphysical importance. The land speaks a language that must be respected and understood. Bernard, enthusiastic and perfectionist as ever, was particularly fervent about the quality of his ingredients. Most chefs insist on ripe, juicy tomatoes. Bernard insisted that a tomato "squirt blood."

Unfortunately, most products that Bernard needed were not available in the backwoods of Burgundy. Part of the problem was seasonal. Fresh vegetables do not grow in the frigid Burgundy winter, and the region produces almost no fish and few fruits. In Dumaine's day, the only fish on the menu throughout the year was *truite meunière,* trout in butter sauce. He bought his trout direct from local fishermen. If he was lucky, some perch was also available. But he could never be sure. No fish farms existed in local lakes, and fresh ocean fish could not be transported so far inland. There still is no *poissonnerie* in the entire Morvan, making it necessary to travel to Dijon, an hour away, to procure almost all seafood.

Saulieu has an open-air market only once a week, with a limited selection of fresh produce. Burgundy chefs such as Jacques Lameloise and Jean-Pierre Silva buy from the open-air marketplace in Chalon-sur-Saône. Its maze of stalls offers a wide array of fresh vegetables and spices, everything from thin, young, pale green zucchini, virginal white asparagus, and bright young carrots to fresh fennel, dill, rhubarb, turnips, and giant tuliplike artichokes. But Chalon is about an hour by car from Saulieu and is fully stocked only during the summer.

Bernard's solution was to buy direct from the giant Rungis market outside Paris, next to Orly Airport. In 1969, Rungis replaced the antiquated Les Halles, in the center of the city, and it has become the world's largest single market, a city unto itself, where the freshest and most exotic products are gathered under one enormous roof and then shipped throughout the Continent. Rungis covers 440 acres of blacktop and is home to sixteen hundred sellers who dispatch about 2.2 million tons of food each year. It doesn't sell only French food, either. There's pork from Poland and, believe it or not, even chanterelles from America's Pacific Northwest.

During his years working in Paris, Bernard assembled a list of the quality producers working out of Rungis. For crayfish, the type he hunted in his youth, he turned to Faisel Vanikoff, who imported them from Greece. Vanikoff also supplied his perch—direct from Holland. "We've tried to get these products in France," Vanikoff said. "But we find better quality abroad." Despite repeated attempts to locate fresher local substitutes, Bernard admitted that Vanikoff's seafood was the best available. "It's better than anything in Burgundy," he said.

Jean-Marie Thiercelin's family had imported spices from around the world since 1809, making Jean-Marie the fifth generation of Thiercelins to run the business. For Bernard, he supplied basmati rice from India, vanilla from Madagascar, cinnamon from Sri Lanka, and five types of pepper, including "long" pepper from Indonesia and "green" pepper from Brazil. All told, Thiercelin bought products from thirty countries around the world. "We import only the best," Jean-Marie said, "from no matter where."

Great French cooking follows the seasons, and accordingly, Bernard changed his menu at least four times a year. In January, he featured a truffle menu, just at the moment when the famous fungi sprout. Few activities are as mysterious and unscientific as hunting for Périgord truffles, perhaps the world's most expensive product, worth up to five hundred dollars a pound. Stories abound of chefs heading off to midnight rendezvous with mysterious truffle dealers. But at Rungis, Bernard met the patriarch of truffledom, Jacques Pebeyre, and the Pebeyre family ensured him—for a steep price, of course—a regular supply of the blackest, tastiest truffles.

During his first few years in Saulieu, Bernard got up three times a week at three in the morning and drove two hours north to Rungis, to be in time for the five o'clock opening. There he filled a pickup truck with everything he needed. He would have preferred to order by telephone, but his boss, Verger, bought in bulk for all his restaurants and needed Bernard to pick up the products in person.

When Bernard bought La Côte d'Or, he stopped traveling to Rungis. Four hours was too much time to waste going back and forth to Paris just to save a few francs. Patrick, the chef de cuisine, placed almost all his orders by telephone and fax. In the mornings, he drew up a list of what was needed for the upcoming week. In the afternoon, he sent in his orders, and two days later a giant truck rolled into the yard next to the kitchen at La Côte d'Or. The staff unloaded the meat and fish and began the arduous task of skinning and cutting into serviceable portions.

The gastronomic historian Philip Hyman says spices and other nonperishable goods have been transported since the Middle Ages. Fresh food has a different history. A study of eighteenth-century Limoges showed that fresh vegetables were distributed only within a radius of forty miles. As late as the mid nineteenth century, even after train transport became the norm, seafood remained a luxury in Paris. The rapid convoys from Dieppe, the closest port, took up to fourteen hours.

Although France played a leading role in the discovery of methods of preserving and refrigerating, it was slow in adapting to this knowledge. The founder of the first food-preserving factory, in Massy, outside Paris, died in poverty in 1804. The first strawberries to be sold in the capital arrived only in 1870. As late as the turn of the century, the French canning industry was still only about one-sixth the size of America's, and England, the master of the refrigerator ship, dominated the meat-carrying trade from South America. Eventually, improved transport and preservation techniques allowed chefs in the far reaches of the countryside to obtain most of the same products as their city rivals.

The celebrated recipes for *coq au vin* and *boeuf bourguignon* may well have resulted from the difficulty of obtaining fresh ingredients. Both dishes are stews, one based on gamy chicken, the other on thick rounds of beef. When well made, they contain pickling onions, lightly smoked bacon, mushrooms, garlic, marc, and bouquet garni, as well as red wine. (Many recipes advise using the same wine in cooking as you drink at table. Given the price of a good Burgundy, no sane chef would ever follow such advice; he uses ordinary table wine.)

At La Côte d'Or, Dumaine marinated his chicken for at least twelve hours before cooking it. His personal touch was to add a tablespoonful of uncooked wine to the sauce at the end. Many chefs insist that a good *coq au vin* or *boeuf bourguignon* should be eaten only after being reheated the day after it is made. Dumaine served sauces and stews that were as much as five days old. Such recipes were well suited to the age of slow transportation and poor conservation.

Bocuse, Troisgros, and the other nouvelle cuisine liberators freed themselves from the slavery of stews. Modern transport allowed them to telephone the fishing boat at the port and have the freshest fish on the menu a day later. The nouvelle cuisine chefs emphasized natural flavor and initiated a hunt for the most expensive, exclusive products. Today, foie gras, caviar, and smoked salmon are found on menus throughout France. Regional variety has been watered down, and a gourmet meal in Marseilles often resembles a meal in Lille.

Worse, nouvelle cuisine chefs began experimenting with strange combinations of ingredients. Dishes such as duck in chocolate sauce appeared on some of France's finest tables. Side portions of raw green beans were offered. The ultimate symbol of nouvelle cuisine excess became the kiwifruit, first imported into France from New Zealand in the mid 1970s. Originally a delicacy prized for its appealing green color, it degenerated into a staple accompaniment to any meat or fish. From being seen as liberators, the practitioners of nouvelle cuisine ended up being criticized for serving up pretentious, if pretty, dishes of food. Little wonder Bocuse, Troisgros, and the other inventors of the new cooking have begun to flee the label. "Nouvelle cuisine degenerated into pretty paintings on the plate," Bernard complained. "All too often, it means little food and little taste."

Bernard cultivated local producers in an effort to restore authenticity to his cooking. The process required patience. He worked with the producers until they reached his exacting standards. Whenever they let him down, he let them know, immediately, by telephone. Whenever he had an idea for improvement, he or one of his assistants called.

Once again, Georges Blanc, the chef who had turned his simple auberge into a grand country hotel, had shown the way. Blanc was the first to organize a group of local producers and to feature their products on his menu. Blanc even opened a food shop across the street from his restaurant where, at great profit, he sold the products under his own label. "We saw how Blanc employed locals to create an additional element of charm," said Hubert. "So we worked hard to find a guy for snails, for rabbits, for pigeons, for almost everything."

★ ★ ★

Bernard's problem was finding farmers near Saulieu who could deliver the highest-quality produce. Like Pepette the baker, many of the best locals didn't want to stretch themselves. They were too set in their ways, weighted down by tradition and by the snail-like pace of the region's "slow civilization." Obviously, this you-owe-us-a-living type of peasant could never meet Bernard's standards.

But Bernard found dynamic innovators in what appeared to be a monolithic landscape, farmers such as Colette Giraud, who rejected the idea of subsidies and set out on her own to produce top-quality cheese. Like her, most of these new Burgundy peasants were forty-something graduates of the 1960s. Many were refugees from cities who, while most of their fellow students entered the establishment, refused to trade in their T-shirts for three-piece suits and transform themselves from yippies to yuppies. They preached instead a revolutionary return to the countryside.

Jacques Sulem was among the first of these rebels. When the May 1968 student demonstrations erupted, he was a high school teacher living in the drab Paris suburb of Créteil. The revolt changed his opinions. In particular, he was attracted to the burgeoning ecology movement. He decided to move to the provinces with his wife, a nurse, and their three children. The cheapest farmhouse they could find was in the middle of the Morvan, west of Château-Chinon. Madame Sulem got a job in the local hospital. Jacques began looking for a profitable way to farm his land. He thought of cultivating vegetables, but the growing season was too short.

Jacques didn't give up. His parents emigrated from Tunisia. He was of Sephardic Jewish origin, although his religious identity had nearly disappeared in Roman Catholic

Burgundy. Perhaps his outsider's position explained his stamina. He was full of energy, and even now, just past the half-century mark, his bushy mane of curly hair remained a youthful jet black.

But the ravages of age did exact their toll. Jacques had begun to lose his eyesight and made his way about his farm by memory. When he met a stranger, he looked hard at him, his head bobbing a bit in a vain effort to focus his failing eyes. Jacques, the perpetual optimist, never complained. "My lack of sight is an advantage," he said. "If I didn't have a handicap, I would be too rushed. I would not take the time necessary to create the best possible product."

Jacques began producing jams as a hobby. In France, almost every grandmother makes her own jam, and Jacques never thought he could make a living with such a simple item. But he started selling his jams at local open-air markets. He sold to Saulieu's crêperie. One day, he knocked on the front door of La Côte d'Or. Before, he never dared approach Bernard. "I could never imagine supplying such a gourmet restaurant," he said.

Bernard explained that he made his own jam for the restaurant. But yes, of course, he was willing to taste some samples. Jacques opened up jars of chestnut, raspberry, apricot, cassis, and strawberry jam. Bernard took out five spoons. One after another, he tasted. Until he was finished with all of them, he didn't say a word.

"Impossible," he said.

Jacques thought he had failed.

"Impossible," Bernard repeated.

The chef stood up and, in a triumphant voice, announced, "Your jams are better than mine."

Bernard snapped his fingers. A waiter came running.

"Champagne," he commanded.

After the toast, Bernard placed an immediate order for 500 bottles of jam. The contract was Jacques's big break.

Before he had done only $8,000 total business in a year. Bernard alone bought $12,000 worth of jam each year from him. Bernard also proved an invaluable reference. When Joël Robuchon visited La Côte d'Or, he tasted the jam and asked, "Where did you find this?" Bernard gave him Jacques's address. Within days, Jacques had signed a new contract to supply Robuchon's new Paris hotels with 4,000 bottles per year, worth about $11,000. His total annual sales were now $80,000. Jacques's wife had quit her nursing job and joined him at the farm.

"Imagine," Jacques said with wonderment. "At the age of fifty-three, I'm finally able to support my family!"

★ ★ ★

Not all of Saulieu's back-to-nature stories have such fairy-tale endings. Michel and Jacqueline Marache were living in the suburbs of Paris when the 1968 student revolution broke out. They watched on television and thought, "We don't want to end our days here in the city, commuting to dull, boring jobs."

Michel's father had grown up on a tanning mill in the Morvan, a few miles from Saulieu. When the mill went out of business, he had left for the city, to become a policeman. "He traded his farmer's hat for a gendarme's cap," Michel said. "It was the typical thing to do."

Michel and Jacqueline decided to return to the Morvan and restore the mill. The setting was picture-perfect, by a stream in a forested valley. The couple was also picture-perfect: he rugged and handsome, she a brooding, dark-haired beauty. Their two cute young children made the portrait even more appealing. Michel and Jacqueline renovated the old stone mill, doing most of the work themselves.

The problems started when they tried to build a profitable venture in this out-of-the-way spot. A friend suggested fish farming. Michel researched the idea and found that the lakes in the Morvan resembled those in Canada, where salmon trout farms were big business. In 1979, Michel and Jacqueline pooled their life savings and launched the venture.

It wasn't easy. Freshwater salmon take three years to reach maturity. During that time, Michel continued renovating the family living quarters. Once the fish matured, he could produce only about seven tons a year—about a tenth the annual output of the competing fish factories in Norway, Scotland, and Brittany.

Michel aimed to compensate with top quality and took his fish for inspection to the local restaurateurs, including La Côte d'Or. Bernard liked the idea of restoring local trout to his menu. But he told Michel that big fish were more tender and easier to cook. Michel promised to supply his largest fish, three-year-old, six-pound salmon trout, but by Bernard's standards still small.

For Michel, Bernard represented a good endorsement, more an advertisement than an important customer. When Michel couldn't get a stall in the weekly open-air market in Autun to sell his salmon, Bernard telephoned the mayor. The following week, Michel had his space.

Michel was not given to easy compliments and simple expressions of gratitude. After he got his stall at the Autun market, he forgot to thank Bernard. When Bernard found out, he was furious. He telephoned Michel and bawled him out. A few days later, Michel showed up with a gift for Bérangère. But the damage lingered.

Michel's infant fish farm was soon submerged in debts. In an attempt to survive, he built a wood-shingled restaurant next to his farm. He called it a *guinguette,* an echo of the lively riverside cafés frequented and painted by the Impressionists at the end of the last century. The setting was magical, the atmosphere convivial, and the food simple yet appetizing: a single menu of smoked salmon salad, grilled salmon, cheese, and a caramelized apple tart called *tarte Tatin.*

But business was slow. Michel opened only on weekends in the summer and sometimes closed without warning. The cooking was irregular and the wine list unimpressive. Michel was bad at publicizing his restaurant. He began dreaming of building rustic lodgings and opening up a fly-fishing camp. Hubert at La Côte d'Or was skeptical about his future. "Michel can't make up his mind whether to be commercial or not," he said. "Is his restaurant open? Or not? You can never tell."

★ ★ ★

Many of Bernard's suppliers faced similar problems. Although they sold their products at Saulieu's Saturday market, the villagers weren't prosperous enough to provide steady support. To help, Bernard came up with an ingenious idea: a gastronomic fair to be held over an entire weekend.

The Journées Gourmandes du Grand Morvan exuded the good-time atmosphere of an American county fair. About sixty producers of everything from buckwheat honey to Vézelay wine set up stands in Saulieu's sparkling new meeting hall, built with millions of francs of regional subsidies, next to the unused train station. Colette Giraud, looking hip in a black leather jacket and pants, sold goat cheeses. Bernard Poisot, who baked La Côte d'Or's spice bread, wore a flour-covered apron. He set up an electric oven and baked five different breads "live." Jacques Sulem spooned out samples of his sumptuous jam. A second, smaller room was piled high with local antiques.

Only Michel Marache, the trout farmer, stayed away.

Bernard was named president of honor. He dressed up in his best Sunday suit and led the dignitaries around to taste the offerings. The agriculture minister showed up. So did several local deputies to the National Assembly and a few local senators. Bernard basked in the attention. In speeches and in private conversations, the politicians described him as a "shining star" in the galaxy of French gastronomy and the dazzling successor to Dumaine. To everybody, Bernard repeated his message of "Quality, quality, and quality."

"I never ask the price of a product," he explained. "I just ask that it be the best—*le top*."

The event was a great success. More than ten thousand home cooks, restaurateurs, food industry professionals, and the idle curious came in search of something new. The visitors filled their baskets with purchases and collected suppliers' names and addresses.

But privately, Bernard was disappointed.

"There are too many goat cheeses," he said as he passed four straight stands of homemade fresh and aged *crottins*.

There also were too many honey producers. Bernard's own supplier, Daniel Blanc, was there, offering liquid acacia and lime blossom, chestnut, sunflower, and other flavors. But five other honey makers came. In contrast, there were no suppliers of free-range chickens or fresh vegetables.

Worse, there were too many foie gras stands. Bernard tasted one substandard pâté after another. Traditional foie gras comes from the southwest of France. Now it is being produced all over the country, with decidedly mixed results.

"Not enough variety," Bernard concluded.

By promoting his local suppliers, Bernard promoted the quality of the ingredients used in his cooking. And by advertising his growers and breeders, he displayed his boyish enthusiasm and generosity. He genuinely wanted to help them.

But there was more to the story. Bernard also acted out of an acute sense of public relations. He had watched how his mentor Bocuse took journalists with him to the market in Lyons, and he said to himself, *I need a similar scheme*. With his local producers, he found his answer. They made great television.

One morning, the French television station M6 made an appointment to do a feature on the business of haute cuisine. Bernard proposed a visit to Michel Marache at his fish farm and to Jean-François Vadot, his snail supplier. The journalists jumped. Great idea, they said. What began as "realistic" reportage ended up as an orchestrated media event.

The three-man crew arrived the night before the scheduled shoot in a rented Renault Espace van. They wore leather jackets; Bernard joked in private that they looked a little like Mafia hit men. But to Bernard, a journalist is a journalist and must be treated well. He offered the TV crew a free five-course dinner. The next morning, the journalists woke with hangovers. Filming started at eight-thirty. Bernard wore his Barbour jacket and led the way in his BMW to Michel's mill.

Michel greeted them in his fisherman outfit, a vinyl jacket and hip-length rubber boots. He handed Bernard a fishnet, and the two posed by the water. The cameraman focused. Michel jumped into the rushing stream, plunging his net into the current. A wriggling fish emerged. He handed the catch to a smiling Bernard. From dry ground, Bernard plucked another fish. They held up their catch for the camera. Bernard explained how he paid 40 percent more for a Marache salmon than for one from an industrial fish farm.

"These fish have been swimming free for three years," Bernard explained. "They don't come from some giant factory. I don't care that they cost more. For me, the only thing that counts is quality."

Bernard looked at Michel and said, "These days the star is the producer, not the cook."

"Perfect," the journalist said. "Bernard, you are made for television."

Michel and Bernard threw the fish back into the water. Of course, Bernard never caught his own fish. Patrick ordered by telephone, and Michel delivered to La Côte d'Or by truck.

"Bernard comes to visit only three times a year," Michel said, "with television cameras."

Michel had a thick book of clippings showing photographs of Bernard and him in the German magazine *Stern,* the Israeli newspaper *Ha'aretz,* and many other publications. "When it comes to publicity, Bernard's an absolute genius," Michel said. "He knows what makes a good picture and a good story. No wonder all of his producers are like him, around forty years old, and not your ordinary peasant."

Jean-François Vadot, the next subject in the television shoot, was one of the few producers in Bernard's stable who was born on his own farm. In the village of Blancey, fifteen miles from Saulieu, he raised snails. Battalions of escargots roamed the region during the nineteenth century. The author Henri Vincenot claims that engineers building the original Paris-Lyons railway line considered laying the tracks over the ridge west of Dijon separating the Rhône and Seine river basins but feared that thousands of snails would be squashed and make the rails slippery. The locomotives might slither to a halt. Instead, the engineers decided to construct a tunnel.

The Romans were the first to prepare snails for cooking. They built "snaileries" where the snails were fattened on wine and bran. Pliny spoke of grilled snails, eaten with wine as a snack before or after meals. In the Middle Ages, the church permitted the eating of snails on days of abstinence. They were nourished on flour and fried with oil or onion, cooked on skewers, or boiled. The consumption of snails decreased in the seventeenth century. But Talleyrand brought them back into fashion by asking the great chef Marie-Antoine Carême to prepare them for the dinner he gave for the czar of Russia.

Since then, weedkillers have destroyed the snails of France, and 90 percent of those eaten in France are imported from Eastern Europe. The snail is a strange animal, with a complex sex life. All are male except for a brief period when they lay eggs. The large white Burgundy snail, which can be up to 1¾ inches long, is impossible to farm, and only a few amateurs still roam the forests hunting it. The Burgundy snail grows slowly, taking two to three years to reach maturity. However, the small *petit gris* snails can be farmed. Bernard believed the petit gris tasted better than the local Burgundy species. When it came to regional authenticity, he talked a good game. But his first priority remained taste.

For a long time, Bernard's efforts to locate a fresh snail producer in Burgundy were unsuccessful. Then, in 1985, Jean-François approached him with a proposal: if you support me, he told the chef, then I will invest in a snail farm.

Bernard agreed.

Jean-François proved to be one of his most reliable producers. Every Thursday evening at seven-thirty sharp, he showed up with sixty pounds of live snails. In five years, he had never missed a date or raised his prices. "Bernard can count on me," he said proudly.

Jean-François was a big, broad man, soft-spoken for his size and reflective for a Burgundian. With his high, domed forehead, floating, wispy hair, and large hazel eyes, he projected the aura of a Wordsworthian romantic. His father raised cattle and pigs on 290 acres. But when Jean-François took over, the pigs were a losing proposition and the farm was too small to allow him to make a living.

Before settling on snails, Jean-François considered several other options. He thought of breeding ostriches. They thrive on sparse grassland in Africa, and he expected them to do well in the lush pastures of Burgundy. He was convinced there would be a brisk demand for plumes, at more than twenty dollars a feather. The meat also might be good. And imagine ostrich egg omelettes! Unfortunately, few chefs shared his fervor for the birds.

He proceeded to hunt truffles. White truffles grow in Burgundy. But they are not nearly as tasty as the Périgord black truffles, and Jean-François soon discovered that the market for Burgundy truffles was too small to support him. He finally turned to snails. When he investigated, he was surprised to find that he faced almost no competition. Snails, even the petit gris, are difficult to breed. They are born in a heated barn and kept during their infancy inside under large, moist plastic blankets. Constant attention is required to guard against infections. Later, the mature snails are moved outside.

La Côte d'Or was the second restaurant Jean-François approached about buying his snails, and it took 80 percent of his production. He needed no additional marketing efforts, since he refused to increase production. Hiring a staff ran against his Burgundian sense of self-reliance—and cost too much, especially when a 50 percent social security charge was added onto the basic salary.

Jean-François was waiting when Bernard arrived with the M6 television crew. He had set up a temporary snail-breeding farm in a field outside his main barn. That fit the ecological image Bernard wanted to project. In Bernard's mind, snails should come not from a heated farmhouse but straight from the earth.

Bernard greeted Jean-François with a giant hug. With the camera whirring, the two men looked at snails. Bernard held one up to his nose and pulled its head out of its shell. Jean-François smiled. He knew the entire performance by heart. The television journalist smiled. He had pictures of quaint Burgundy snail farming.

"It's a giant act, making it look like there are snail farmers all over Burgundy," Jean-François said. "Really, I'm about the only guy in the entire region left in the business."

★ ★ ★

Bernard rushed back to the restaurant for lunch. He fed the TV crew again and then sat for an interview in front of a roaring fire. Like an animated, well-rehearsed tape recording, he reeled off his personal history, starting out with only a toothbrush in Clermont-Ferrand, arriving in Saulieu, and finding the run-down restaurant. He disclosed the size of the loans he had taken out to rebuild La Côte d'Or and outlined his quest for the third, magical star.

"Hello there, microphone," he said during one break, turning to his interviewer. "I love television and radio."

The journalist returned the compliment. Bernard spoke with verve and enthusiasm. He framed his answers in colorful sound bites. The interview was finished in a quarter of an hour, and Bernard rushed off to his next appointment: an advertising photo session.

The Hennessy cognac house was photographing the great French chefs posing with a bottle of their brandy. Bernard agreed to appear, free of charge. He thought that his appearance in the luxury advertisements would be good for his image.

No expense was spared for the shoot. The crew came to La Côte d'Or in two large vans and numbered eight, including three makeup artists. More than $10,000 had been spent just on dresses for the female models. Pascal Chevalier, one of the hottest names in fashion photography, took the pictures. An extra power generator had to be installed. Technicians rolled gigantic strobe lights into the Dumaine room and focused them on a table. From the wall behind, Papa Dumaine's portrait stared down on the scene, with a skeptical smile. In his day, he never had to deal with television interviews or take part in fashion displays.

An elegant couple, the man in a dinner jacket and the woman in a glittering evening dress, sat at a table sipping cognac. Bernard, dressed in a double-breasted blue suit, held a Hennessy bottle up to the camera as if he were ready to serve the models. The female model smiled at him seductively. Bernard, a bit embarrassed, returned the smile. For more than two hours, the scene was repeated until the photographer shouted: "Bravo! Bravo!"

*Bernard inspects Michel Marache's salmon*

# CHAPTER 12

★ ★ ★

# The Triumph

*Bernard and La Côte d'Or staff in the garden*

BERNARD suffered frequent bouts of nervousness as the March Michelin publication date approached. He feared that his renovation had been completed too late in the season to earn him the third star. He thought the guide might make him wait another year to see how the new, enlarged restaurant functioned.

The anxious chef telephoned his brother, Rémy, who worked at the tire company, to see if he had any inside information. Rémy had none. Bernard telephoned his friends in the restaurant business and found out that Michelin printed its guide in the city of Bourges. He made inquiries. But none of his efforts turned up anything.

As judgment day drew near, gastronomic critics began visiting to write their own, pre-Michelin reports. Bernard was buddies with most of the French press. Most had enjoyed numerous pleasant stays at La Côte d'Or and he could hope for their positive reviews. Typical was Michel Piot of *Le Figaro,* who enjoyed good food and was generous about handing out compliments. He visited La Côte d'Or just after the renovation was completed and turned his next column, "Gourmet Agenda," into a manifesto for his favorite candidate. "Loiseau's new dining room surpasses anything one could have expected," Piot wrote. "His cooking already is worth three stars."

Bernard was more nervous about Patricia Wells. The American critic had called to reserve a table for dinner and a room for a night at the end of February. Bernard thought Wells had the same demand for perfection as the judges from the Red Guide. His enthusiasm and food produced giant smiles of pleasure on almost all diners. Not with Wells. When she was eating, she almost never smiled. Bernard could not tell whether she liked what he was serving. And when he spoke to her, she never laughed at his jokes. "An intellectual," he said.

Even though Wells had eaten homemade breads, pies, and garden-fresh produce as a child, she was, after all, an American. Bernard was both impressed with and frightened by her success as an outsider in the tough gastronomic world. He desired success on the other side of the Atlantic. But he didn't speak English and didn't understand their critical culture.

When it came to Wells, Bernard had a specific worry: her closeness to his colleague Robuchon. Wells was preparing a cookbook with Robuchon that would be published at the end of 1991, and began all her lists of top chefs with Robuchon. Bernard thought Rubochon was lucky to be friends with Wells. But Bernard didn't know her well, and that made him anxious.

When Wells arrived at La Côte d'Or, Bernard greeted her with a giant smile, revealing none of his doubts. Hubert was not working that night, so Franck stepped in as maître d'hôtel. He placed Wells and her husband at the best table at the restaurant, in the main dining room right in front of the giant bay windows that looked out onto the garden. Eric was assigned to serve.

He proposed the following menu:

*Les filets de sole à la vinaigrette de pommes de terre*
*Les jambonnettes de grenouille à la purée d'ail et au jus de persil*
*Les noix de Saint-Jacques aux endives et au jus de ciboulette*
*Le sandre rôti à la fondue d'échalotes au vin rouge*
*La pintade de ferme rôtie*

"Sounds wonderful," Wells said, genuinely enthusiastic.

The menu included many of Bernard's specialties, variations on traditional Burgundian classics, such as frog legs with a garlic puree of parsley juice, and perch in red wine sauce. And it wasn't even complete. Only the appetizers and main courses were listed. Cheese and dessert would naturally follow.

Back in the kitchen, Eric told Bernard about her menu.

"Good," Bernard declared. "At least she will see what dishes made me famous."

Lyonel glided over to Wells's table. He was determined to make an impression on the difficult American. Although sommeliers usually are required to first address the most senior male at table, Lyonel ignored Mr. Wells. "My target was Madame," he said, "not Monsieur." Turning directly to Wells, he suggested a white Meursault, 1984 vintage, from Jean-François Coche-Dury.

"Madame," he said, "this Meursault has a direct, mineral taste, perfect with the strong parsley and garlic puree on the frog legs."

Wells nodded.

For the main course of perch in a red wine sauce, Lyonel proposed a red Savigny-lès-Beaune, a first growth from the Jarrons La Dominode field. The vintage was 1985. The producer was Jean-Marc Pavelot.

"Pavelot is a resonant name in Savigny," Lyonel explained. "His wines are rich, intense, elegant—just right for the perch."

"But I am eating fish," Wells said. "Shouldn't I continue with white wine?"

"No, the perch is in a red wine sauce," Lyonel responded. "That requires a red wine. Savigny is a tender, fruity wine, not overpowering."

"Oh," Wells said, interested. "You taught me something there."

But Lyonel could not stop with a simple home run. He wanted to hit a grand slam. So he kept on speaking.

"Yes, this Savigny is a charmer," he promised. "It's a typically feminine wine."

Wells looked shocked. The sommelier had never heard about political correctness and didn't understand what he had done wrong. But he tried to recapture his momentum. He rushed back with the bottle of Meursault, uncorked it, and poured himself a quarter of a glass. Theatrically, he raised the wine to his nose to smell it and then to his mouth for a taste.

"Ahh," he said, thinking that Wells would not resist such refined beauty.

He was right. After he poured her glass, he waited to see her reaction. She put the wine to her mouth and slowly tilted it to take a taste. After she swallowed, a small smile broke through her previously stern face. Lyonel walked away satisfied.

*I've got her,* he said to himself.

Eric arrived with the frog legs.

"Monsieur and madame," he announced. *"Les jambonnettes de grenouilles à la purée de l'ail et au jus de persil."*

Then he stood in the back of the main dining room to judge Wells's reaction. She took a taste of the frog legs and hesitated. Her face remained passive and revealed nothing. When Eric returned to the kitchen, Bernard grabbed him.

"What's she think?" he asked.

"I don't know," Eric responded.

Bernard was more worried than ever.

Lyonel next entered the kitchen with a promising piece of information.

"She's on her second glass of wine," he said.

Bernard smiled with satisfaction. He wasn't surprised that Lyonel got along well with the American. Both considered themselves intellectuals. They approached food as a science, with the pleasure of eating only a secondary issue.

"Keep up the good work," Bernard commanded his sommelier. "I think she's enjoying herself here."

Lyonel uncorked the red Savigny-lès-Beaune and poured a glass. Eric glided in behind him to serve the perch in red wine. He stood behind Wells and watched as she tasted. He still could not discern whether she approved. But at least Wells was enjoying the wine. Lyonel poured generous refills.

The cheese course was next. A nervous Eric, thinking of his months of cheese tasting, wheeled his cart over to her table. Colette's white rounds of fresh goat cheese sparkled. The Epoisses was ripe, golden, and runny. Eric recommended both. Wells nodded in agreement.

"Great," Eric said as he wheeled the cart off. "She took my two best cheeses."

By the end of the meal, the Wellses had polished off both bottles of wine.

"I'm pretty sure she's going away happy," Lyonel told Eric as he carried off the second empty bottle. As Wells left the table, Bernard approached her and put on his most scholarly face. He explained that he caramelized the frog legs by a quick sauteeing in butter, then patted the butter off with paper towels. Wells nodded in approval. The parsley, he said, was liquid pureed with salt, pepper, and a little lemon. The garlic was cooked in ten changes of water to remove all the harshness.

"You taste frog leg, garlic, and parsley, each in its turn," he said. "That's what I mean by respecting the purity of each taste."

Wells had planned to eat only one meal. But the next morning, she announced that she would stay for lunch. When Bernard heard the news, he was delighted. He ordered the staff to prepare the controversial all-potato menu, *Pommes en fête.*

"We've got her," he announced with pleasure. "If she's staying for a second meal, she loves us."

The published version was indeed encouraging. "Next Monday, the 1991 Michelin Guide for France will publish its annual restaurant ratings," Wells began, "and gastronomes and chefs are betting on a new name in the top three-star roster, that of Bernard Loiseau of La Côte d'Or."

Wells admitted that she hadn't always loved Loiseau's food. But she emphasized that "over the years, he has changed styles, discarding a holier-than-thou conviction that food without fat tastes great. You need a little bit of butter, a touch of olive oil to bind the flavors of food and transform the good and the ordinary into something heavenly and spectacular." After "two recent meals in his newly enlarged dining room," Wells was now convinced that Bernard had "paid his dues and can be counted among the top chefs in France." In particular, she said, "what I remember most from his meals is not the dishes themselves but the ingredients: the plumpest and freshest of scallops; a thick filet of sandre that's sweet and cloudlike; the freshest of sole bathed in a remarkable vinaigrette. And I could sample his 'pommes en fêtes' menu once a week, if only to savor once again his remarkable purée studded with minced truffles and bathed in a rich jus de queue de boeuf."

She speculated that some "might suggest that extensive restorations completed in December—lavish new hotel rooms and huge, airy new dining rooms—are simply a way of buying into the three-star elite." But she praised the new main dining room: "a tasteful 'old Burgundy' look mixed with practical modern . . . a place that makes you feel perfectly at home." She saluted the "reassuring" staff—"you feel as though they actually want to be there"—and especially the "expertise" displayed by sommelier Lyonel Leconte. "He has been in the cellars of most of the wine makers on the wine list and can graciously lead you to some real treasures, such as J. F. Coche-Dury's lush, unfiltered Meursault or Jean-Marc Pavelot's charming, cherry-rich Savigny-lès-Beaune.

"I admit that many will gasp at the prices: 370 francs [about $60] should buy a ton of potatoes," she concluded. "Unless you calculate the pleasure per bite."

Bernard was pleased. "The review won't hurt me," he said. Eric was relieved because Wells did not mention the cheese platter. "At least she didn't attack me," he said.

The team at La Côte d'Or was convinced that it had overcome the final hurdle. If Wells, formerly negative in her comments, went away pleased, then Michelin couldn't be far behind. Bernard was confident. He promised to take his entire sixty-person staff to Paul Bocuse's restaurant if they won the third star. "We'll celebrate like we've never celebrated before," he said.

The fateful telephone call came a week before the March 4 publication date. Bernard Naegellen, the director of the Michelin Guide, was speaking. Trembling, Bernard picked up the phone. It was the first time the director had ever called.

"Don't tell any journalist," Naegellen commanded. "We're only making the announcement in a week."

Bernard promised not to tell any journalist.

"You have the third star!"

Bernard let out a giant sigh of relief.

"You must be happy," Naegellen said, dry as ever.

"Of course, I am happy," replied Bernard, ecstatic.

Naegellen conveyed a final message. It was serious, and he waited until Bernard had calmed down to deliver it. He wanted no misunderstandings about the reason for La Côte d'Or's success.

"Don't think your renovation helped," the guide director said. "We had already decided to give you the third star."

Bernard didn't believe Naegellen, and he couldn't keep the secret. He told Dominique. He called his parents in Clermont-Ferrand. In the kitchen, he confided to Patrick. Soon the entire staff knew. Still, no one celebrated. No one was willing to anticipate Michelin's decision until it became official. Everyone first wanted to see the new edition of the guidebook. Then, on Saturday morning, March 2, Agence France-Presse published a scoop.

"The closed club of three-star Michelin chefs has a new member in 1991, Bernard Loiseau of Saulieu," the agency announced. "He becomes only the nineteenth chef with three stars."

AFP added that Bernard was the only chef that year to win the sacred third star. Within minutes, the phone began to ring. Telexes and faxes of congratulations poured in from actors, singers, rival chefs, and even heads of state. Albert René, the president of the Seychelles Islands, sent a telegram. François Mitterrand faxed a brief note saying "Bravo for the star." Bernard replaced his roll of fax paper three times. The restaurant phones were jammed all day long. Soon, trucks arrived from the local vintners with complimentary cases of wine.

By lunchtime the next day, so many television stations had dispatched reporters and cameramen that Bernard sent one of his waiters out to buy extra electrical plugs for their lights. Happy and smiling, Bernard posed for the cameras. He remembered all the bottles uncorked at Troisgros to celebrate the third star, and he ordered free champagne, his favorite, Veuve Clicquot Grande Dame, for everyone: journalists, clients, and staff. With all the interviews, he found no time to eat, just a spare moment to grab a yogurt.

"I feel fabulous," Bernard repeated to interviewer after interviewer. "I started with nothing but my toothbrush, and now it's all mine."

Hubert returned that day from a two-week vacation on the beaches of Ivory Coast with his wife, Françoise. He had tried to fax the restaurant and find out about Michelin's decision. But the message never made it through the terrible African phone lines.

At Paris's Charles de Gaulle Airport, while Hubert was buying a newspaper, Françoise saw the English actress Jane

Birkin with tears in her eyes. When Hubert came back with the *Journal du Dimanche,* she understood why. The headlines announced the death of Birkin's husband, singer Serge Gainsbourg. Together they started reading the article about him. When they looked at the bottom of the front page, they discovered another headline:

"MICHELIN HONORS LA CÔTE D'OR."

CHAPTER 13

★ ★ ★

# Flying High

*Bérangère, Bernard, Bastien, and Dominique*

BERNARD SOON HAD more to celebrate.

On March 13, a week after the announcement of the third star, Dominique gave birth to their first son, Bastien. The delivery was at twelve-thirty at the Sainte-Marthe clinic in Dijon. Dominique said the timing was wonderful, "at lunchtime." Bastien weighed 6 pounds, 11 ounces, and received the middle name of Alexandre, in homage to Alexandre Dumaine.

The picture now was perfect. Guests not only ate the perfect Michelin meal at La Côte d'Or, they met the perfect family: the smiling chef, the smiling wife, and the two adorable babies. The future of the restaurant seemed assured, and the path cleared for establishing a Loiseau dynasty. If Bernard ever retired, he could pass the establishment on to either of his children, Bérangère or Bastien, and the trademark BL logo would remain unchanged.

Before going to the hospital, ever-thorough, precise Dominique had prepared press releases in French, English, and German. Once La Côte d'Or won the third star, she dispatched them around the world. The publicity wave was astounding. Praise showered upon Bernard. Most critics judged his award long overdue. "MICHELIN 1991, LOISEAU FINALLY," headlined *Le Figaro*. "A WISE MICHELIN," said *Le Monde*. Many pointed to his renovation as the reason for his success. "Loiseau's cooking is not better this year—one doesn't know how to do better—but the ambience, thanks to the costly renovation, is magnificent," wrote Robert Courtine, the newspaper's venerable critic. "The third star last year would have crowned the cook; this year, it seems to award the architect."

In his few public comments, Michelin Guide director Naegellen repeated what he had told Bernard on the phone, that the renovation had nothing to do with La Côte d'Or's award. Bernard revised history, telling questioners that he would have made the investment even if the Michelin Guide did not exist.

"For haute cuisine today, you need to eat in a garden, in a beautiful room," Bernard insisted. "Before you could be a road stop. Today, you sell dreams."

When asked, Naegellen confirmed that no simple bistro would ever again win three stars. "You can't have paper napkins and aluminum forks and knives. People these days demand a certain luxury from a restaurant."

A certain luxury. Not ostentatious luxury. The guide has begun punishing ambitious chefs who engage in expensive renovations. Marc Veyrat spent millions creating a sumptuous palace in a sublime setting on Lade Annecy. He still had two stars. Pierre Orsi renovated his Lyons restaurant, and he was relegated to one star and eventual bankruptcy.

Dominique came up with a different theory for Bernard's success. She felt the renovation was "necessary but not sufficient" for obtaining the third star. In her opinion, fatherhood clinched his success. "Before, Bernard seemed to be passionate and emotional, but not a stable person," she said. "The fact that he has children impressed them. It makes him appear more stable than before."

Bernard credited Dominique. "Some wives have foolish dreams, but she is serious," he said. "To Michelin, that meant I would be stable."

"Yes," Dominique agreed, "Michelin searches above all for stability. Stability."

Overall, the Michelin rankings remained steady: 19 three-stars, 87 two-stars, and 495 one-stars, out of a total of 10,722 restaurants and hotels listed. The only innovation in the 1991 edition was the addition of seventy-one new city maps showing starred restaurants. Restaurants in the provinces gained 29 new stars, compared with only 7 in Paris, reaffirming the supremacy of cooking outside the capital. Said Courtine in *Le Monde:* "Michelin's new guide conforms to its style, steady, newsworthy with wisdom, and skeptical of all fads."

Business boomed at La Côte d'Or. For the entire month of March, the restaurant's main dining room was full, lunch and dinner. April also was terrific—double the previous April's sales. Without the third star, Bernard hypothesized, his renovation would have increased business by 15 percent. But if things continued at this rate, sales would shoot up by a whopping 75 percent.

"All of a sudden, everyone comes with a camera," Bernard said, amazed. "They'd say things like, 'Monsieur Loiseau, could we please have a photo with you? Today is my mother's eightieth birthday and we're at a three-star restaurant.'"

Of course, Bernard knew all about the Michelin effect. Still, its power surprised him.

"You work sixteen years and overnight everything changes," he said. "Sixteen years of work, you fight and fight and nothing. Michelin is slow. Then all of a sudden, everything is so fast. Parisians make day trips just to come here, a hundred and fifty miles to lunch, and return home. All because there are three stars."

Bernard was grateful and a bit puzzled by Michelin's attitude. Not once since he had won the third star did anyone from the company contact him. "They fill the restaurant and ask nothing from you," he said.

In mid April, Dominique returned to the restaurant. She too was overcome by the Michelin effect.

"It's crazy," she said, standing next to her husband. "When I speak with the clients, the first thing they mention is the three stars."

Ever-worried, Bernard hastened to add, "The restaurant wasn't full last night. There were two or three free tables."

"But Bernard," Dominique responded. "There were twenty-two people at one table, an entire research laboratory from Dijon."

"They came for the third star?"

"Yes, Bernard."

To whoever would listen, Bernard said little would change at La Côte d'Or because of the third star. He would not add elaborate silver serving domes. No waiter would ceremoniously unveil a dish before a customer. "We can never do something so pretentious here in Saulieu," he said.

Even before Bernard won the third star, his prices had soared to an average of $200 a person for dinner. Bernard said that he would not add a third-star surcharge. He increased his breakfast tariff by only $2, which he justified as payment for the creamy goat yogurt. Coffee, tea, croissants, cakes, a soft-boiled egg, and a little glass of goat yogurt topped with some Jacques Sulem jam now cost $20. "It's worth every penny," Bernard said, in a tone that showed he was trying to convince himself.

Despite the high prices, reservations became necessary for the first time. Weekends needed to be booked at least a week in advance. Because the hotel was full on Friday and Saturday nights, Bernard began sending clients across the street, to sleep at Guy Virlouvet's Hôtel de la Poste. Virlouvet never said thank you for the extra business. He had fought with Bernard's first wife, Chantal, and considered Bernard a pretentious upstart. Like many in Saulieu, he was unprepared for the town's newfound fame and was envious of Bernard's success. "We don't need any help," Virlouvet said. "We already have enough business."

But the third star raised great expectations at the other twelve restaurants in town. Most of them were struggling to make ends meet. "The gastronomic renown of Saulieu will be re-created," said Jean Berteau, chef at La Borne Impériale. Even the newspaper stand next door to La Côte d'Or reported a 50 percent increase in sales.

Bernard began planning the promised staff trip to Bocuse's restaurant. Bocuse, ever the showman, agreed to host everybody, on the condition that he could invite "two impressive guests."

"Who are the guests?" Bernard asked.

"You'll see," Bocuse answered.

*Who could the special guests be?* Bernard wondered. He thought hard about it and figured it could only be President Mitterrand and his wife.

The date was set for April 24, and by that time signs of spring began to peek out of the frozen wintertime. Burgundy's interminable fogs lifted, and the cold, biting Morvan winds quieted. Big, lazy Charolais cows and friendly ivory sheep once again grazed on the velvet-green hillsides.

Bernard rented a bus for the trip to Lyons, and on the Nationale 6 south, the staff celebrated like one big happy family. Most of the time, the chefs and the waiters lived in two different worlds. On the way to Lyons, however, everyone laughed and sang together.

It took a little less than two hours to reach Bocuse's, sandwiched between the Saône River and the Paris-Lyons train line. The great chef greeted them with a big smile. Next to him was Pierre Troisgros.

Between the two stood two giant elephants.

One elephant was named Saba. He weighed three and a half tons. The other was named Dehly. She weighed four tons. The elephants were on loan from the Pinter circus, which was performing in Lyons that weekend. Bocuse climbed up on one of the elephants in his white kitchen uniform and tall white toque. He signaled Bernard, dressed in his best city suit, to climb up on the second. Both men held up bottles of Mumm champagne. Bocuse had an advertising contract with Mumm. Television cameras whirred away—the event later would be transformed into a champagne commercial. Without quite realizing it, Bernard was making his debut in the high-flying world of three-star advertising.

"Imagine that," Bernard said afterward, in a bit of a daze. "Elephants."

★ ★ ★

Hubert reorganized the work shifts to keep up with the new business. In the past, the entire staff had worked only on weekends, and it was easy to give days off on slow weekdays. Now the restaurant was busy all week. Until Hubert could hire more staff, everyone would work seven days. Few complained, and the waiters, in particular, rejoiced. While the kitchen staff was paid a flat salary, the waiters' wages depended on tips. Hubert, Eric, and the others soon were pocketing 50 percent more than in the pre-three-star era.

Before the third star, Hubert had found it hard to persuade possible employees to come live in Saulieu. Afterward, he received hundreds of applications. "We used to hear, 'Sorry, it's a small village in the country,'" he said. "All of a sudden we get letters every day asking for a job."

Bernard believed that three-star status called for at least one extra service: a doorman. Thierry was hired. When guests drove up, he parked their cars in the underground garage. While they ate upstairs, he washed their vehicles by hand. "You should see their faces when they leave and find their cars gleaming," Bernard said. "Three stars means offering something extra."

Thierry soon found himself parking Mercedes and BMWs, not to mention Rolls-Royces, Lamborghinis, and Ferraris. One client returning to Paris from a car rally on the Côte d'Azur drove up in his Porsche. Thierry parked it but could not open the door. Florence the receptionist kept ringing her bell for Thierry without an answer. After more than a half hour, she walked down to the garage and discovered Thierry trapped in the driver's seat of the fifty-thousand dollar car.

"Competition Porsches don't have door handles," he explained.

The receptionists thought this was the funniest thing that had happened all year. For the next few weeks, when anyone asked them "How are things at the restaurant?" they laughed and asked, "Did you hear about Thierry and the Porsche?"

Many of La Côte d'Or's new customers were from as far away as Japan. Their arrival confirmed the maxim that a third star above all attracts foreign customers. One April weekend, the crowd included the Ellises and the Lanes from Tulsa, Oklahoma, and the Pelsmaekers from Leuven, Belgium.

The Pelsmaekers were a family of four from the university town of Leuven. They arrived in a Mercedes-Benz driven by the father, Raymond, a Luciano Pavarotti look-alike, complete with bulging stomach. Raymond explained that the family was on a gastronomic tour of France. No matter that the children were in their early teens. Introduction to the good things in life starts early in Europe.

The Belgians are even more fanatical about eating than the French. "Food is a religion in France," Belgians say. "It's an obsession in Belgium." Belgian food is classical French cooking, heavy, overflowing with cream and butter.

The Pelsmaekers picked their itinerary according to the Michelin Guide. They preferred one or two stars. As Monsieur Pelsmaeker saw it, the more modest establishments gave the best value for the money. In his opinion, the three-star establishments were often overpriced.

When the Belgian saw three stars next to La Côte d'Or, he hesitated. Still, Saulieu was right on his route south. He and his family were agreed that "the taste was the best of our lives." But the bill horrified them. For two rooms and four dinners, one night came to a whopping eight hundred dollars.

"Maybe we should have settled for two stars and a lower price," he said, patting his belly as he and his family piled into the Mercedes.

The middle westerners, the Ellises and the Lanes, came to La Côte d'Or after reading a front-page article in the *New York Times* about Bernard's three stars. They looked like quintessential upper-middle-class Americans in their L. L. Bean corduroys and cotton turtlenecks. They also were on a gastronomic tour of France. First they ate at Troisgros, in Roanne. Then they headed north to Saulieu. Afterward, they planned a stop at Michel Guérard's three-star, in the village of Eugénie-les-Bains. Money was no object. Stars were.

Throughout their weekend in Saulieu, the Oklahomans ate lunch and dinner at La Côte d'Or, sampling "strange but wonderful vegetable dishes," wild asparagus with truffles, the bass, the sole, and the pigeon. They marveled at the artichoke puree in the tomato coulis and the caramelized onions. They even found room for desserts and left with particularly fond memories of the chocolate chocolate cake.

The prices "were terrifying." But when perfection is the goal, they asked, what's money?

"Some people ski in the Alps or buy a vacation house in the Caribbean," Nancy Ellis explained. "We eat."

★ ★ ★

The famous soon made their own three-star pilgrimages. On a Sunday morning in early June, the minister of culture came to Saulieu to inaugurate the city's new regional museum, dedicated to the local nineteenth-century sculptor François Pompon. Pompon, a follower of Rodin's, sculpted the animals that ran wild in the Morvan. Until Dumaine, Pompon had been Saulieu's most famous citizen. He carved graceful storks, powerful moose, the entire panoply of the local animal kingdom, but never the human figure. Like a true native of the Morvan, he preferred the raw truths of nature to the complexities of civilization.

Pompon had sculpted a massive bronze bull just to the side of the main road into Saulieu. After Bernard won his third star, he posed there, grabbing the bull's horns as if to steer the animal. The photographer wanted to suggest that Bernard finally had mastered the gastronomic universe.

The minister and his entourage arrived at nine o'clock, their black limousines, sirens blaring, racing into the quiet of Saulieu. Police blocked off the center of town. Mayor Lavault greeted the minister, a small, balding man dressed in a strict, uptight grey suit, and his wife, a tall, elegant woman draped in a couture suit. The official delegation moved through the new museum at TGV speed, not waiting for the explanations.

"*Magnifique, magnifique,*" the minister kept repeating.

The entourage moved on to the museum's second floor, where an exhibition celebrated Saulieu's gastronomy. Madame de Sévigné's famous seventeenth-century meal was described. A menu from Dumaine's day was displayed. A 1939 Michelin Guide was there under glass, showing three stars for La Côte d'Or, two stars for the Hôtel de la Poste, and a star for Le Petit Marguery. In the final room, one of Bernard's menus was on exhibit, alongside a page from the just-released Michelin Guide listing La Côte d'Or's three stars.

At the cathedral, Father Hablezig greeted the minister. He lectured the distinguished guests on the art in the cathedral, pointing out the sixth-century marble tomb carved with pagan and Christian symbols. The nave's fifteenth-century pictorial capitals, he explained, portrayed pure Romanesque symbols: an eagle with outstretched wings represented spiritual striving; a phoenix symbolized eternal life; bees building a nest in arum leaves was a sign of solidarity and companionship. Elsewhere, grotesque heads peered out of acanthus leaves and griffins devoured a wolf. The gruesome sculptures seemed to disgust the minister. He was more interested in a nineteenth-century choir loft, painted bright blue for the occasion.

During Mass, the minister and his wife sat in the front row. At the restaurant, Bernard rushed back to the kitchen to make sure everything was in order. Dominique was already rearranging the minister's seating arrangements. "The minister should have a good view of the garden and the dining room," Dominique told a waiter who had already set the table. She began moving the place cards around. With a wave of his hand, Hubert motioned the waiter to leave. Then he offered Dominique a smile that seemed to say, "OK, if you like, play at being important." The minister arrived at La Côte d'Or at twelve forty-five. Before he could sit down, he told Dominique that he had a four o'clock appointment with a French rock star named Johnny Hallyday in Paris. He must leave Saulieu no later than two o'clock.

*What a sacrilege,* Bernard thought. *The uptight minister is trying to rush perfection.*

Hubert and Eric and the other waiters scrambled to serve the meal. As one sumptuous dish after another disappeared, the minister wolfed them down, showing little pleasure. To him, this was just another official lunch, a duty rather than a pleasure. He wanted it over—quick.

At two, the minister began looking at his watch. He hadn't yet had his cheese and dessert. Before coffee could be served, he said, "Let's go, let's go," signaling to his bodyguards.

He rushed out without shaking Bernard's hand. Or paying his bill. He needed to be back in Paris.

Bernard sighed.

Why did the minister have to go to Mass? he asked. Why couldn't he have spent the time at La Côte d'Or?

Later in the afternoon, 150 leather-jacketed, long-haired bikers roared up in front of the restaurant. The national Harley-Davidson foundation had just finished its annual meeting at nearby Lac des Settons. Some of the bikers began looking at the menu posted outside. They hooted with scorn at the high prices.

Bernard appeared at the front doorway. He watched the aging hippie bikers and smiled. One of them, a robust woman, yelled, "Hey, Loiseau, how are you doing?"

Bernard responded with a smile.

"How about champagne?" he asked.

"Who's paying?" the female biker shot back.

"I'm inviting you," Bernard answered, looking hurt at the question.

Eric and the other waiters stood behind their boss, shaking their heads. They thought Bernard was joking. But Bernard was serious. They began fetching champagne.

The bikers filed into the elegant restaurant. Some draped their leather jackets over the expensive furniture. They gulped the champagne. A few asked for pictures with their host. Bernard beamed. After the drinks were finished, he waved a cheerful good-bye to the bikers.

"These people," he said, "they know how to live."

★ ★ ★

Two weeks later, on a busy Saturday morning, Annie the receptionist came running for Bernard.

"The Elysée Palace is on the telephone," she announced. "The president wants a room for this evening. But we're all booked."

"Mitterrand is coming?" Bernard asked.

"Yes," Annie said.

"You find him a room," Bernard ordered.

Annie was lucky: later that afternoon a regular customer canceled.

François Mitterrand had deep roots in Burgundy. He was born into a right-wing bourgeois Cognac family, and it recently was revealed that he spent a good part of World War II as an important Vichy official, even being decorated by Marshal Pétain for his services. But when the war ended, Mitterrand was among the maquis who fought the Germans in the Morvan. The region became a left-wing bastion, in large part because its relentless poverty fed deep resentment of the rich, conservative winegrowers to the south. In 1946, at the age of thirty, Mitterrand was elected a deputy to the National Assembly, and until his presidency he made his political base in the region. From 1959 until 1981, he served as the mayor of Château-Chinon.

Mitterrand learned he had been elected the first socialist president of the Fifth Republic in the Hôtel du Vieux Morvan in Château-Chinon. For years, he had stayed in room 15; he was particularly fond of the manager, Ginette Chevrier, and had invited her, among many other Morvan friends, to the Elysée Palace to celebrate his first decade in power. Even as president, Mitterrand returned frequently to see old friends. In his book, *The Builder and the Bee,* Mitterrand declared: "I love the forests: my path in life often brings me back to the forests of the Morvan."

His loyalty became legend. When one friend, the mayor of the tiny village of Gouloux, was up for reelection in 1989, Mitterrand sent him a postcard saying "Good luck for tomorrow." Earlier, when the mayor was ill in the hospital, the president had called with a word of encouragement. From wherever his worldwide trips took him, Mitterrand always sent notes back to his friends, addressed by hand. All his gifts from foreign heads of states are stored in a new museum in Château-Chinon.

In 1990, Madame Chevrier of the Hôtel du Vieux Morvan retired, and Mitterrand now needed another hotel in the region. Bernard hoped he would choose La Côte d'Or. Not for the money, of course. Bernard would never think of asking the president to pay. But he wanted the prestige of being able to say, "The president stays here."

When, a few weeks before, Bernard had heard that the president would attend a summit with German chancellor Helmut Kohl in nearby Beaune, he wrote to the Elysée Palace inviting both the French and German delegations to La Côte d'Or. "What an opportunity for great publicity, especially in the German press," he enthused. "All next year I will be full with rich Germans."

But the president declined the invitation. There would be no time during the summit. Bernard suspected that the German chancellor, preparing for his annual slimming trip to a spa in Austria, had vetoed the idea. Still, Mitterrand had promised that he would soon make "a private visit" to La Côte d'Or.

So Bernard was not completely surprised by Mitterrand's call. When he had read in the papers that the president was attending a ceremony at nearby Mount Beuvron, he thought there might be a surprise visit. In contrast to an American president, whose visits are planned weeks in advance, the French president can still decide on his destination at the last moment. Security guards say flexibility is the best form of safety.

Mitterrand was known to adore the pleasures of the table. But he detested what he called "false chic," pretentious service and elaborate decor. In Vézelay, he preferred the reassuring conservatism of the Hôtel de la Poste et du Lion to the flashy modernity of Meneau's L'Espérance. Bernard knew he would not like La Côte d'Or's new main dining room. In his past visits, he had chosen a seat in the back of the Dumaine room, from which he could view all the pretty women in the room. So Bernard ordered the Dumaine room set for dinner this one evening.

"Oh my God," moaned Eric, panicked.

The restaurant was packed. Even without a celebrated guest, the kitchen would have trouble keeping up. If Bernard insisted on serving the president dinner in the Dumaine room, the harried waiters would have to traverse the entire length of the hotel. Keeping his food hot would be almost impossible.

"We have a hundred and sixty reservations this evening," Eric muttered. "Bernard is playing with fire."

Worse, Hubert was away. He almost never took Saturday evening off. But this was his wife's fortieth birthday. Earlier in the week, he had gone home to his family's farm near Lyons. For the occasion, his parents killed a pig. Hubert brought it to Saulieu in the back of his Renault station wagon. For four days, he stored it in the refrigerator. On Saturday afternoon, he set up a spit in his backyard. The theme of the dinner was a desert festival, no matter that Muslims don't eat pork. Hubert prepared a North African–style barbecue. Most of the guests arrived wearing Arab headdresses and tunics. But this was Burgundy, and that meant defying Arabic abstinence with generous supplies of alcohol, starting with a powerful punch and followed by a Burgundy red offered by Simon Bize. Almost the entire town of Saulieu was invited, leaving La Côte d'Or short-staffed for the presidential visit.

At six o'clock, three black Renault 25 sedans pulled up in front of La Côte d'Or. Mitterrand stepped out, surrounded by seven bodyguards. He was dressed in rubber walking shoes and English country clothing. In the bright sunlight, the aging, balding president looked pale, his skin an unhealthy, pasty yellow. Not long afterward, his doctors would reveal that he was suffering from prostate cancer. He already seemed smaller and thinner than on television. In one hand, he held a plastic sack. Bernard rushed out to greet his illustrious guest.

"Please keep these fresh," the president said, handing him the sack. Bernard looked inside and saw that it was full of *girolles*. The president had spent the afternoon mushroom hunting.

"I do not eat a big dinner," Mitterrand announced. "Now that's original: coming to Loiseau without an appetite."

That evening, the president put on a dark blue jacket and a white shirt and tie and took his favorite seat at the back of the Dumaine room, with his doctor and his security guard. From there, he had a direct view of the décolletés of the elegant women sitting at the next table. His wife, Danielle, had stayed in Paris. According to Bernard, the president had never come to La Côte d'Or with either his wife or another woman.

The president started dinner with an oyster salad. If there was one thing Mitterrand loved, it was shellfish. He could make an entire meal of raw oysters and clams. As the main course, Bernard served a simple plate of cèpes sautéed in garlic and parsley. Bernard knew this light dish was another presidential favorite. To accompany the meal, Lyonel offered a 1985 red Volnay from Michel Lafarge. The president took only one glass.

"He's not a big drinker," Lyonel said, and he offered no white wine or dessert wine. For dessert, Eric served a solid chunk of Epoisses.

In the front hallway, Bernard served the bodyguards aperitifs and a meal. When a few guests were led to the Dumaine room for dinner, far from the main dining room, they looked pained, as though they were being sent into exile. Then they saw the president. Nobody spoke. They all just stared.

By ten, the president had finished eating and retired to his room. Outside his door, two guards, replaced every few hours, stayed awake all night. The rest of the security crew slept at the Hôtel de la Poste.

At Hubert's house, the party continued through the night. Dominique showed up around eleven. Almost everybody was drunk. An informal striptease show, starring some of the more inebriated guests, was under way. Dominique, impeccably dressed, looked out of place. She nibbled on grilled pork and a little salad prepared by Hubert and sipped a glass of wine. As soon as she finished eating, she began looking around for a way to escape.

"I must get home to take care of the children," she said.

Bernard showed up at the party at two, still full of energy. The president's visit had given him an extra shot of adrenaline. He stayed until five, leaving only when Hubert began serving morning coffee, and went straight to the hotel to make sure everything was in order. At eight o'clock, the president called downstairs for a Sunday newspaper. But at ten he was still in his room.

"He's working," a security guard reported.

"There was a call from Washington this morning," Annie the receptionist said. "From the White House, I think."

At ten after ten, the president emerged for his breakfast. He was dressed in his informal country outfit, ready for a morning hunting mushrooms in the forest. He stopped at the reception desk.

"May I pay my bill?" the president asked.

Bernard came rushing out. "There is no bill," he said.

"I want at least to pay for my telephone," the president said.

"Make out a bill for three hundred francs," Bernard told Annie, the prettiest and youngest of the receptionists.

"No," the president said, taking out a 500-franc note, about $100. "I owe more money."

"No, the bill is three hundred francs," Annie said.

"Is Monsieur Loiseau intimidating you?" the president asked.

"No, no," Annie said. Bernard interrupted and asked if the president could autograph a copy of the menu as a souvenir. Annie took a deep breath. She thought her trial was over.

"*Au revoir, Monsieur le Président,*" she said.

Then the president turned to her.

"Are you from Saulieu?" he asked.

Annie turned red. The waiters stood in the background chuckling.

"No," she said, "I'm from the Cher," a region of delicate watercolor landscapes dominated by majestic châteaux in the Loire Valley.

"Oh, what a pretty region," the president replied.

By now it was obvious that he was flirting with her. The other receptionists began paying attention. Mitterrand smiled as he headed for the door. Bernard followed. A photographer from the local paper was standing outside. The next day, a picture of Bernard escorting the president from La Côte d'Or led the front page. Inside the restaurant, Annie collapsed.

"If he had said another word," she said, sighing, "I would have melted."

★ ★ ★

Bernard began getting invitations from all over France, including a request to speak at a conference of academics at the University of Lyons. To the professors, the uneducated three-star chefs were near-gods, masters of the universe, cherished and revered. When Bernard heard that Paul Bocuse and Pierre Troisgros would attend, he decided to go. He was proud to be on the same stage as his heroes. "Thank you, Bocuse and Troisgros, thank you," he told anyone who asked. "You are the best ambassadors for French cuisine. You were the first to understand the media, the first to take the chefs out from behind the stoves."

The University of Lyons hosted the conference in its main auditorium, a majestic Napoléon III building overlooking the Rhône River. The amphitheater had been renovated in French high tech; electronic window shades "read" the amount of outside light and regulated themselves, closing as the sun rose and opening as it faded.

Bernard arrived in the middle of the morning session and spotted Paul Bocuse. He waved. As he sat down, he noticed a smart-looking hostess dressed in a striking red miniskirt uniform that showed off her long, lean legs. An elegant silk scarf, made in Lyons, added to her allure. As the speakers droned on, discussing such subjects as the transportation of turnips in the eighteenth century, Bernard began to stare at his pretty neighbor. Soon he became bored. After a half hour, in full view of the crowd, he buttoned his jacket and left the lecture hall.

"I came for Paul," Bernard said. Bernard didn't like academics. How could you intellectualize good taste? In his opinion, you didn't need to know the history of garlic to know that Bernard Loiseau's garlic puree exploded—*wham-bam*—in the mouth.

Lunchtime arrived, not a moment too soon. Bernard headed out with Troisgros and Bocuse to a boat anchored at the river's edge, just in front of the university. In the dining room, a stereo piped in loud, doctor's-waiting-room music. Bernard winced. If there was one thing he detested, it was music that distracted him from his food and from the table conversation.

The meal was a disaster. It started with a liver pâté that was cold and hard to cut. Some suggested it had been taken straight from the freezer, unfrozen. The accompanying Beaujolais was also frigid. Next came salmon in a cream sauce, a version of the famous Troisgros dish that helped launch nouvelle cuisine. But what a sacrilege: there was no sorrel in the sauce. Instead, the dry, overcooked fish was drowning in cream. "You see what happens when you raise fish on farms," someone snickered. "This is what you get."

The conversation turned to the deterioration of eating habits in France. Both Troisgros and Bocuse were pessimistic. "When we were children, you went home for lunch every day at noon and you mom cooked a great meal," Troisgros recalled. "Now you don't have any time, you eat in school, and in cafeterias."

Dessert arrived, a dish of tasteless strawberries. "It's impossible to find a real strawberry these days," Bernard said. "I've taken all the red fruits off my menu."

The other chefs nodded in agreement. When the coffee arrived, weak and filtered instead of strong espresso, they snickered one last time.

"Ugh, this tastes like American coffee," someone said.

When they returned to the auditorium, Bernard and Troisgros were ushered onstage. Bocuse was in the audience, waiting for his turn on another panel. The moderator introduced the two chefs as "the leading warriors of French haute cuisine." Troisgros described his role in the creation of nouvelle cuisine. "Our goal was not to provoke," he began. "It was to preserve French cooking for future generations." He argued that Escoffier's codes needed to be modernized. "We thought we were starting an evolution," he explained. "Instead, we unleashed a revolution."

Like all revolutions, he said, nouvelle cuisine proved both constructive and destructive. It taught chefs that they must always create. But Troisgros warned against excess; he insisted that creation should always respect tradition. "We don't want Dover sole in chocolate sauce," he said. "Sole is a beautiful product. Chocolate is a beautiful product. But they do not go together." Troisgros ended his speech with a plea to end the "abuses" of freedom while "maintaining the advances of new French cooking."

Next Bernard took the microphone. As usual, he spoke with no notes, enthusiastically and cheerfully, his words rolling rapid-fire out of his mouth. He started by expressing his fidelity to Alexandre Dumaine. "The principles of my cooking are to take classical cooking, revising and correcting it," he declared, detailing his recipe for frog legs that used no butter or other fat. "Nouvelle cuisine became too much for the photo. It looked pretty but it had no taste. I want to remind people of the dishes their grandmothers made. My motto is 'Let things have their taste.'"

After he finished, the moderator called for questions. A well-dressed matron rose in the audience.

"Why are there so few women among the great chefs?"

"Cooks are macho," Troisgros said. "They think women can't endure the hours we put in or the heat of the kitchen."

"I always have a woman in the kitchen," Bernard said, exaggerating. "Whether she succeeds or not, that's something else."

Bocuse stood up in the audience.

"If we talk about women, that's a subject I know well," he said. "All of us learned to cook from our mothers and yet almost none are in our kitchens. It's a shame."

Another spectator rose and directed a question to Bernard. "Why don't you have a cheese menu?"

"We pay a lot of attention to the cheeses," Bernard responded, describing Eric's long hunt for the strongest, ripest Epoisses.

"At my restaurant," Troisgros added, "we are doing a lot more with cheese, placing straw over the tray to give a rustic air to its presentation and developing new types of bread that give the product extra value."

Again, Bocuse stood up and stole the show.

"French cheese makers try to export Camembert and by the time it arrives, it has spoiled," he said. "The Dutch make only five cheeses and they are all lousy, but at least they are of uniform quality."

"One final question," the moderator said.

A motherly-looking woman stood up in the back row.

"Why does only McDonald's provide a good atmosphere for children?" she asked.

The audience applauded.

"You are right," admitted Troisgros. "Our profession must do more to introduce children to good taste."

"Most families don't cook for themselves anymore," Bernard said. "The success of McDonald's proves that good taste begins at the bottom."

Bocuse stood up for a final word.

"Let's admit it," France's most famous chef said. "McDonald's does everything for children. We should learn from them."

The session ended with a great round of applause and a standing ovation. John Merriman, a professor of French history at Yale University, was among those cheering.

"Wow," Merriman said afterward. "That was like watching Don Mattingly hit a fastball out of the park."

★ ★ ★

Just as an ambitious son wants to surpass his talented father, Bernard aimed to take over the great Bocuse's mantle. But he knew he still had much hard work ahead before he entered the culinary Hall of Fame beside his hero. His immediate goal was to make himself the leader of a new generation of cooks. Bocuse had persuaded the other nouvelle cuisine chefs to found a group called Bande à Bocuse. Bernard, with the gastronomic critic Gilles Pudlowski, decided to create the Bande à Loiseau. "Bernard," Pudlowski said, "you are the biggest celebrity of your generation of cooks. You must take over from Bocuse!"

Pudlowski invited a group of talented forty-something chefs to join the Bande à Loiseau. Most had two Michelin stars and were shooting for the precious third. Only Joël Robuchon was a longtime three-star holder. Bernard talked him into accepting a secondary role in the Bande à Loiseau and soothed his ego by anointing him the group's godfather. Robuchon accepted.

Together, the bande totaled an impressive twenty-two Michelin stars. Most came from the provinces: Antoine Westermann from Alsace, Marc Veyrat from Savoy, Michel Bras from Auvergne, Olivier Rollinger from Brittany. The chefs from Paris included Robuchon; Guy Savoy, an old friend of Bernard's from the Troisgros days; and Alain Passard, chef at the Paris restaurant Arpège, across the street from the Rodin Museum. In selecting his bande, Bernard aimed to promote regional cuisine.

Pudlowski convinced the Sygma photo agency that the creation of Bande à Loiseau was a news event. A photo session was scheduled in a Paris studio near the Champs-Elysées, close to the Arc de Triomphe. Haute cuisine rises to its apogee in the provinces, and these chefs lived all over France. But almost everything else is centered in Paris, and any occasion designed to win press attention had to take place in the capital.

The famous restaurateur Raymond Thuillier died the day before the photo shoot. At ninety-eight, he had seemed indestructible. For nearly half a century, he had presided over the magnificent Oustau de Baumanière, at the edge of the medieval Provençal village Les Baux-de-Provence. When Thuillier arrived in the village after the war, it was dead. Its medieval ruins stood on a mighty spur of rock high above the olive trees and quarries of the surrounding countryside. Few could imagine coming to such a remote place for a vacation. But Thuillier created the concept of Relais et Châteaux, rural inns combining urban luxury with country beauty. He took a lost village and made it fashionable.

Thuillier's setting was idyllic: guests luxuriated in sumptuous rooms overlooking the village's chalky white cliffs. He was never a cook, and many doubted that the cuisine at Oustau warranted three stars. Even before his death, Michelin had reduced the inn to two stars. "Thuillier was a visionary," Bernard said. "He was the first to understand Relais et Châteaux, the new sense of luxury, the need to relax when you eat well."

France's entire gastronomic universe converged on Les Baux for the funeral. Bernard drove an hour and a half to

Vonnas to meet Georges Blanc. Together, they made the four-hour drive to Provence in Blanc's Mercedes sedan. Blanc also owned a Mercedes convertible and a Porsche. Bernard was amazed at his wealth. "A chef really can make it big-time," he said.

After the funeral, Bernard and Blanc drove to Lyons. Paul Bocuse, who had also attended the funeral, had invited them in for a snack. By car phone, Paul ordered up a simple roast chicken, and they ate it in his kitchen. When Bernard arrived back in Saulieu, it was almost one-thirty in the morning. The whole staff was assembled in a nearby village meeting hall for the engagement party of one of the workers, and Bernard decided to make an appearance. When he walked in, the entire room exploded with the cry "Loiseau, Loiseau," meant half in admiration and half in fun.

Bernard went home only to change his clothes. Without any sleep, he left for Paris at five-thirty, speeding north to the capital at about 120 miles an hour. On the highway, his eyes darted back and forth, looking out for police radar checks. "I can smell the police like a good meal," he boasted. As the BMW hurtled along, the sun slowly rose. The weather was turning hot.

When the Eiffel Tower appeared in the distance, it glowed. The car clock read 8:30. Bernard's first appointment was at the Europe 1 radio station, where he was appearing on the morning show. Before going on air, he rushed to the café next to the studio and ordered a coffee and a croissant.

"Ugghhhh," Bernard moaned when the breakfast was served. "This croissant tastes like chewing gum."

Bernard perked up in the studio. Some of the journalists saluted him with a thumbs-up sign. "Congratulations on the third star," one said. "Boy, did I enjoy eating in Saulieu," said another. The compliments stimulated the chef more than the caffeine. As he prepared to go on the air, he was back in form. He wore a Hermès tie and a double-breasted blue jacket and gray pants and looked every bit the picture of success—a true Burgundy star.

"We have the new three-star chef with us, Bernard Loiseau," the announcer began, and she told the history of La Côte d'Or and Bernard's quest for the third star. Bernard explained how he attended Raymond Thuillier's funeral the day before and afterward dined with Paul Bocuse.

"I told Paul, 'You can relax now,'" Bernard said. "'Bernard Loiseau will take over for you with the media.'"

Everyone in the studio let out a giant laugh.

The radio show over, Bernard hailed a taxi and headed to his photo session. He didn't feel confident driving in the city. Like him, most of his fellow chefs were starved for sleep. They had worked the previous evening and left for Paris in the morning. Those near large cities, such as the Alsatians from Strasbourg, had flown and looked somewhat fresh. But the others had had to drive or take the train. Marc Veyrat, from the Savoy Mountains near Annecy, had finished his service at three in the morning and boarded the 5:45 TGV.

Michel Bras, a small, wiry man with glasses, ended his service at one in the morning, rose at four, and drove the six hours to Paris. He came from the forgotten country called the Massif Central, which includes some of the least populated parts of Western Europe. High above a little village called Laguiole, on a forlorn peak in the middle of nowhere, Bras pioneered a cuisine that glorified herbs. Bras encouraged local growers to return to vegetables that had long disappeared from the markets. He could recount the detailed differences in texture and taste of thirty different cabbages.

After his La Côte d'Or fiasco, Larry, the American stagaire, found a job with Bras. This time, he wanted a paid position as a commis. When Bras made him an offer, Larry grabbed it.

But the experience turned out to be a disaster. "Laguiole made Saulieu look like a metropolis," the American moaned. The atmosphere in the kitchen was authoritarian. "If you made the smallest mistake, like letting the milk boil for a second too long, one of the sous chefs would start screaming," Larry said. "They kept telling me time after time that I was a *connard*—a stupid, fucking idiot."

Larry found Bras distant and lonely, untouched by all the tension in his kitchen. When Henri Gault showed up one day, Bras told the rest of the staff, "I don't care." He instructed his staff not to tell him what table Gault was sitting at. "One of the most famous critics in France comes and he doesn't care," Larry said, incredulous.

By the time the Bande à Loiseau was formed, Bras had decided to fire Larry. "We made an agreement that he'd leave at the end of July," Bras told Bernard, with little emotion. "He just didn't have the necessary experience."

"Yup," Bernard agreed, his own feelings about Larry confirmed.

"What's the American going to do afterward?" he asked.

"He doesn't know," Bras answered. "Perhaps he will go back to the States."

The chefs had time to talk. They were waiting for Joël Robuchon, who was in Bordeaux that morning. Bernard was happy that Robuchon had agreed to take part in his bande and delighted that he had offered to treat the participating chefs to a post-photo meal at his restaurant. But the others, many of whom were on tight schedules, were upset by the delay. "I have to get back to my restaurant for lunch service," said Alain Passard. "This guy Robuchon thinks he is above everyone."

While they were waiting, Bernard called La Côte d'Or. Dominique told him that the health inspectors had paid a surprise visit that morning.

"How did it go?" Bernard asked. He didn't sound worried. After all, no state bureaucrat could find anything wrong when the Michelin monks had already given their seal of approval.

"The inspectors criticized Lyonel for putting an Aligoté on the wine list as a wine from the Côte Chalonnaise," Dominique reported. "They said it is wrong."

"No," Bernard said. "There is an Aligoté from the Côte Chalonnaise."

"They also checked the fish to make sure it really was fresh. And they said we should post the prices of the bedrooms on the front door."

Bernard hung up.

"Nothing serious," he said. "They need to show that they are big guys and that they can give Loiseau a problem."

Robuchon finally arrived, all apologies. The photographer told the chefs to put on their white uniforms with toques. When Bocuse and his bande had been photographed, they had imitated Rembrandt's *Anatomy Lesson,* except that instead of a human corpse, the chefs dissected a giant steer. For the Bande à Loiseau picture, the photographer handed out black leather jackets. "To give you a gang look," he said. The "gang" of chefs gathered around Bernard, who stood stirring a large copper casserole.

"Here they are, the cooks of the year 2000," announced Gilles Pudlowski with theatrical fanfare. "Robuchon is the godfather, but Bernard is in the center. Everything happens around him."

Bernard beamed. A television team from France Television arrived. As the photographer and cameraman took turns shooting the scene, the reporter asked, "Why are there no women in the bande?"

The chefs burst out in embarrassed laughter.

After the photo session, Michel Bras said he had to rush back to Auvergne for his evening service. Bras wasn't the type to enjoy a celebration anyhow. Alain Passard returned to his restaurant for lunch. The other chefs gathered at Robuchon's Jamin. As they sipped Dom Perignon champagne, Bernard turned to Pudlowski.

"We have to do something about this woman situation," he said.

"Yes," the critic agreed.

A few months later, Ghislaine Arabian, the new chef at the Restaurant Ledoyen, on the Champs-Elysées, joined the bande. Since she was from the north of France, her specialty was cooking with beer. Her arrival in the all-male preserve produced a wave of desired publicity—more than the creation of the group—including a picture of Bernard hugging her in *Time* magazine.

By the time the lunch at Jamin ended, Bernard was exhausted. He had not slept in thirty hours. But he couldn't yet go home. He had scheduled an appearance on the late-night news. It ended at one in the morning, and he wasn't back in Saulieu until three.

The next morning, he was at the restaurant at seven, ready for another photo shoot.

CHAPTER 14

★ ★ ★

# Flying Higher

*Bernard with scallops and truffles*

ALTHOUGH THREE STARS meant more clients coming to experience La Côte d'Or, the restaurant could never be more than a showcase for Bernard's talents. With its kitchen staff of twenty-five and a total of sixty employees, profits would still be small even if every table was full at every meal and every room reserved for every night.

Bernard's hope for real wealth would be realized only through endorsements. Here again his model was Bocuse. When you ordered a Beaujolais, Bocuse hoped you would order a Paul Bocuse Beaujolais. The next time you wanted candy, he hoped you'd try Paul Bocuse candy and that when you bought pots and pans they'd be Paul Bocuse pots and pans. If you happened to need an apron—well, yes, he had Paul Bocuse aprons. Paul Bocuse meals could be had at his Tokyo branch, as well as at the Epcot Center. Bocuse showed that like a team built around one superstar, a culinary conglomerate could rest on the fame of a single talent.

Over the years, competitiors and gastronomes criticized Bocuse for diversifying and not spending enough time in the kitchen. During the mid 1980s, Gault-Millau downgraded his restaurant because the Great Paul was too involved in his outside interests. "We take away a toque from Bocuse for his red snapper and all the other unmemorable dishes that were served during the year, in his presence, or in his absence," the guide explained.

Bocuse was sensitive to such criticism. He insisted that he had assembled a top-notch team and that the cooking in his restaurant did not suffer because of his outside activities. His motive, he insisted, was to make gourmet foods available to everyone, not only to the elite that could afford to eat in great restaurants. Other chefs followed his lead. Michael Guérard became the first three-star chef to sell his own line of frozen food. Frozen gourmet food, that is; after all, it's France. Put the package in the oven or on the stove and, half an hour later, out pops a TV dinner French-style, such as *savarin de poisson à l'océan* (a light fish mousse with a vermouth sauce decorated with four crab legs). "Why not frozen food?" asked Guérard. "We cannot cook just for the few who come here."

Michel Oliver created two chain restaurants (Assiette au Boeuf and Bistro de la Gare) selling inexpensive but highly praised dishes. Oliver developed precooked food for an equally unusual endeavor: a gourmet employees' cafeteria for a large supermarket chain. Why not chain restaurants? he asked. "Why should you have to eat badly because you can't afford a three-star restaurant?" Oliver never made any pretense of spending much time in the kitchen. He revised the menu at his restaurants every month or so and checked in, time permitting. "People understand that it is my team, not my personal touch," he said.

Bernard was not convinced. Although he himself almost never stood behind the stoves, he knew that his clients wanted to see the star in person. La Côte d'Or is my restaurant, he proclaimed. I am responsible for everything that comes out of the kitchen. Guérard closed his restaurant six months a year so he could work on his other projects—and still be able to supervise every dish that came out of his kitchen. "To be good, you have to concentrate on one or two things at a time," Guérard said. Bernard could not afford to shut down for six months. He pledged, except in the case of an unforeseen crisis, not to be away from Saulieu for more than one meal on any day.

Then he plunged into a series of alluring projects. His first plan was to open a bistro in the building he owned next to his kitchen, the Bistro du Morvan. As recession loomed over France and the rest of Europe, many of the famous French chefs were beginning to forget about haute cuisine—fancy, five-course feasts—and instead were concentrating on informal, inexpensive restaurants, serving traditional, simple dishes, so-called bistro food.

The chefs preferred bistros because costs are low and turnover high. Bistro decor is cheap—simple wooden tables will do—and only a few chefs are needed to turn out more than a hundred meals, made from moderately priced ingredients. Blood sausage, a bistro favorite, costs a tenth of what foie gras does. "I don't think any of the grand restaurants can make money anymore," said Henri Gault. "The only profitable formula is the bistro."

The bistro trend had started in Paris. Guy Savoy, Michel Rostang, Jacques Cagna, and, more recently, even Robuchon opened inexpensive restaurants alongside their highly rated, high-priced flagships. Often they were more restaurant than bistro, charging as much as fifty dollars a dinner. But that was still about five times less than a meal in the flagship. The common denominator was a new simplicity, both in the decor and the menu.

Dominique Versini, one of the few top-ranked female chefs, closed her expensive gastronomic restaurant and reopened as a bistro. She served pâtés, lamb stews, and other standards, all spiced with her inimitable creativity. Her trademark ravioli were on the menu, but filled with guinea fowl, not foie gras. "Haute cuisine has become too stiff and too snobbish," she said. "I want to show that you can do things in a simple fashion."

At La Côte d'Or, not every guest wanted to eat three straight meals in three-star heaven. Many wanted a simple lunch, and Bernard hoped they would prefer his reasonably priced franchise to other modest local restaurants. He also hoped to attract Saulieu residents, intimidated by three-star prices and three-star formality.

In Vonnas, Georges Blanc again had shown the way, opening a bistro across the square from his three-star establishment. Instead of elaborate food, he served a stripped-down menu of such dishes as frog legs and chicken livers Grand-mère Blanc. At lunch and dinner, Blanc's bistro was full. When President Mitterrand invited Mikhail Gorbachev to his wife's home in Cluny for a weekend, he chose to entertain him at Blanc's bistro in Mâcon. If Blanc could make a go of it in isolated Vonnas and Mâcon, Bernard thought, he couldn't miss in Saulieu.

As Bernard saw it, the Bistro du Morvan would breathe Burgundian authenticity, with a tiled floor, wooden beams, and a roaring fire. Bernard pored over the figures for the new restaurant with his accountant, Bernard Fabre. He talked to Hubert about how to organize the kitchen, splitting it in half, one side for three-star cuisine and the other for bistro fare. Eric was interested in becoming the maître d'hôtel.

But after six months of study, the project was dropped. Hubert didn't believe there were enough local customers, nor did he think that rich Parisians or clients from abroad would travel hours to eat simple food in simple surroundings. And if they did choose the bistro, it would be at the expense of La Côte d'Or. "We'll cannibalize ourselves," he said.

Finally, Fabre was not sure how to separate the two operations. He did not want a bankrupt bistro to sink a three-star success. For tax purposes, this meant that La Côte d'Or and the Bistro du Morvan could not share the same kitchen or personnel. This constraint sent budget estimates soaring. "Perhaps you should consider opening an outlet in Paris," Fabre suggested.

Ever energetic, Bernard turned his attention to other projects.

★ ★ ★

The chef who had not finished high school and who said he never read books—but who strangely had an acute knowledge and sensitivity about current events—was suddenly a best-selling author. He had written a cookbook titled *L'Envolee des Saveurs* (Flavors in Flight), in which he expounded in his philosophy of water cooking, or, as he now insisted on calling it, "truthful cooking." Most of his star recipes, including snails fried in nettles and frog legs floating in a parsley puree, were included. The publisher Hachette had contracted for the work with modest expectations. But after Michelin awarded La Côte d'Or three stars, Hachette expanded the print run from ten thousand to fifty thousand, an enormous number for a forty-dollar cookbook. When it came out in the fall of 1991, it soared to the top of the French best-seller lists.

Now Bernard was offered a column in the Sunday paper *Journal du Dimanche*. The editors asked him to write six hundred words each week on a specific product, describing its history and presenting a recipe. The product could be anything from pumpkins to snails to Christmas capons.

For his cookbook, Bernard had hired a ghostwriter. This time, Dominique suggested that she write the newspaper articles. Bernard agreed. He realized that with the renovation done, she needed a new role. While Dominique could continue to help Hubert receive guests on weekends, she never could replace him. One evening, after forty-five minutes at the restaurant, she asked Bernard, "What should I do?"

"I don't know," Bernard answered.

Dominique went home.

"There is no role for her," Bernard mused. "She must have more of her own career."

Dominique soon decided that she needed to step back from daily restaurant obligations and redevelop her journalistic skills. She began returning to Paris for a day every other week to see old friends. She signed a contract with her former employer to edit a new version of her book about kitchen sanitation and nutrition. And she took over Bernard's column for the Sunday paper.

At the beginning of the week, Dominique would interview Bernard, asking him questions about the product to be covered. Then she researched its history and tested the recipe. She liked the job because she could set her own hours. She spent most days with the children. After dinner, when Bernard was at the restaurant and the children were asleep, she had time to concentrate. Although Dominique enjoyed the work, she also was a bit ashamed of it. Before, she had written under her own name. Now she was ghosting for her husband. Bernard understood that she needed to have her own identity, but he did not know how to help.

"I asked *Journal du Dimanche* if she could sign the articles," he said. "They said no. They wanted me."

The couple skirmished over another subject, too: vacation. From her time working for Club Med, Dominique had become fond of long sun-drenched holidays. During his sixteen years in Saulieu, Bernard had never taken any time off. In his entire life, he had never been outside of France. "Every time I earned a hundred francs, I said we needed to buy another rug or painting for the restaurant," Bernard said. "I was too obsessed by three stars to see anything else."

Bernard agreed that he should slow down. In the past, he had kept the restaurant open 365 days a year, except during the renovation. Now, he decided to close La Côte d'Or for a month, from mid November to mid December. The idea of a vacation, of seeing something other than Saulieu, both excited and frightened him.

"When the restaurant is closed, we'll go to Venice," he promised his wife at the end of a busy summer weekend.

But Dominique still wanted to take a summer vacation. She proposed a week on the beach in Spain or in Brittany. Bernard was horrified. Summer was his high season. The restaurant was packed. He had never been to the beach in his life, and the idea of crawling around in the sand with his small children did not appeal to him.

"I don't have the time," Bernard said.

Dominique ended up going to Ibiza with the children and some friends from Dijon.

★ ★ ★

Bernard's first big-money offer came not from France, but from Japan.

As usual, the Japanese were intent on learning from the best. Bocuse opened his Tokyo restaurant with the giant Japanese distiller Suntory in 1970. Troisgros soon followed, sponsored by Sony chairman Akio Morita. In a typically farsighted move that made him the model of Japanese management, Morita gambled that top-flight French cuisine would project the kind of first-class image he wanted for his electronic goods. As Japan boomed during the 1980s, every major hotel company felt obliged to create its own French restaurant. Talent scouts from the Japan Travel Bureau spotted Bernard, whose creative, light cooking appealed to their oriental tastes. So did his colorful personality. "The Japanese wanted someone like Bocuse, strong enough to carve out an image with the media," said Pierre Béal, director of a Japanese cooking school outside of Lyons and the go-between in the negotiations. "And they loved Bernard's cooking."

In 1987, the Japan Travel Bureau offered to finance a La Côte d'Or restaurant. Bernard refused. He needed to concentrate on Michelin and said he would not accept any foreign contracts until he won his third star. Every year the Japanese returned to Saulieu, and every year Bernard turned them away.

"I didn't mean no forever," Bernard said. "I just meant no for the time being."

In 1990, the Japanese arrived in Saulieu, this time with an ultimatum: now or never. Expensive French cooking had already peaked in a Japan about to fall into recession. Cheaper Italian cooking was making inroads. Spanish tapas houses were springing up. So were cheap French bistros: Brasserie Flo, the successful Paris chain, had just opened a Tokyo branch. But the Japan Travel Bureau was building a new Sheraton skyscraper in Kobe, just outside of Osaka. It needed a prestigious restaurant for the top floor.

Bernard, drowning in debts, made stiff demands.

"I want my own chef," Bernard said.

"Yes," the Japanese replied.

"I want the same products used in Saulieu."

"Yes."

Bernard named Jean-Jacques Belin, from nearby Semur-en-Auxois, as chef and began training him at Saulieu. Jacques Sulem jam, Michel Marache fish, and even Jean-François Vadot snails were shipped to the Orient. "Once Bernard said yes to the idea, everything became negotiable," Béal recalled. "Including the money."

For ten days a year in Japan, Bernard would receive $100,000. The new restaurant would bear his name. When Fabre heard about the deal, he said, "Sign."

Bernard signed. After he won his third star, the Japanese were ecstatic. La Côte d'Or's Kobe branch was scheduled to open in June 1991, only two months later, and a ten-day trip to Japan was planned for the restaurant inauguration. Bernard boarded the plane with trepidation. He had not done much flying, and the trip from Paris to Tokyo took twelve hours. The Japan Travel Bureau bought him a first-class ticket. It cost $10,000. Hubert went along with him, but in economy class. "Lucky they didn't put you in the baggage department," Bernard joked.

In Japan, Bernard reveled in his VIP treatment. He was surprised by the quality of the cooking at the restaurant. "It's an exact copy," he marveled, "as good as Saulieu." He had only one problem: everywhere he went, his hosts wanted to treat him to sumptuous platters of sushi. But Bernard was allergic to raw fish. On the second night of the trip, he was overcome with violent stomach spasms. He survived the full ten days thanks to Hubert. Their relationship began to resemble that of a prince and his butler. After the sushi disaster, Hubert tasted every dish to detect any hidden raw fish before Bernard ate.

"Dominique says we are becoming an old couple," Bernard laughed.

★ ★ ★

Once he returned from the Orient, Bernard received another appealing offer, from giant Unilever, the world's second-largest food and consumer group, which planned to launch a new line of soups. It would be called Bernard Loiseau Souper d'Or—Soup of Gold.

Back in 1953, Unilever had been the first in France to sell an instant soup. As the 1990s dawned, it still held 70 percent of the market. In recent years, however, competitors began air packaging soups, using a technique first developed for fruit juices. The new product tasted better than instant soup. Unilever conducted marketing studies that showed a niche for a new luxury brand. Who better to promote this image than Bernard?

"Bernard had the allure and the charisma," said Jean-Christophe Malrieu, the brand manager. "Of course, he had also just won the third star."

Unilever got in touch with Claude Lebey, who was expert at marketing haute cuisine chefs. Silver-haired, smooth, aristocratic—he looked a little like an English lord and drove a luxurious Rover sedan—Lebey presented himself as a gastronomic impresario. He started out as a critic, writing for ten years for *L'Express*. Then he put out a guide to Paris restaurants called *Guide Lebey*.

Lebey had grown up with the Holy Trinity: Dumaine, Pic, and Point. But he was not a nostalgic traditionalist. When he went to New York, a frequent destination, he didn't go to fancy French restaurants. His favorite American food was pastrami. "I dream about it," he said. He criticized Dumaine for using five-day-old sauces and canned goods. "He was a great cook, but all those sauces, it was real old-style stuff. Dumaine was rich, rich, rich, too rich."

Then in 1980, Lebey began to publish cookbooks by the great nouvelle cuisine chefs, Bocuse, Troisgros, and Guérard.

"I saw the paychecks of these great chefs and choked, they were so low," he said. "So I went to Nestlé and said, 'Hey, guys, why not do a line of frozen food with Guérard?'"

Until that time frozen food had a poor reputation in France. The new Guérard dishes were gourmet—and good. Although they were expensive, as much as fifteen dollars for a single portion, they helped change the image of frozen food, useful for Nestlé's inexpensive, mainstream Findus brand. "Guérard put value into the idea," Lebey said.

Lebey invited Bernard to Paris to discuss the Unilever offer. While Dominique stayed in Saulieu to work on the article about radishes for the coming week's *Journal du Dimanche,* Bernard set off for the capital, arriving first for a guest appearance on a TV talk show hosted by Christophe de Chavanne, France's version of Johnny Carson. De Chavanne was a regular customer at La Côte d'Or and paid for his meals with invitations to his show. In front of the cameras, he blindfolded Bernard, pinched his nose with a rubber swimmer's clip, and put two glasses in front of him. Tell me which is whiskey and which is gin, he said. Bernard tasted. He identified the whiskey as gin and the gin as whiskey.

"They tricked me," he told Lebey later. "After three glasses blindfolded, you can't tell the difference between red wine and white wine."

Bernard was a little smashed by the time he arrived at Lebey's spacious apartment overlooking the Parc Monceau. He was impressed.

"Wow, he's made it," Bernard told Dominique afterward. "I hope one day I will have the money to do something like that."

Lebey served champagne. His wife, a cookbook writer, showed Bernard her most recent work, a handsome photo work praising the glories of chocolate.

Lebey suggested dinner at Le Grand Véfour, in the magnificent Palais-Royal, one of Paris's prettiest restaurants, with gleaming Napoléon III decor. Founded in 1784, it is one of the oldest in Paris. After World War II, the young chef Raymond Oliver took it over and achieved three stars. Then Oliver died, and the monument declined. In the late 1980s Véfour was bought by Taittinger, the champagne house. A new chef, Guy Martin, had just put it back on the upward path, with two Michelin stars. Bernard was eager to try Martin's cuisine.

As soon as Bernard and his agent arrived, the maître d' came running.

"Monsieur Loiseau, Monsieur Lebey, so wonderful to see you."

He led them toward a table in the back, next to an ornate mirror and with a clear view of the splendid dining room. The restaurant was full.

"Wow," Bernard said. "This must be one of the few two-stars to do such a great business."

"What would give you pleasure?" the maître d' asked.

"To begin with, foie gras," Bernard said.

"How about *ravioles de foie gras et crème truffée,* ravioli filled with foie gras and topped with truffles?"

"I'd prefer plain foie gras," Bernard said.

"I'll try the ravioli," Lebey said.

"I like to see how a restaurant does the simple things, whether it can achieve a true taste without camouflage," Bernard said.

"For your main course, how about the baby lobster, *les langoustines?*"

"I'll try the *langoustines,*" Lebey said.

"I've heard your sweetbreads are terrific," Bernard said.

For wine, the sommelier suggested a "modest Bordeaux," and a 1985 Château Lafite was placed before them.

"A modest wine, right!" Bernard exclaimed, a grin spreading across his face.

The appetizers arrived, and Bernard began smearing his foie gras on toast. He tasted Lebey's ravioli and smiled.

"Good but not paradise," he said.

The next courses came, and the judgment was the same.

"The food is not worth three stars," Bernard said. "It's very, very good but not quite paradise."

"Oh, Bernard, half the three-stars aren't worth three stars," Lebey said. "Go and eat at all nineteen three-star restaurants. Then come back and tell me which half to get rid of. It won't be hard."

When desserts had been served—a chocolate mousse and a mille-feuille filled with mocha and topped with caramelized pears—the talk finally turned to business. Lebey warned Bernard that despite Guérard's success with Nestlé, most chefs didn't like dealing with big business and most big businessmen were skeptical of chefs. The chefs were focused on taste and forgot about the price of their raw products. But a big company had detailed budgets for ingredients calculated down to the last centime.

"Chefs don't understand business," Lebey explained, "and the businessmen don't respect the chef's creativity."

"You know," Bernard said, "I think this is pretty simple: if you freeze something good, you get something good. If you freeze shit, it comes out as shit."

"We'll taste everything and you get final approval," Lebey assured Bernard. He explained that old-fashioned stews generally proved to be successful. Such "mother's cooking" was invented as a way of preserving food. Soups, too, froze well.

Bernard didn't need too much convincing.

"OK," Bernard said. "I'll sign."

Lebey, smiling for the first time that evening, called for the bill. The maítre d' arrived, looking horrified.

"No, no," he said. "It's on the house."

Lebey took out a five-hundred-franc bill and left it as a tip.

★ ★ ★

Dominique studied the Unilever proposal. Prudent as ever, she was worried that the arrangement might hurt La Côte d'Or's image. When Unilever said that they would not put Bernard's name on ordinary vegetable soups, she was relieved. The Souper d'Or items would be gastronomic: a "cream of salmon soup," a "Provençal *pistou,*" an "old-fashioned mushroom." Dominique approved of the plans to produce soups that were "a little original, but not too original, a little in advance, but not too far." She also approved of the decision to avoid dehydrated ingredients. The new line of Bernard Loiseau soups would contain chunks of fresh food, unlike most of the competition.

What worried her most was the advertising. The plan was to put a portrait of Bernard, stirring a pot of soup, on the package with the words "I, Bernard Loiseau, three stars."

"That's too direct, too American," Dominique told her husband. "You don't have the right to use the Michelin trademark, three stars."

"But Dominique," Bernard replied, "Michelin doesn't have a patent on the word *stars.*"

"Perhaps you're right," Dominique conceded. "Still, it's so American."

Bernard went ahead anyway. He traveled to Poitiers to visit the Unilever factory. He tasted the soups. He recommended adding dill and onion to give the salmon soup a stronger taste. He suggested that a veal stock in the mushroom soup would bring out the flavor better than a beef stock. The fish soup was improved by adding some tomatoes and green peppers. And cauliflower was added to the vegetable soup. The final recipes were prepared for a marketing test. During the next few months, the company would offer samples to consumers. Do you like the soup? they would ask. If so, would you like to buy it? At what price? A meeting was set for mid August in Paris to review the marketing results and taste the final recipes.

The Unilever offices were in a block of faceless office buildings beyond La Défense, in the western suburbs of the city. Bernard arrived at ten, right on time. Jean-Christophe Malrieu, the ambitious, fresh-faced brand manager, was there, along with his boss, marketing director Stéphane Régnault, smoother and more sophisticated. Claude Lebey represented Bernard.

The day before, the Unilever president had studied the marketing plan. He had asked tough questions about introducing a new brand in the brand-aversive 1990s. Régnault had replied that food was not the same as cigarettes. "People need to feel an emotional, personal attachment to what they eat."

"The marketing results are positive," Malrieu had reported. "Customers say they are willing to pay twenty percent more for a soup endorsed by Bernard Loiseau." After a long silence, the president had given his go-ahead.

Malrieu called the meeting to order and announced the president's approval. "The launch is set for January," he said. But he added that the campaign was provisional, depending on the success of continuing marketing tests.

Bernard let out a sigh.

"We're going to kill them," he boasted.

Bowls of soup were brought out one by one, starting with the salmon. Bernard took a big spoon and dipped into the simmering, bright orange mix.

"Ugggggh," he said. "I need to work on this."

"We had some problems mixing the dill and the onion," Malrieu admitted.

"It's too liquid," Bernard said. "It doesn't explode in your mouth."

"We'll work on it," Malrieu promised.

Samples of the mushroom soup were next. Instead of the usual creamy beige color, the liquid looked dark brown. Bernard tasted.

"Not enough mushrooms," he suggested.

The fish soup was better. Bernard judged the vegetable soup "well balanced." A "Mediterranean" vegetable soup received an even higher grade.

"It's top, top." Bernard smiled. "I'll improve the other soups and the press will love it."

Bernard's approval calmed the nervous Unilever executives. They promised to improve the soups, and they outlined how the marketing would proceed. Burson and Marsteller, the giant public relations firm, had just been hired. Bernard would soon film a promotional film in Saulieu. Television ads would follow. The samples would be distributed in the supermarkets.

"Bravo, bravo," Bernard said as things wound up.

Bernard walked out of the meeting a rich man. In a couple of hours of tasting, he had made more money than in his sixteen years running La Côte d'Or, working twenty hours a day.

★ ★ ★

A few weeks later, Unilever invited fifty journalists to Saulieu. The writers worked for women's and family magazines, not for gastronomic journals. All but one was a woman. "The haute cuisine critics with their noses up in the air are men," said Mauricette Clement of the magazine *Famili.* "Women only get to write about new products."

"The only exception is Patricia Wells, but she is American," Dominique interrupted. "Elsewhere, women gastronomic critics are accepted."

In La Côte d'Or's conference room, Unilever officials presented Souper d'Or, saying that the first reaction in the supermarkets was positive. More than 60 percent of the country's giant *hypermarchés* had agreed to carry the line, twice as many as predicted. "Brands still are powerful," said Stéphane Régnault. "You just can't sell blah, blah, blah and pretty pictures. You must sell real recipes, real quality."

"For me, this is a dream," Bernard chirped. "We chefs should work with the masses, bring our savoir faire to the greatest number of people."

Then the lights dimmed. A camera whirred, and Bernard's promotional film appeared on a television screen. When the film was over, the lights went up and Bernard lifted up a red velvet cover to reveal giant boxes of Souper d'Or.

"Ahhhhhh," the audience sighed.

"The packaging is great," said Bernard. "A class act."

"Monsieur Loiseau?" a voice called out.

"No," Bernard said. "Call me Bernard."

"OK, Bernard, are the soups frozen?"

"No, they are air packed, though the vegetables are frozen."

Nervous laughter moved through the room.

"But," Bernard continued, "as another great chef used to say, when you freeze something good, you get something good; when you freeze shit, it comes out as shit."

Dominique broke into the conversation.

"I was concerned that the soup not be made from dehydrated ingredients," she said. "It should be real food all cooked together."

"Yes," Bernard said. "I could never have done this project without Dominique."

Dominique's involvement and Bernard's praise for her pleased the women in the audience.

Another journalist asked Unilever's Régnault, "Will this be a long-term relationship between you and Bernard?"

"We are getting married," Régnault said with a smile. "We hope to stay together for many new products—many children."

"But I already have two children," Bernard joked.

Everyone moved into the Dumaine room for aperitifs. Gasps of pleasure greeted Bernard's new invention, fried artichoke chips. The lunch opened with a tasting of the soups. When the first sample was served, a journalist summoned Eric Rousseau.

"Salt, please," she said.

Eric looked shocked. Bernard never put salt and pepper on his tables. His dishes were spiced to perfection, and any alteration was sacrilege. In all his years at La Côte d'Or, Eric had never been asked for salt. But the Unilever soups did need spicing. Eric brought the woman a salt shaker.

There was a good response to the vegetable soups. Then came the cream of salmon.

"This is terrible," one woman said as she took a sip.

Before anyone could complain further, Lyonel poured glasses of a Simon Bize Savigny-lès-Beaune. As the journalists sipped the wine, smiles returned. Bernard's own cooking sealed the pleasure, and the women left satisfied. Bernard promised them that further work would perfect his mass market soups.

Everything was soon ready for the promotion campaign. A film crew, including a makeup artist, descended on Saulieu. Bernard asked her to pay special attention to his bald pate.

"No problem," she said. "I do Sean Connery's makeup."

Bernard smiled.

"Only the best," he said.

In front of a roaring fire—imitating a cold winter day—Bernard recounted his quest for three stars. Once more he started by saying that he set out to make his fortune "with nothing more than a toothbrush." He told about uncorking champagne as an apprentice when Troisgros won the third star. Bernard needed no script to tell the story of his arrival in Saulieu, his trek through the culinary desert, and the ultimate consecration. "Here we sell a dream," he announced. "I am going to let you be part of this dream."

In the kitchen, the film director ordered all the ventilators shut down. The chefs began to sweat in the summer heat. The ingredients for each soup were placed before Bernard, and he recited a florid text. For the salmon, Bernard intoned, "I wanted to exalt the richness of the salmon by the finesse of the endive, this marriage lightly spiced by a trace of onion, white wine, and garlic." For the vegetable soup, the freshness of the vegetables from the garden was "heightened by a hint of garlic and thyme." The mushrooms came "straight from the forests of my childhood." And for the Mediterranean vegetable soup, Bernard pointed to each of the various ingredients, the tomatoes, leeks, saffron, basil, garlic, potatoes, and onions, all enhanced by fresh olive oil. "Here is a taste of the sun," he announced.

During a lunch break, Bernard served the entire dozen-man crew a five-course meal, free of charge, of course. Afterward, filming continued in the main dining room. Bernard stood before a giant poster promoting his soups and stirred a giant pot. "I will be the ambassador of Souper d'Or," he promised. "I will be on television, in the newspapers, in short, everywhere for Souper d'Or."

He got his lines right on the first take. The crew broke into a round of applause when he finished.

"Perfect, Bernard." The director smiled. "Did you ever think of going into the movies?"

*Bernard and Bastien*

CHAPTER 15

★ ★ ★

# *A New Burgundy Star*

*Lyonel Leconte, sommelier*

SAULIEU SIMMERED in the mid-August heat. For these few weeks each year, tourists filled the town, tripling its off-season population. The only French indulgence that rivals cuisine is vacation. Few other countries display such an annual urge to get away from it all. In New York, people work through the dog days of summer; in Paris, by the end of June, people are talking of nothing but *les vacances*.

The August getaway is sacred. Shops and restaurants shut down in the big cities, leaving behind an urban desert. Year after year the government has urged the public to spread holidays throughout the year. Yet the summer holiday seems one of those traditions almost impossible to change. About three quarters of the French go away between July 14 and September 1. Industrial production falls by 40 percent in August, against only 10 percent in Germany, where holidays are staggered.

Before the war, long holidays were the province of the well-to-do. These days, French workers enjoy the longest paid annual leave in Europe. In 1936, the Popular Front legislated the legal right to two weeks' vacation. A third week was added in 1956, a fourth in 1965, and a fifth in 1981. When tourism began in the nineteenth century, city-dwellers often felt ill at ease in the country. They preferred such resorts as Biarritz, Deauville, or the Côte d'Azur, with their casinos and promenades. Now more and more of the French want to lose themselves in the far reaches of the provinces.

Bernard worried that this back-to-the-country movement could cause a backlash against three-star restaurants. As the vogue for bistros suggested, Frenchmen wanted a return to "true values." Bernard believed that his style of haute cuisine, taking traditional recipes and modernizing them, satisfied this appetite for true tastes. For the time being, his strategy was working. La Côte d'Or was full almost every night.

The summer rush pressured the kitchen. One evening, a young waiter named Sylvan played a practical joke on Paul, the American stagaire, smearing a dab of Epoisses behind his ear. Paul didn't find this funny. He took the casserole simmering on the stove in front of him and turned around to confront the waiter. The pan was full of red wine sauce, ready to be poured over Bernard's famous fresh perch. In one motion, Paul poured the sauce over his tormentor.

"It was war," Paul said. "Sylvan looked like he had been wounded in battle, covered with all that red sauce." The sauce splattered over the dishwasher and splotched the wineglasses. Lyonel and his assistants had spent hours making the glasses sparkle, wiping each one with a wet rag. Now they would have to do it all over again in the middle of a busy dinner service. Lyonel never forgave Paul.

Sous chef Olivier mediated the combat, and everybody returned to work. Later Olivier told Bernard, who was not in the kitchen at the time, about the incident. At the end of the evening, Bernard spoke to Paul. Although he liked the American, he would never permit discipline to slacken in the kitchen. "Don't be a *con*—a fucking idiot," he warned Paul.

"That was just the last straw," Patrick, the chef de cuisine, said. In Patrick's opinion, Larry, the previous American intern, didn't have the necessary three-star talent or drive. Paul was different. "He had talent and never stopped working," Patrick said. "You could see that he had real training, that he knew the rules and did it by the book."

Olivier tried to explain to Paul that paid workers would never, never take criticism from stagaires. "They know you're going to leave soon," he explained. "They have to stay."

"I get it. A French guy can get away with murder, but an American should shut up," Paul said. "That's bullshit."

Tensions continued off the job. After dinner service, most of the young French workers went out drinking at the Café du Nord, across the street. They were noisy coming back to their rooms. One chef jingled his keys and kept waking up Paul. "He has as many keys as a janitor," Paul complained, "I can't get back to sleep afterward."

Earlier in the summer, his mother had visited. She stayed in a suite at La Côte d'Or and ate almost all her meals at the restaurant. The night before she left, she and Paul arrived for dinner at ten-thirty. They were the last customers. That night Franck was having his engagement party, and the staff was eager to go to it. Suddenly the word spread through the kitchen: "The American stagaire is in the dining room." The news was greeted with a giant moan. To serve Paul and his mother, the entire kitchen staff had to stay well past midnight.

Paul attempted to avoid further confrontations by moving out of his cramped worker's quarters above the restaurant into a room in Saulieu. But the rent took up most of his $375 monthly salary. Paul wasn't enjoying himself and he wasn't getting rich. So he decided to quit. He called his girlfriend, Patricia. She said he could stay at her parents' home in Mulhouse. Paul could go back to work for her father, the owner of a prosperous charcuterie business, and look for another internship on the Côte d'Azur. After a fruitless yearlong job search, Patricia had settled into a job with her father.

On August 13, Paul went to see Patrick in his apartment and announced his decision. Patrick was shocked. Most times, he told staffers to leave. Few had the gumption to take the initiative themselves. Patrick hadn't expected the problems with Paul to end so abruptly.

"No hard feeling," he said, offering Paul an aperitif.

"No hard feelings," said Paul.

The next day, Patricia picked Paul up. His precipitate departure surprised most of the kitchen staff. Only Bernard seemed to understand. He gave Paul the addresses of friends on the Côte d'Azur where he could apply for a job. He even called one or two chefs to see if they had any positions open then. None did, but Paul was touched by his efforts.

"This is a sad day for me," Paul said. "If you need me, I'll stay until you replace me."

"Don't worry," Bernard said. "You have learned everything you can learn here. Go and be successful."

"I went out in style," Paul said afterward.

★ ★ ★

Bernard had another worry: Saulieu's annual August festival, the Charolais Fair, was approaching. The three-day show was a chance for the Charolais cattle breeders to show off the right stuff. Like the American conquerors of the Wild West, the Burgundy cattle raisers believed that their calling was noble. Farmers who grew things were mere farmers. Cattlemen were cowboys.

Of all the nations in Europe, France consumes the most beef. And of all the different types of beef in France, the Charolais is considered king. Until about twenty years ago, the beef growers were richer than their Burgundy wine cousins. On their pilgrimages to Saulieu, they stayed at La Côte d'Or and ran up fabulous bills. One of Dumaine's best-loved specialties was *côte de boeuf,* a thick T-bone cut, which he grilled to perfection.

Then, as it did everywhere else in the western world, red meat became associated with cholesterol and heart attacks. Since 1980, French per capita consumption of red meat has plummeted by about half. In addition, big supermarkets began driving small-town butchers out of business. The supermarkets sold on price, not quality. After the fall of the

Berlin Wall, they began to import cheap meat from Eastern Europe. These days, French cattlemen find it harder and harder to make ends meet.

Bernard loved beef. Sometimes he took his entire kitchen staff to a gas station cafeteria just north of Saulieu that served fabulous côte de boeuf. But the steak house closed, in part because the prices were too high to attract locals. First-quality beef costs much more than poultry, veal, or even fish, because it takes years to breed cattle compared with weeks for chicken. Also, the cholesterol factor cut the demand for red meat, even in this beef-loving district of this beef-loving country.

As much as Bernard loved to eat steak, he hated to cook it. "What can one do that is interesting with a lump of meat?" he asked. "With fish you can show much more creativity."

Bernard complained in particular about the decline in quality of Charolais cattle. In the 1980s, the greedy Charolais breeders began to use hormones, which let them produce bigger steer in less time—to sell more beef with less effort. The hormones took a lot of the taste out of the tender Charolais. It cut like butter and tasted of nothing.

This artificial blandness revived Bernard's interest in the ancient breeds growing naturally, the natives of remote areas. In private, Bernard said the beef from the Aubrac region, high in the Massif Central, produced without hormones, surpassed the local Charolais. In the kitchen, the Englishman Michael Caines had lobbied for Scottish Angus beef. He thought it by far the best raised in Europe.

Bernard could not bring himself to put a non-French meat on his menu. Many products could come from abroad—but not something as basic as beef. The local Charolais growers might decapitate him. So Bernard chose a third solution: he took beef off his menu. Until the local growers improved their product, he would not offer their trademark côte de boeuf. He also began using a butcher in Paris. Local butchers could not obtain the choicest cuts of veal, lamb, and other meats. Since no one else in Saulieu bought such luxury products as tender milk-fed veal and delicate nuggets of venison, no local butcher carried them.

The Charolais farmers wrote letters calling Bernard a traitor. They held press conferences denouncing the "tyranny" of "so-called" great chefs. Once when Agriculture Minister Jean-Pierre Soisson was staying at la Côte d'Or, a group of angry farmers drove up in their tractors. They wielded pitchforks and threatened to burn the restaurant down. Luckily, the police intervened and prevented a disaster.

In 1981, the Charolais farmers gathered for the first Charolais Fair, modeled after the wine makers' famous Les Trois Glorieuses. The success of that event convinced the Charolais growers to stage their own festival.

Gradually, the Association of Charolais Growers acknowledged that there was some truth to Bernard's criticism and began to improve its product. They created a Red Label for high-quality beef. In order to receive the label, growers certified that they used no hormones. When Bernard tasted Red Label beef, he agreed it was an improvement and returned côte de boeuf to his menu.

Still, tensions simmered. Bernard continued to worry about the varying quality of beef that he received from his suppliers. The growers continued to fear the bad publicity he could generate, particularly in the wake of his third-star victory. As a gesture of goodwill, Bernard decided to visit the Charolais Fair on its opening day.

The fair was held in Saulieu's convention hall, around the corner from La Côte d'Or. Mayor Lavault had received government subsidies to build the new auditorium. The mayor's goal was to make up for the loss of traffic to the new highway and to revive Saulieu as a small convention center. But the hall was much too large for the town. Except for three days in the spring, during the regional gastronomic fair, and three days during the summer, it was empty.

Early on Saturday morning, after checking on breakfast service at the restaurant, Bernard walked to the convention hall. The use of public funds to construct the hall nagged him.

*Who's the biggest single employer in Saulieu?* he asked himself.

*Me,* he answered.

*Did I ever receive a penny in subsidies?*

*No!*

It was a beautiful sunny day. Many of the visitors to the fair wore shorts. Outside, a circus atmosphere reigned. A Ferris wheel whirled in the air. Children squealed with pleasure as they drove model stock cars against each other. Near the entrance to the fair, local artisans sold their wares. Bernard observed that many of his suppliers were not present. "Their customers don't go to events like this," he snickered. "Only the mediocre producers are here."

When Bernard entered the hall, the sharp smell of animal sweat, spiced with manure, greeted him. He took a deep breath of the pungent air. "Smells good," he said. But he looked around and was surprised by the small number of visitors. At wine festivals, the streets of the host village were packed. Saulieu's Charolais Fair could not compete. *It's calm—too calm,* Bernard thought.

He strode down the aisles, looking at the large, powerful steers. Again he was disappointed. "There are fewer animals to sell than ever before. It's nothing like the old days."

A friend, Gérard Mazis, greeted him. Two of his animals were entered in the fair. Bernard began examining the larger one, an enormous, robust-looking cow. He put his hand on its jaw and pulled it open, revealing three large white teeth—one for each year.

"Three years old," he proclaimed.

"Yes," Mazis said.

Bernard continued his inspection, moving backward along the animal's body, until he reached the behind. Then he thrust his hand under the hind leg and squeezed.

"Almost there," he said. "Give him a year more and he'll be ready."

The conversation turned to the fate of the local slaughterhouse. Not long before, it had failed to pass the new European Community hygienic standards. Unless millions were spent to renovate the building, local farmers would have to send their animals far away for slaughtering.

"If that happens, we'll have even less control over quality," Mazis said.

Bernard agreed. If a steer has a stressful death, its muscles become tense and the meat will be tough. After butchering, the animal must be refrigerated and hung for three weeks. "It needs to become a little rancid to have the best taste," Bernard explained.

For Bernard, the only beef worth eating came from cornfed cattle. Corn produces a meat that is violet and ribbed with fat, which gives the meat its flavor. He criticized the farmers for feeding their animals the cheaper soy imported from America.

"You guys try to rush nature," Bernard told Mazis. "Instead of waiting four years, you want everything done in nine months."

By now, a group of growers had gathered around Bernard. Many recognized him.

Bernard looked around the room. Most of the cattle were enormous. The biggest weighed almost two thousand pounds. Some could hardly stand. Their buttocks were so large that they spread out like a truck. Their breasts drooped with excess poundage.

"They're so full of hormones that some of these guys are radioactive," Bernard said.

"Bernard, now, that's just not true," Mazis interrupted. "You know, under the Red Label, we're not allowed to use hormones anymore."

Bernard was silent, but only for a moment. He led Mazis to a corner of the room, where the Association of Charolais Growers had put up a display of cuts of meat. They were white and showed little fat. Bernard took one look and exploded.

"This isn't beef," he shouted. "It looks like veal."

The cattle breeders around him became embarrassed.

"Real meat should be violet, *violet,*" Bernard continued. "You should be able to see rings of fat."

"But to many customers, the fat means cholesterol," one grower said.

"Don't talk to me about this cholesterol," Bernard responded, continuing his harangue. He became so worked up that he began to resemble the violet, fat-filled animal he wanted to devour.

"I don't want veal when I buy beef," he kept repeating. "I want my meat *violet, violet, violet.*"

By the time he stopped, the entire room around him was silent. Everybody was watching. None of the growers tried to contradict him. Bernard stormed back to La Côte d'Or for lunch and didn't return to the fair for the rest of the weekend. On Saturday night, he missed the awards dinner; on Sunday, the ceremony for the best cattle.

But not long afterward, Bernard was only too delighted to receive a visit from another company in the beef business—McDonald's. The top managers of McDonald's France chose La Côte d'Or to host their annual three-day retreat. "This is a perfect place to reflect and study," said McDonald's personnel director Jean-Paul Brochiero.

The McDonald's men proved tough bargainers. They negotiated a special discount, room and three meals, all for three hundred dollars a day. At that price, Hubert grumbled, Bernard was giving away meals. Dominique disagreed. She pointed out that the McDonald's party would help the cash flow. In addition, she enjoyed discussing business with the Big Mac man, Mr. Brochiero.

"I was a consultant for Club Med," she told him. "I'm sure that we can learn about professional management techniques."

"Yes, of course," he replied. "Obviously, we cannot work like you, but there is a lot we can learn from you—for example, an attention to detail."

"There's also a question of personal contact," Dominique said. "We don't put mini-bars in the bedrooms, because we think everyone should be served personally."

"McDonald's is not self-service for the same reason," Brochiero said.

Bernard overheard this conversation and said he was proud to be chosen by McDonald's. "In your field, you are the best," he told them. "In my field, I am the best."

★ ★ ★

During Dominique's vacation in Ibiza, she telephoned Bernard and told him that everything was wonderful, particularly for the kids. "There's a terrific Baby Med," she told him. "Even Bérangère is learning to swim."

Then, before hanging up, she said in her most suggestive voice, "I have a surprise for you." Bernard wondered what she meant. When Dominique returned, she showed him a tattoo of a bird on her breast. Bernard was shocked.

"You did this for me?" he asked, worried. "Doesn't it hurt?"

Dominique smiled.

"The tattoo washes off," she said, laughing.

Bernard began looking for new ways to strengthen Dominique's ties to the hotel. He put her in charge of a new renovation. Almost as soon as the kitchen and dining room were done, Bernard began dreaming of adding more rooms. Having to send guests across the street to the Hôtel de la Poste on busy weekends was doubly distressing, because the profit margin on his hotel rooms was much higher than on the dining room, even at $200 a meal. Bernard had only nine renovated Relais et Châteaux suites and duplexes that cost $150 to $200 a night. The rest of his rooms were $50 specials left over from Dumaine's day. "In the restaurant, you have to pay for all the cooks and the food," Bernard said. "With hotel rooms, you just sell air."

Catonné, Bernard's architect, drew up plans for twelve new rooms. In order to renovate the rooms on the second floor, Catonné said, he needed to raise the roof. The complicated procedure drove the total cost up to $2.5 million. Fabre gave his approval. So did the banker Schneider.

Dominique directed the decoration of the bedrooms. With the architect, the accountant, and the contractors, she sat through afternoon-long lunch meetings to work out the details. Catonné drove to Saulieu in his sleek silver BMW for frequent meetings. Fabre arrived, usually late, from Auxerre. "What's that fathead doing now," Catonné complained, as they waited for the accountant.

Dominique soothed the architect. When Fabre finally arrived, wearing his usual loud purple suit, they pored over the plans. At lunch, a fabulous red Burgundy cheered everyone up. Hours were spent arguing over details. Dominique wanted traditional shutters for the new rooms. Catonné preferred shades.

"Shutters are prettier," Dominique said.

"Shutters don't add anything," Catonné replied.

"You're going to make the restaurant look like a hospital," said Dominique, ending the discussion.

Then, a week before construction was scheduled to begin, the project was delayed. The banks demanded that Bernard take out more life insurance. After Bernard arranged for the insurance, Fabre asked for another delay. Given France's deteriorating economy, he was not sure an ambitious renovation made financial sense. Next Schneider demanded a less expensive plan. Bernard was forced to revise his dream downward and settle for only five new rooms.

Dominique began to spend more time away from La Côte d'Or, concentrating on her own writing and editing career. She finished a new edition of her kitchen sanitation book. A journalist friend at her Europe 1 radio show suggested they put together a proposal for a new show. These outside activities excited her. She had three more book deadlines the following spring. But in Saulieu she found it hard to concentrate on her writing. She told Bernard that during the winter she wanted to spend two or three days a week in Paris to write. Too much fresh country air emptied her mind. She needed some Paris pollution to energize her brain cells.

Bernard was understanding. Although for a long time he had wanted Dominique to become *la patronne,* he approved of her decision to revive her own career. "She'll go crazy if she only stays here," he said.

Dominique had feared the worst when she made up her mind to split her time between Saulieu and Paris. But Bernard's positive reaction encouraged her. So did a big check she received on signing her next book contract. She rewarded herself by buying a new car—a bright red Renault convertible.

"Everybody at the restaurant was a little surprised," Dominique said. "They say we are asked to watch our wallets and then I buy this fancy car. But my books, not the restaurant, paid for it."

For her, the message was clear.

"I need a part of my own life outside of La Côte d'Or."

★ ★ ★

house Ruinart had started in 1978. Its goal was to revive the profession of sommelier—and, not incidentally, to sell more of its high-priced champagne.

Previous winners had gone on to great things. One became the director of a Relais et Châteaux hotel, another starred on a television food show, another opened a popular wine bar in Paris, and another vaulted into the high-paying world of wine consulting. One even soared to the ultimate heights: he won the title of Best Sommelier in the World.

Not surprisingly, the number of entrants increased dramatically. The first year, only a dozen had competed. In 1991, there were 397 candidates from all over France. Seventeen made the quarterfinals, and six were invited to Reims for the finals. Before, Lyonel had just missed making the semifinals. Later, he had gone to Reims but finished a poor fifth. "I choked," he said.

The competition was open only to French sommeliers aged twenty-six or younger. Lyonel had just reached the age limit, and if he lost, his wife, Christine, feared for their marriage. He had swept through the preliminary rounds. But he knew the competition in Reims would be tougher. In the weeks leading up to the event, Lyonel came home from the restaurant after lunch service and skipped his afternoon siesta, instead memorizing obscure facts about wine. To save time, he ate sandwiches. His apartment was so small and, with two toddlers crawling about, so crowded that he often worked in the bathroom, sitting on the toilet.

The profession of sommelier is a strange one. Some say it started with the Greeks, who appointed one person in the family to take care of wine. The actual term first referred to the monk who was in charge of the crockery, linen, bread, and wine in a monastery. During the Ancien Régime, the king's household included several sommeliers, whose function was to receive wine shipped in the cask. *Sommelier* also applied to the officials who took care of royal furniture, and later to any bearer of burdens. Under Louis XIV, the sommelier was wine in a monastery. During the Ancien Régime, the king's household included several sommeliers, whose function was to receive wine shipped in the cask. *Sommelier* also applied to the officials who took care of royal furniture, and later to any bearer of burdens. Under Louis XIV, the sommelier was in charge of baggage when the court moved. In the household of a great lord, he was the official who chose the wines, table settings, and desserts.

During the nineteenth century, the term came to mean the wine waiter in a large restaurant. There were 4,000 registered sommeliers in Paris by 1920. The 1930s confirmed the wine steward's high status. But after the war, as city restaurants faded, so did the sommelier. Widespread introduction of wine shipped in bottles further diminished the position. By 1955, only 150 sommeliers were left in Paris.

The modern wine boom revived the profession, but today sommeliers continue to receive less recognition than great chefs. More and more grand restaurants do without a sommelier, assigning the maître d'hôtel the responsibilities of choosing and serving the wines. Even Bernard toyed with this option, since Hubert had "a good nose." But in the end, Bernard decided that he would have a better chance at three stars with a special wine steward, although it was a close call. While almost all of the three-stars have a sommelier, Michelin is not doctrinaire about the issue. In the champagne capital of Reims, the three-star Les Crayères still did not have a sommelier.

Young sommeliers find themselves in a difficult position. Clients want to be reassured when they choose a wine. But they have more confidence in a bald, paunchy veteran than in a slim newcomer. Lyonel tried to compensate by dressing so that he appeared at least a decade older than he was. His seriousness, which rubbed his colleagues the wrong way, hid a gnawing insecurity, a deep inner tension about his ambitions. Lyonel wanted to command respect. "I didn't get my baccalaureate and go to university to end up washing glasses at age forty," he said. For him, the path to a bigger and better career depended on the Ruinart.

The contestants gathered on a Sunday afternoon at the Ruinart headquarters, a grand brown and white château in Reims. Ruinart prided itself on being the first champagne house ever founded. Dom Ruinart, a seventeenth-century monk, perfected the means of sealing the sparkle in the bottle, using a stopper of cork. Ruinart had a long history, but like most champagne houses, these days it was owned by a large conglomerate, Moët Hennessy.

The industry still has a sense of noblesse oblige. Ruinart's director, Roland de Calonne, carried himself like an aristocrat, wearing a tight gray suit, silver hair framing a bronzed, balding pate. He spoke in a high voice with a slight lisp, and everyone addressed him as "the count." Not long before, workers angry over impending layoffs repeated a scene straight from the French Revolution. They locked the count in his office for two full days, releasing him only after the police threatened to storm the building.

De Calonne greeted the past winners of the Trophée Ruinart, all men but for Anne-Marie Quaranta, the 1980 winner. She was a striking, outspoken blonde who directed a large hotel in Nice. Wine was no longer her profession, only a hobby. Over flutes of champagne, the former winners greeted each other like best friends, hugging and kissing, sharing recent exploits, gastronomic gossip, and wine discoveries. Lyonel watched in awe. "What a club," he said. "I would do anything to join it."

The contest began with the six finalists sitting for a two-hour written exam. "It was tough," he told Christine afterward when the couple went to their hotel room to change for dinner. Lyonel put on his sommelier's tuxedo. The dinner was at the Ruinart headquarters, in a room decorated to resemble a wine cellar. Cynics might have compared the room, full of elaborate wrought iron tributes to champagne, to a dungeon. But for Lyonel, the setting was "grand."

Ruinart champagne, rosé and regular, including a spectacular 1976 vintage, was poured throughout the entire meal, from appetizer to dessert.

At the end of the evening, Jean Frambourg, the president of the French Sommeliers' Association, announced the names of the three contestants who, on the basis of the exam, would advance to the ultimate round.

"Frédéric Robello of Provence–Côte d'Azur," he began.

"Emmanuel Pajot of Savoie Rhône-Alpes," he continued.

In his seat, high on champagne, Lyonel took a deep breath and turned beet red. He was frightened.

"And the last finalist is"—the president paused—"Lyonel Leconte of Burgundy."

Lyonel's entire body sagged. Christine gave him a big kiss. The crowd broke into applause. That evening, Lyonel relaxed by drinking until three at a local disco.

The competition resumed early the next morning. Lyonel, the two other finalists, judges, and spectators gathered in the cellar dining room, which had been transformed into an auditorium. On one side, there was a stage decorated with three giant wine barrels. The judges included all the past winners of the Trophée and other distinguished professionals, including the former European and World Sommelier champions. They sat at a table—like customers in a restaurant—with glasses and microphones set before them. Water, not wine, was placed on the table. A television camera recorded the event.

Lyonel was the last finalist to compete. He walked onto the stage, his steps unsteady. "I was in the clouds," he said later. "When I got to the stage I thought I would continue out the door and keep going."

But he stopped and bowed. As he listened to the instructions from Frambourg, he nodded his head slowly. For the first eight minutes, he would be graded on his recommendations for the wines to accompany a set meal.

"*Bonjour,* messieurs, madame," Lyonel introduced himself.

"We understand that your new chef hopes for a Michelin star," the judge said. "Well, we are six friends who love wine. What do you recommend for our meal?"

"As a starter, I propose champagne," Lyonel began. "It is the king of aperitifs, after all."

The jury nodded.

"I like a 1986 Ruinart," he said, to chuckles from the Ruinart employees in the audience. "That year has a fine taste. I think it will put you in a good mood for the rest of the meal."

The hors d'oeuvre was an autumn mushroom salad. Lyonel recommended a 1985 white Beaune, "a very good year and already fully developed." For the next course, a white turbot fillet in a butter sauce, he suggested a 1983 Alsatian Riesling. "It has a perfect bouquet for the fish."

"Let me stop you," interrupted the lead judge. "Our friend here is Alsatian and would like to try something other than an Alsatian wine."

Lyonel nodded.

"Would a wine from the Loire Valley please you?" he asked, and before anybody could answer, he called for a 1982 Vouvray.

The next course was roast guinea fowl with chestnuts. Lyonel advised "a return to Burgundy with a Vosne-Romanée, 1985 Premier Cru Henri Jayer." Or, he continued, "if you want something spectacular, try a 1969; it's the best in two decades, rich, round, and spiced, not too heavy, bringing out the value of the fruit without crushing it."

"No," the judge snapped. "Burgundy is too expensive."

The audience broke into laughter. Lyonel did not smile.

"Burgundy winegrowers have been making an effort to offer excellent products at reasonable prices," he countered, ever serious.

"We would prefer a Bordeaux," the judge said.

"If you want a full-bodied Bordeaux," Lyonel said, "I propose that you taste a Château Lynch-Bages, 1982."

For the cheese dish, a creamy Chaource from the Champagne region, Lyonel made a bold suggestion. He proposed "a light, fruity red wine" from Savoie Rhône-Alpes. "It's a much misunderstood vintage," he said. He followed with a recommendation for a sweet Muscat from the southwestern Minervois region, "perfect" to accompany an apple cinnamon puff pastry.

Finally he asked, "Would you like a little mineral water?"

He proposed a bubbling Badoit, lighter than Perrier but still a naturally carbonated fizz.

"At the end of the meal, I would be delighted to show you our menu of digestives," Lyonel concluded. "And, of course, there is our cigar list."

He turned, and the audience gave him a round of applause. The next part of the contest would be the most difficult for Lyonel. It was the English test. A Swedish judge explained that he did not speak French.

"What wine do you suggest with codfish?" he asked, in English.

Lyonel looked at him without understanding. The judge repeated his question. Lyonel still did not understand. Finally, somebody rescued him by asking the question in French.

"Sometimes eet izzzz diiiffiiicult to find the right wine with monkfish, but we can try," Lyonel stumbled. "Maybe you could try a white wine. Yes, a Puligny-Montrachet 1985, Domaine Sauzet. One of the finest."

"No, I'd like something from this region," the Swede said, impatient with Lyonel's poor English.

"We are in a lovely region," Lyonel answered, not understanding the comment. "If you like, I can set up some champagne tastings. If you like, I have a half day off, and we can make a taste at Ruinart."

Thankfully, the buzzer rang, ending the English test before Lyonel could make any more mistakes. He moved on to the next stage, the serving of wines. He had five minutes to serve a bottle of champagne—Ruinart, of course. Like a dancer, he set out the champagne glasses. He took out his napkin, wrapped the champagne bottle in it, and presented the bottle. He drew out his corkscrew and cut the gold foil capsule protecting the cork.

"I do not want to disturb the wine," he explained, holding his thumb over the corkscrew to avoid a shock. Slowly, slowly, he rolled the bottle from the bottom, turning the cork with his hand, softly and smoothly, until it came out. He held the cork to his nose. It smelled fine. He poured himself a glass of champagne, smelled and tasted it. "Perfect," he announced. He poured a glass for the only woman at the table. She tasted and said, "Perfect."

"May I serve the rest of the table, madame?" Lyonel asked.

"Of course."

Next Lyonel set out large glasses for red wine. He picked up the bottle, a 1967 Château Margaux, cut away the lead capsule, snapped his corkscrew open, and in one motion, like an accomplished cheerleader whirling a baton, uncorked the bottle. He smelled the cork, then looked at the wine intently and poured it carefully into the decanter. He poured a glass, wiped the lip of the decanter, and smelled the wine. Finally, he put down the bottle and took a taste.

"Madame and messieurs," he proclaimed. "This is a miracle of nature!"

A burst of laughter broke the silence in the auditorium.

Lyonel served the wine, pouring smoothly and slowly into the glass.

"You said 1969 was a great year?" asked one of the judges.

"Yes," Lyonel replied. "The other great years after the war were 'forty-seven, 'fifty-nine, 'sixty-one. All of them provide great pleasure."

Lyonel bowed and bid his guests good-bye.

The tasting came next. Lyonel took a glass of water and swished his mouth clean. He picked up a glass of white wine and began.

"It has a beautiful color, light and golden. Tears appear on the glass. This is a young wine of high quality."

He put the glass to his nose and smelled. He swirled the wine inside and smelled again. Four times he repeated the action.

"The aromas are good and clean," he said. "It's a little young. There are white fruit and flowers"—he took another smell—"a little apricot."

Finally, he took a sip. He swished the wine into his mouth, rolling it back and forth before he spit it out. He swirled the glass again and took a second, larger taste of the wine.

"A beautiful attack combined with a soft velvety touch," he said. "It has a wonderful framework." Another taste and he smacked his lips. "Yes, a good aroma, with some smoky notes and finishes with aromatic new fruits."

He stopped and hesitated. Now came the big moment, when he had to tell where the wine came from. Lyonel was unsure.

"The origin is difficult to discern," he confessed. "It could be a Loire Valley wine. But I think it is a Côtes-du-Rhône, a Crozes-Hermitage."

The judges sat stony-faced, revealing no clue. The wine was neither from the Loire Valley nor the Côtes-du-Rhône. It was an obscure vintage from the Haute-Vallée de l'Aude. Neither of the other finalists had known it, either. So Lyonel did not lose any points.

A red wine came next. Lyonel gave his elaborate description. It had an "excellent transparency," an "open, powerful, and complex bouquet," and "an elegant attack." He concluded that it was a Bordeaux, either a "Château Lynch-Bages or a Graves, probably a 1982."

The judges smiled. Lyonel's answer was close to the truth. It was a Graves, a Smith-Haut-Lafitte, 1986.

The next glass was filled with champagne. For five full minutes, Lyonel analyzed the structure of the foam, finding it "light," "persistent," "fine," "full of finesse," "perhaps a little gassy." It took another few moments to describe the color. Finally, he swirled the glass of wine and tasted. "Soft but fresh." He took another sip and concluded, "soft with a nice finish, a Dom Ruinart."

The judges smiled again. It was a Dom Ruinart 1981.

Lyonel moved to the final tasting of cognacs, Armagnacs, and other digestives. The competition ended with a review of a menu to find any errors. A 1984 Château d'Yquem was listed. Lyonel spotted the error: Château d'Yquem had not been harvested in that year. The menu contained an Appellation Controlée 1985 Maranges. Lyonel knew that the Maranges appellation had not been created until 1990. He said a 1989 Pauillac was too young to be put on the menu. He ended by telling the judges that a Vacqueras should not be listed as a Côtes-du-Rhône-Villages.

At last it was over. Lyonel turned to the audience, let out an audible sigh, and said, "Thank you."

Everyone moved down to the Ruinart wine cellar, a magnificent cave called Les Crayères carved deep into the chalky soil. Count de Calonne made a speech praising the Ruinart awards. Lyonel stood in the back listening, shuffling his feet, moving his hand over his face, trying to hide his nervousness.

Christine assured him he had done well. But Lyonel wondered whether he had achieved the right tone, whether he had appeared subservient enough without being obsequious. Had he cut off the judges when he should have listened? Had he defended Burgundy wines too fervently? Would his terrible English ruin his chances? As all these questions and doubts ran through his mind, the winner was announced.

Lyonel Leconte had triumphed.

He looked ready to faint. Shaking, he moved to the front of the room and hugged his colleagues. Anne-Marie Quaranta, the winner from 1980, wrapped a sommelier's apron around him. It read TROPHÉE RUINART, 1991. Lyonel shook the hand of Count de Calonne, who handed him a trophy—an oversize bottle of Ruinart champagne.

"Bravo, bravo," the crowd shouted.

"It's not quite over," the count said. As Lyonel lined up with past winners for photographs, a small smile played across his lips.

When he heard the news of Lyonel's victory, Bernard was delighted. "Three stars and the Best Young Sommelier in France," he beamed. "We are the top!"

Bernard asked Lyonel to help turn the barren Bistro du Morvan into a shop selling products featured at La Côte d'Or. Lyonel would be in charge of the wine and spirits section. The idea appealed to him, and he borrowed $100,000 to buy and renovate an abandoned farmhouse in nearby Liernais.

"There can be no greater compliment," Bernard observed. "Now that Lyonel is buying a house, he is staying with me for life."

*The dining room*

EPILOGUE

★ ★ ★

# A Fourth Star?

*A final toast*

BERNARD WAS SMILING.

It was July 1994, three summers since he had won the third star, and La Côte d'Or was full almost every day of good weather. Construction was proceeding on the five new rooms. Bernard's new cookbook was selling well. Then, on Bastille Day, President Mitterrand awarded him the Legion of Honor, making the forty-three-year-old the youngest chef ever to receive the award. For the first time since he had arrived in Saulieu, Bernard took a few days of summer vacation. He visited his parents at La Bourboule, where he went crayfish hunting. "It was still like poetry," he said, "just as good as when I was a kid."

His happiness was heartfelt, the more so because the years following his third star had proved harder than expected. In the early 1990s, a recession pummeled France. Unemployment soared to 12 percent. Growth vanished. Worst of all for Bernard, French interest rates remained at a punishingly high level. The halcyon days of the 1980s were gone, perhaps forever.

Bernard watched as luxury restaurants around France collapsed. Bordeaux's Jean-Pierre Amat, possessor of two Michelin stars and a striking, supermodern steel structure, declared bankruptcy. The luxurious two-star casino in the Paris suburb Enghien-les-Bains shut down, and other prestigious restaurants were also rumored to be near to closing.

Once the initial Michelin effect subsided, even Bernard's business began to slow. In 1993, he suffered a 3 percent drop-off in sales. That year, he arrived at the restaurant one winter day and found that there was not a single reservation. He asked Annie to do a calculation.

"I must pay back three hundred fifty thousand dollars a year," he said. "How much is that per day?"

The receptionist took out her calculator.

"It's ten thousand dollars," Annie answered.

"Ten thousand dollars," said Bernard, looking sick.

He laid off thirteen workers. The first year he had three stars, Bernard closed La Côte d'Or for a month, from mid November to mid December. Now he could no longer afford such a luxury. "We will stay open three hundred sixty-five days a year," he told the staff. Some employees grumbled, but no one said anything to Bernard. They wanted to hang on to their jobs. Bernard realized that success would never be assured in Saulieu. "Every winter will be a struggle," he said. "No one wants to come here when it's so cold."

Signs of mortality frightened Bernard. After the untimely death of Alain Chapel, in 1993 another three-star chef, Jacques Pic, succumbed in his prime to an unexpected heart attack. Bernard was also no longer the most recent three-star winner. Michelin awarded three stars first to Pierre Gagnaire in St. Etienne and then to Antoine Westermann in Strasbourg. Both were young chefs, around Bernard's age, and both received large amounts of publicity. Suddenly, Bernard no longer felt alone at the top of France's competitive gastronomic world.

Meanwhile, Bernard's partnership with Unilever provoked unexpected scorn and sarcasm. Angry phone callers demanded to know how a three-star chef could sell out to greedy capitalists. Letters arrived at La Côte d'Or addressed to Restaurant Unilever. Bernard began to worry that he might have erred by cashing in on his fame.

One French television station offered to make him its regular food commentator. That would have meant traveling to Paris each Friday and missing lunch service. Bernard was tempted. But criticism of his frequent appearances on television was mounting. Christian Millau wrote that Bernard was spending more time in front of the cameras than behind the oven. The barb stung. Bernard turned down the TV offer and decided, for the first time ever, to refuse interview requests from journalists.

Worried, Bernard began to have trouble sleeping. He tried homeopathic medicine, then sleeping pills. His fears of insomnia grew, and signs of depression emerged. A few times Bernard could not drag himself out of bed. Other days he didn't want to see his children. He even stopped eating regular meals. Customers began to notice that he had lost a lot of weight. Dominique suggested he see a doctor and spend a few weeks with his parents in Clermont-Ferrand.

"You have to calm down," she said.

Through the ordeal, Dominique proved indispensable. She finished her book and began a new one. Despite her desire to spend a little more time in Paris and concentrate on her own career, she took on additional responsibilities at La Côte d'Or and she never complained. When Bernard was absent, she ran the restaurant. Customers didn't notice that Bernard was missing. Dominique's quiet perfection paid off.

Slowly, in 1994, as the cold winter gave way to a balmy springtime, Bernard's infectious energy and enthusiasm returned. The recession retreated, interest rates came down, and customers again started to fill La Côte d'Or. The Japanese restaurant and his soup contracts assured Bernard's financial future. He seemed mellowed, matured, able for the first time to joke about himself.

One day, a journalist and a chef showed up. Both would be offered a free meal.

"Why don't you serve them the Unilever salmon soup?" Eric Rousseau said. "They're not paying anyhow."

Bernard instead served a sample of one of his new ideas: leek soup, spiced with truffles. He watched each guest taste.

"Good?" he asked.

"Delicious."

"I told you," he said, breaking into a small smile. "There is Loiseau soup, and there is Unilever soup."

Eric smiled, too. After fulfilling his cheese mission, he had hoped to become the maître d'hôtel at the Bistro du Morvan.

The project's cancellation proved a great disappointment. But his spirits were lifted by a trip to Japan for the special gastronomic week at Bernard's restaurant in Kobe. The cooking and service at the Japanese La Côte d'Or impressed him, and he found Japan fascinating. The only problem was with the bread and cheese. "The Japanese use terrible white bread. And they can't import any cheese made of raw milk." That excluded Epoisses.

Lyonel prospered as well. When La Côte d'Or experienced financial difficulties, Bernard shelved his plans for turning the Bistro du Morvan into a luxury food shop. Lyonel still hoped the project would be revived and he would become director. Meanwhile, he stayed on as sommelier. Burgundy wine prices began to fall. In 1992, they plunged about 25 percent. Lyonel now could begin to breathe easier about stocking La Côte d'Or's cellar. He began preparing for another competition, for Best Sommelier in France. This time, he no longer had to study in his bathroom. His new farmhouse had a big garden outside and plenty of room inside. In June 1994, he won. The victory made him the French representative in the upcoming Best Sommelier in the World contest. "I think I can win that too," he said.

Bernard's best suppliers also thrived. Colette Giraud bought twenty more goats, took on an employee, and increased production, investing $50,000 to build a small cheese-tasting house. "In the recession, people are searching for a return to true values," she said. "That's great for me." Jacques Sulem the jam maker, Jean-François Vadot the snail breeder, and Jean Gaugry the cheese maker all flourished. And Pepette continued to make the world's best bread, if only for a privileged few.

All in all, the report card was positive, so one day Bernard decided to celebrate. He made a reservation for himself and Hubert at a restaurant called Greuze in Tournus, a small town on the Saône River about an hour south of Saulieu. Its seventy-three-year-old chef, Jean Ducloux, had apprenticed with Dumaine in the 1930s. He still used Dumaine's recipes to produce such old-fashioned classics as *pâté en croûte Alexandre Dumaine, quenelles de brochet Henri Racouchet,* and *grenouilles sautées en persillade.* Ducloux's establishment had two stars. He had never tried to get the third star by lightening his cooking or renovating his out-of-date restaurant.

Bernard considered Ducloux a monument to another gastronomic age. For him, trips to Tournus were like pilgrimages to a great museum, like that of a modern artist to the Louvre. "Ducloux is the best classical cook left in France," Bernard said.

The morning of the visit, Bernard rose at seven and arrived at La Côte d'Or, as usual, at eight. He read through his mail and saw that the preparations for breakfast were under way. But when he went back home, he felt ill and began to sweat. Dominique put him to bed, called a doctor, and telephoned Hubert.

"I don't know if Bernard can go today," she said.

"I'm not feeling well either," Hubert replied.

The doctor diagnosed a mild flu.

"I'm going," Bernard told his wife. "I wouldn't miss those quenelles for anything."

When Hubert heard that Bernard still wanted to go, he summoned all his energies. The two sped south in Bernard's BMW along the Nationale to Tournus. When they arrived, it was twelve-thirty. Ducloux's restaurant was almost empty.

"Not counting you, I only have two reservations for lunch," the chef told Bernard. "And you don't count because you don't pay."

Ducloux looked thin and trim, in excellent health for his age, except for poor eyesight. He needed thick glasses, but he still wore his tall white toque with pride. His restaurant resembled a shrine to the Middle Ages, with dark brown wood furniture and paneling.

"Fewer and fewer great chefs are going to survive," Bernard said. "No one wants the great meal anymore. They want simple food served in a congenial atmosphere."

"Don't worry so much, Bernard," Ducloux said. "I've been in this business for fifty years and learned not to take it so seriously."

Because there were so few other guests, Ducloux ate with Bernard and Hubert. He ordered champagne. A waiter followed with the traditional Burgundy accompaniment—cheese popovers called *gougères*. The exquisite mixture of Gruyère and pastry melted in the mouth.

"The best *gougères* in the world," Bernard pronounced.

"Remember," Ducloux said, "there are only four universal things in life, things that you don't need words to explain: tennis, opera, sex—and eating."

Bernard laughed. Ducloux's ribald humor cheered him, and he forgot about his flu. Lunch continued with a stupendous red Chassagne-Montrachet.

"I don't cook anymore," Ducloux said, joking once again. "There are eight chefs in the kitchen and nine in the photo."

The first course was the *pâté croûte Alexandre Dumaine,* a supple pastry crust filled with liver.

"Just like Dumaine's pâté," Ducloux said.

Next came the famous quenelles. A thumbful of cognac added an unforgettable accent to the delicate, soft fish dumplings.

"How much cognac do you use?" Bernard asked.

"Enough," Ducloux answered.

Golden frog legs, dripping in butter, followed. Bernard started talking about his dream of finding local frogs. Ducloux laughed.

"These come from Greece," he said, "and they are much better than any of the local variety."

For his main course, Bernard chose kidneys in a brown sauce. He took a taste.

"Perfectly rosé," he proclaimed.

Hubert ordered the chicken in vinegar sauce. When it was served, Bernard leaned over and cut himself a piece. He tasted and grimaced.

"Tough," he said.

"Nobody's perfect," Ducloux reminded him.

For the rest of the meal, through the *soufflé au Grand Marnier,* petits fours, chocolates, and coffee, Bernard reflected on the overcooked chicken. Ducloux's response bothered him. Nobody's perfect, he thought. Bernard hoped that Ducloux would cook his unique traditional style as long as possible. But as for himself, Bernard knew that the moment he stopped striving for perfection was the moment he should retire.

Of course, Bernard himself wasn't ready to hang up the pots and pans just yet. Even as he mellowed, he retained an unquenchable thirst for improvement. Back at La Côte d'Or, he still watched every mouthful that a diner ate with a searching gaze. In his kitchen, he surveyed every plate that came back and knew exactly which guests left part of their meal uneaten. My God, table 12 didn't eat the parsley puree. What's wrong?

Unlike many great chefs, Bernard hated to tour his dining room during the meal. In his opinion, that practice was distracting. Instead, after each service, Bernard would stand next to the reception at La Côte d'Or and greet his guests as they were ready to leave.

"How was everything?" he would ask.

When asking the question, he would manage to look enthusiastic, happy, and worried all at the same time. Invariably, the guests would assure him that their meal had been wonderful. But even as Bernard listened to the compliments, his eyes would dart around the room looking for the slightest error, a crinkled rug, for example. He would snap his fingers and a waiter would come running.

"Fix it," he would command.

The guests would shake his hand and reassure him once again about their meal. But Bernard never could be sure. He always wanted to know how he could continue to improve.

Now he took a chunk of Ducloux's classic Grand Marnier soufflé. He sipped an espresso. Lunch was over. He began thinking of new challenges, new recipes, new projects. He had reached the top, and yet he wanted to go higher. He wanted a new goal. As they prepared to drive back to Saulieu, he looked at his friend and colleague Hubert and asked, entirely serious: "Don't you think Michelin should create a fourth star?"

*Colette's goats*

★ ★ ★

# Acknowledgments

*Three-star goat cheeses*

*Burgundy Stars* recounts the events of 1990–91. That was when Bernard Loiseau rebuilt his restaurant in hopes of winning gastronomic glory. That also was when wine steward Lyonel Leconte entered the Best Young Sommelier in France contest and waiter Eric Rousseau undertook his quest to uncover the most pungent cheese in France.

In November 1992, my wife and I settled in Burgundy. This was when I went hunting with Bernard, wine tasting with Lyonel, and cheese tasting with Eric. I also included in the narrative some incidents and minor characters drawn directly from my experience in 1992–93, especially the attempt by the two American interns, Larry Knez and Paul Lynn, to integrate themselves into the French world of haute cuisine.

We rented a small stone house in a village called Sussey, about eight miles south of Saulieu. Some two hundred people populated our new hometown. The hills around Sussey also were home to a thousand white Charolais cows and ten thousand sheep, not to mention an array of chickens, geese, goats, rabbits, cats, and dogs. Sussey was a village outside of time, a collection of centuries-old stone houses and barns perched on a gentle green slope.

Our landlady, Marie-Paule Garreau, brought us fresh eggs laid by her chickens, fresh yogurt made by her brother, and even honey cultivated by a son-in-law. Her husband, Pierre, regaled us with stories about the village's ten centuries of history. They were always generous to a fault—and proud of their land and its traditions, nourished over the centuries with love and care. For us, they were certainly Burgundy Stars.

Of course, thanks go first to the original Burgundy Star, Bernard Loiseau. For more than a year, he let me follow his routine. No matter how much I intruded, he never complained. No matter how many questions I asked, he answered with endless patience and boundless enthusiasm. And then, on my way out of the kitchen, he would often command, "Tonight, you eat here."

Into the dining room my wife and I went, strolling through half a museum's worth of polished oak, wrought iron, antique furniture, shimmering brass, and ancient tile, to a table adorned with silver and crystal. A kir royale—champagne and cassis—would be placed before us, followed by various other golden nectars and irresistible aphrodisiacs. Three hours later, we would stumble away, sated and smiling.

The rest of the staff—Hubert, Franck, Patrick, Lyonel, Eric, Annie, and all the others—were equally generous. They invited us not only into the restaurant, but into their homes, where we enjoyed their three-star taste in good food and wine. Hubert was one of the best cooks I have ever met; he and Franck also were both wonderful tennis partners. Patrick showed me the insides of a great French kitchen. Lyonel taught me about wine and used his influence to get me into the best vineyards. And Eric's talent was not limited to cheese. He grilled giant T-bone steaks, the best I have ever tasted.

A special word is in order for Dominique Loiseau. More than anybody else in Saulieu, she shared a journalistic complicity and supported it with her considerable talent for research.

Not to be forgotten are Bernard's wonderful suppliers. Every morning, I savored Jacques Sulem's jams. Colette Giraud would ply me with her freshest rounds of goat cheese. Simon Bize and Michel Lafarge would insist on opening vintage bottles of wine.

Back in the United States, my thanks go first to my agent, Michael Carlisle, who understood right away that Bernard's story warranted a book.

Almost fifteen years after my graduation, it was a delightful surprise to rediscover my Yale professor John Merriman, and he generously donated his considerable expertise in reading the manuscript.

Thanks above all to my editor, Jim Silberman, who put his pencil over every word and much improved the first draft. He displayed a great talent for improving rough writing. Whenever I complicated the task, Jim managed to tear away all the unneeded fat and pare everything down to the essential.

Finally, thanks to Anu and Sam, who enjoyed the bounties of Burgundy but also helped me persevere deep in the French countryside through the cold days of book writing.

JULY 31, 1994
SUSSEY, FRANCE